Lonely on
The Mountain

A Skier's Memoir

George M. Henderson

Book design: Jeff Thomas, Keep Climbing Press
Cover design: Muki Kerr
Copy editors: Bonnie Henderson and Jeff Thomas

I want to give special thanks to Linny Adamson, Randi Black, Sarah Munro, and Lloyd Musser for their help and to acknowledge Jeff Thomas, climber, Mazama archivist and author of Oregon High, who has been invaluable to me in researching and planning this memoir – George Henderson.

All photos by George Miller Henderson or Verlinda Miller Henderson unless otherwise noted. Front cover photo by Curtis Ijames: James A. Mount skiing at the future site of Timberline Lodge, circa 1935.
Back cover color photo courtesy of Friends of Timberline: George M. Henderson with his Zeiss Ica Reflex camera purchased used in 1935.
Back cover black and white photo: Timberline Lodge before the headhouse was completed, Autumn 1936.
Title page photo: Hjalmar Hvam passing Illumination Rock as he tested the Crater Rock Downhill Run on Mount Hood before the first annual Golden Rose Race on June 14, 1936.
Page iii photo: Mount Jefferson through frozen trees on Park Ridge, February 28, 1936.
Page v photo by Ray Atkeson: George Henderson skiing on Mount Hood, late 1939. Magic Mile chairlift in the background.

Note for Librarians: A cataloguing record for this book is available from Library and Archives Canada at www.collectionscanada. ca/amicus/index-e.html
ISBN 1-4120-8233-1

Printed in Victoria, BC, Canada. Printed on paper with minimum 30% recycled fibre.
Trafford's print shop runs on "green energy" from solar, wind and other environmentally-friendly power sources.

PUBLISHING

Offices in Canada, USA, Ireland and UK
This book was published on-demand in cooperation with Trafford Publishing. On-demand publishing is a unique process and service of making a book available for retail sale to the public taking advantage of on-demand manufacturing and Internet marketing. On-demand publishing includes promotions, retail sales, manufacturing, order fulfilment, accounting and collecting royalties on behalf of the author.

Book sales for North America and international:
Trafford Publishing, 6E–2333 Government St.,
Victoria, BC V8T 4P4 CANADA
phone 250 383 6864 (toll-free 1 888 232 4444)
fax 250 383 6804; email to orders@trafford.com
Book sales in Europe:
Trafford Publishing (UK) Limited, 9 Park End Street, 2nd Floor
Oxford, UK OX1 1HH UNITED KINGDOM
phone 44 (0)1865 722 113 (local rate 0845 230 9601)
facsimile 44 (0)1865 722 868; info.uk@trafford.com
Order online at:
trafford.com/05-3199

10 9 8 7 6 5 4 3

DEDICATION

To our delightful children,

Donna Cate Henderson
Bonnie Lynn Henderson
Heather Ann Henderson
Randall Wymond Henderson
Darcy Verlinda Henderson

And their equally delightful spouses.

REVIEWS

In the twilight of my failing eyesight a bright new star has appeared. It is George M. Henderson's account of his life from infancy to World War II. The author has a keen memory for those adventures that happened so long ago and a charming way of relating them. This book is history at its best.

Keith McCoy – historian and author of *The Mount Adams Country*

This memoir lovingly recounts the twentieth century history of skiing in the magnificent Pacific Northwest. The hard life, dedication and pageantry of building our scenic national winter wonderland on Mount Hood is told with great care. May this book reach out and touch you as it did me.

Howard Hermanson – past president of Cascade Ski Club

In reading *Lonely on the Mountain* I was impressed by the accuracy with which George Henderson tells of events which he and I experienced together. The book recounts history just the way it happened.

Hank Lewis – first patrol chief of Mount Hood ski patrol, 1938

Anybody with an interest in northwest skiing will want to read and own for his or her personal library, George M. Henderson's new book, *Lonely on the Mountain*. He has brought the subject alive with pictures and prose you cannot forget.

Jack Mills – cofounder and former president of Friends of Timberline

We are fortunate that George Henderson decided to write his memoir. He has been involved with Mount Hood and Timberline Lodge throughout his life. The stories about the mountain and lodge provide a unique and significant record from one of the original Friends of Timberline.

Sarah Munro – historian and coeditor of *Timberline Lodge, 1978*

Historians know the names of the major Mount Hood historical figures, but little about their personality or the character traits that would bring these people back to life. The inclusion of this material in George M. Henderson's memoir, *Lonely on the Mountain* sets it apart from other works.

Lloyd Musser – Curator Mount Hood Cultural Center and Museum

PREFACE

Most of my first thirty years were spent in the mountains: as a youngster in Montana and Idaho logging camps – as a Forest Service lookout and smoke chaser in Oregon – as a pioneer in the early development of skiing on Mount Hood – and as an outdoor writer and ski columnist.

This memoir recounts those years from the beginning of World War I until the beginning of World War II.

George Miller Henderson
Portland, Oregon
2005

TABLE OF CONTENTS

PROLOGUE: MONTANA – 1924...8

1   INDIANA – 1909...9

2   MONTANA – 1885...11

3   A VISIT HOME...17

4   INDIANA – 1919...21

5   MONTANA – 1920...25

6   MISSOULA...43

7   THE PABLO FIRE...51

8   HAYES CREEK...53

9   ACROSS THE BITTERROOTS...63

10   LEWISTON IDAHO – 1927...75

11   KLAMATH FALLS – 1928...79

12   CRATER LAKE 1928 – 2002...83

13   KLAMATH FALLS: FOUR JOBS A DAY...87

14   KLAMATH FALLS TO PORTLAND – 1929...91

15   GOVERNMENT CAMP – 1930...95

16   HIGH SCHOOL DAYS...105

17   MOUNT HOOD CLIMBS – 1933...115

18   MOUNT ST. HELENS AND MOUNT ADAMS – 1934...125

19   SKIING THE SKYLINE TRAIL – 1936...135

20   A DOLLAR HERE, A DOLLAR THERE.................................149

21   A SHINY NEW BADGE AND A MODEL T FORD.....................157

22   SKIING THE SKYLINE TRAIL AGAIN – 1937.......................169

23   INDIANS AND BEADED BAGS......................................173

24   MOUNT HOOD'S SECRET BACKSIDE.............................177

25   YOCUM RIDGE AND CATHEDRAL RIDGE.......................183

26   DOWNS WITHOUT UPS...187

27   PRESIDENT ROOSEVELT DEDICATES TIMBERLINE
      LODGE..199

28   A DAUNTING SALES JOB..205

29   THE 1939 OLYMPIC TEAM TRYOUTS...........................215

30   NORWAY'S SKIER PRINCE...227

31   THE STORMY STORY OF MOUNT HOOD'S SUMMIT
      SHELTERS..233

32   BONNEY BUTTE – 1942...239

33   ERNIE PYLE LEARNS TO SKI – 1942............................247

34   LONELY ON THE MOUNTAIN.....................................257

      EPILOGUE...270

      INDEX..272

Prologue: Montana – 1924

In 1924 hand-logging in the Bitterroot Range of Montana in winter was a dangerous proposition at best and could turn life-threatening if things went wrong. I was only 8 years old, but that is when I learned to swear.

"Let's get the hell out of here," I screamed at my 9-year-old brother, Wymond, who stood beside me along a curve in an ice-filled log chute watching huge logs hurtling from far up Hayes Creek Canyon toward the Bitterroot River far below. He was facing uphill when I glanced down the chute and saw that the string of logs there had come to a sudden stop. I grabbed Wymond's hand and we raced across the icy side hill just before the next log from above rammed into those below with a splintering crash and bounced out of the chute into the clearing where we boys had been standing.

My father had risked the family's bottom dollar by contracting to clear-cut an entire watershed of virgin yellow pine timber and bring the logs down to the railroad through 3 feet of snow-covered terrain too steep even for horse logging.

Father was desperate. He had just lost a modest fortune when his newly built sawmill at Pablo near Flathead Lake, along with millions of board feet of logs and lumber, had burned to the ground in a fire for which the insurance company escaped liability. The post-World War I economy was in shambles, and to win this bid to supply timbers for the mines in Butte had required a desperately low bid.

It was a 15-minute walk back to our log cabin, and Wymond got there first. His news to Mother was "George swore at me today." When I arrived, I reported breathlessly, "A big log fell out of the chute and almost killed us."

Sorting the priorities of our reports quickly, Mother responded, "Didn't Father say never to go onto those trails along the log chutes?"

Our penalty was short lived, and soon we were again trapping ermine along frozen Hayes Creek and adding their soft white pelts to our bundle of winter furs.

It had been five years since our family moved from our Indiana farm to a sawmill site near the Flathead Indian Reservation in Montana, and Father had resumed his long career in the lumber business.

Wymond and me with our downsized canthooks in front of the Pablo sawmill

1   INDIANA – 1909

My mother, Verlinda Miller, and her primary grade school class, Clermont, Indiana, 1908

THE SUITOR

In 1909, after 25 exciting years as a logger and lumberman in western Montana, Father had sold his sawmills and retired with a tidy fortune to the native Indiana he had left as a boy of 19. He bought a run-down farm on a beautiful hilltop near the Indianapolis Speedway and built a showplace home with huge barns and corrals.

Then on Dec. 20, 1912, the 46-year-old confirmed bachelor and the lovely 34-year-old spinster school teacher Verlinda Miller, who lived on the adjacent hilltop, were married in the crystal dining room of the Hotel English in Indianapolis. They boarded a train the same evening to spend the rest of the winter honeymooning in Florida.

A ROCK-SOLID MARRIAGE

Father was a lovable roughneck and Mother a frontier aristocrat. It seemed an unlikely match, but their devotion to one another remained rock-solid to the end of their lives. How predictable their future looked at that moment and how different reality would be!

Mother was born on the Miller family homestead in Clermont, Indiana, on Dec. 20, 1878. She was an amateur botanist and a lover of the outdoors who enjoyed galloping sidesaddle across the fields of their Indiana farm. She sang and played the piano; I still have some of the 78-rpm records which she played on her wind-up Brunswick phonograph with its choice of needles – bamboo or steel. They ranged from Tchaikovsky symphonies to solos by tenor Enrico Caruso, while Father favored Irish jigs and such ballads as "When I Was Twenty-One," sung by Scotsman Harry Lauder. After graduating from teachers' college Mother taught primary grades in Clermont for a dozen years.

Wymond was born on March 10, 1914, shortly before the outbreak of World War I, and I came along on Aug. 19, 1915, two years before the United States entered the war. We both were born on a brass bed in our Indiana farmhouse. A measure of Mother's modesty was that she told me years later that we both were born "under the sheets."

"WAR'S OVER"

"War's over!" I shouted through two rows of corn. Father looked up from the ear he was shucking and saw me running toward him, then saw Wymond, who had arrived a few seconds earlier and who was trying through tears of frustration to stammer out the same message.

It was Nov. 11, 1918. Mother had just gotten word over our Indiana farm phone line that Germany had surrendered to the Allies, ending World War I, and she had sent us boys racing to tell Father. Four-year-old Wymond easily won the foot race, but before he could calm his stuttering, my 3-year-old legs had carried me within shouting distance. Boy was Wymond mad!

THE 1918 FLU EPIDEMIC

We boys had almost died during the war.

Early in 1918 we both came down with the deadly Spanish Influenza, the worst infectious disease outbreak in human history. It is estimated that it killed between twenty and fifty million people worldwide in a little more

than a year, including 675,000 Americans, more than were killed in all the United States' wars of the twentieth century combined.

But Father hadn't been there to share in our care. A few weeks earlier, he had boarded a ship to Guatemala to speculate on a possible logging operation in the forests of Central America. That left Mother and our beloved black housekeeper Maudie alone with two small flu-racked boys.

There was no effective vaccine for the disease. Hospitals overflowed; doctors and nurses who hadn't been called to the war were overwhelmed, and many of them were stricken too. The flu was fatal within a week to one-fourth of those infected.

Our survival would depend upon the intuitive skills inherited from pioneer forebears, the loving care and prayers of my mother, who was a faithful member of the Clermont Christian Church, and motherly Maudie, whose piercing contralto rang the rafters of her Baptist church on Sundays.

TWO FORTUNATE SURVIVORS

We boys both beat the odds.

Mother told us later that as our fevers soared to 105 degrees, we sometimes were delirious for hours and then would lapse into ominous lethargy. I remember only frightening dreams followed by the soothing sounds of Mother singing Stephen Foster songs and Maudie crooning spirituals. The homespun care worked its magic, and by the time Father reached home, we both were on the mend.

The flu epidemic in the U.S. peaked in October with 119,000 deaths that month alone, but then the malady released its grip. Following the November Armistice those Americans whose families had not been decimated set out to begin their lives anew.

2   MONTANA – 1885

Map from Father's 1846 school geography book, which described Oregon as "undefined."

BEFORE THE IRON HORSE

Father was born in Ripley County, Indiana, on Sept. 20, 1866, a year after President Lincoln was assassinated and the Civil War ended. There were no railroads across America then, and the automobile had not been invented, so the only way to cross the continent was to walk, ride a horse, or travel in a horse or ox-drawn vehicle. Electric lights, telephones and radios hadn't been invented either, so the cutting edge of technology was the telegraph, by which messages could be tapped out over wires in Morse code.

Lewis and Clark's Voyage of Discovery from St. Louis to Oregon had opened the West, so settlers were pouring across the Rocky Mountains in covered wagons to take up land or search for gold.

OREGON – "AN UNDEFINED REGION"

I have the geography book that Father studied in school. It describes Oregon as "...an undefined region stretching from the Rockies to the Pacific...occupied by Indian tribes and a few white people from the United States and Great Britain."

Father was born with a spirit of adventure, unbounded self-confidence and unrelenting determination. Fortunately that will to win included scholastics. He won school and countywide spelling bees, wrote near-

My grandparents

Sarah Legg Henderson
born 1835
Milton Moon Henderson
born 1827

Both died in 1907
Photo taken July 1905

perfect Spenserian script, won gold stars for memorizing long passages from McGuffey's Readers, and could do complex mathematics calculation in his head.

A HOMESTEAD ALONG THE OHIO

Both Grandfather and Grandmother Henderson died in 1907 before Wymond and I were born, so we never saw the Indiana farm where Father was born. He said that his grandfather built the house in 1825 on a homestead near the Ohio River and several miles from the county seat of Versailles, where he taught high school one winter term.

Hearing Father's plethora of stories made Wymond and me feel that we had known the members of his family personally, even though we met only a few.

There was no way that the hardscrabble Indiana farm could have contained his exuberance, and in his 19th year he and his older brother Clark boarded the newly completed Northern Pacific Railway and headed for Montana.

FATHER'S BACHELOR DAYS

When Father and Clark first arrived in Montana, Missoula was booming. The first Florence Hotel was being built, and the brothers quickly found work, driving oxen to haul timbers to the hotel site six miles down the Clark Fork River from the Bonner sawmill.

They had walked from Missoula to the mill and were hungry, so after buying blankets at the company store and carrying straw from the barn to the bunkhouse to fill their wooden bunks, they headed for the cookhouse.

When they sat down for supper, no one responded to their requests to pass the food. Finally they realized that all the other lumberjacks were French-Canadians. Of course, the Hoosiers could not speak French, much less that dialect that even the French have trouble understanding. Soon they realized that not only were they being ignored, but also they were being ridiculed in French.

Ben and Clark did not like it. Sure, they were greenhorns in the logging camp, but they had handled horses and oxen all their lives and

"In his 19th year he and his older brother Clark boarded the newly completed Northern Pacific Railway and headed for Montana." Ben Henderson (left), 23, and Clark Henderson, 33, in Missoula, Montana, in 1890.

were expert axe men and sawyers. They had not suffered ridicule gladly in their Indiana schoolyard and were not about to do so here.

One day after they had been at Bonner for a month or so, Ben stood up during supper, rattled a spoon on the pewter water pitcher, and announced, "This is America, and the language is English. From now on anyone speaking French during meals will have to answer to me!

ROUGH AND TUMBLE

After supper, with Clark as his second, Ben was challenged by the French-Canadian bull-of-the-woods and whipped him in a bloody, bare-knuckle, rough-and-tumble fight. From time to time after that, another challenger would tackle Ben, with the same result. From then on when Ben and Clark came into the cookhouse, the cacophony of voices would give way to subdued sounds of supper, then limited conversations would resume, in English!

"I never lost a rough-and-tumble fight in my life," Father proudly told Wymond and me one day as he was describing his early days in Montana, adding that those "fights to the finish" with no rules or referees were the primary way, short of gunfights, in which violent conflicts were settled on the frontier. They ended only when one antagonist could fight no longer or admitted that he was beaten.

His own fierce pride, his rigid personal code of honor and his quick temper must have made him a ready candidate for such battles.

His role models were John L. Sullivan, who in 1889 won the last world bare-knuckle heavyweight boxing championship, and James J. Corbett, who beat Sullivan after the introduction of boxing gloves. Father must have talked about those boxers often, or I would not have remembered their names all these years.

Father was a fine raconteur and graphically pictured for us the Montana scene as it had been in the late 19th century. Wymond was excited by the fight stories, but I was frightened. I did not like to be hurt and did not enjoy seeing others hurt. I was the pacifist of the family.

TENDING BAR ON THE FRONTIER

Father's skill at bare knuckle fighting was sorely tested during a winter he spent tending bar in Libby, Montana, while the Great Northern railroad was under construction. Fighting was an inevitable part of keeping order in a frontier bar. His rule was, "If there is to be any fighting in this bar, I'll do it."

Another hazard of that job was too much whiskey. When Father described his fight with Demon Rum to Wymond and me, it seemed as if I was there. He told us that, near the end of the winter, he realized that he no longer could start a day without a big swig of whiskey.

Father was a follower of the renowned health advocate, Bernarr McFadden, yet there he was on the verge of alcoholism! He told us of the torture it had been to quit cold. Each morning for weeks, he took a five-mile run in zero-degree weather and then spent the rest of the day serving liquor to boisterous barroom customers. The ensuing fights probably served as good therapy.

As I recall he always had a bottle of whisky in the house and would serve a drink to guests, but I never saw him take a second drink – not even a second bottle of beer!

His fighting temper never deserted him. One day when he was nearing 90 a bus driver crossed him and he invited the driver to step out and settle the matter on the street.

PROSPECTING FOR GOLD

Felling tall trees with a double-bitted axe in bitter winter weather while balanced six feet above ground on a springboard was a tough way to make a living, and when summers came Father exchanged the axe for a miner's pick and headed for the glacial peaks of the North

Cascades to prospect for gold.

He had come West to make his fortune, and working for wages was a slow way to do that. Gold hadn't yet been discovered in the Klondike or Father probably would have joined the 1898 gold rush there, but in the 1880s there was a smaller rush to the almost inaccessible mountains bordering the Methow Valley and Lake Chelan on the east side of the Cascades. Streams tumbling down from the peaks carried enough gold to provide a fair living to someone staking a claim, installing sluice boxes to catch the nuggets and sand, and then separating the gold from the black sand by hand with a gold pan.

That gold had to have originated in veins of gold in the hard rock of the mountains above, and it was the hope of finding such a "mother lode" that lured prospectors such as Father.

In early summer he would saddle his horse, lead a packhorse, and ride across the Bitterroots to Spokane Falls and on across northern Washington Territory to the Cascade Mountains. (Washington would not become a state until 1889, and Idaho became a state in 1890.) Father traveled light, for he wanted to leave room to bring back the gold. His supplies were a sack of flour, a sourdough "start," a frying pan and a side of bacon loaded on one side of the packhorse and mining equipment and a gold pan on the other side. Blankets, a slicker and his Winchester were on top along with whatever fresh meat he killed as needed.

It must have been a healthy diet, for he remained vigorous and mentally alert until he died after a hip fracture at age 91.

Father told us that he did his prospecting near the Methow Valley and that he usually stayed in the mountains for several months with only the picas and whistling marmots for company. However, he must have come out for supplies from time to time because he told of drilling and blasting tunnels into the cliffs to follow likely "colors" where a vein seemed to be exposed on the face, and that would have

required more supplies than he would have brought from Missoula on his packhorse.

Father never made a strike, but he said that the nuggets and gold he panned from the creeks were worth much more than he would have made working in the woods in summer.

Many of those streams and towering peaks now are a part of the North Cascades National Park. In the 1950s and 1960s, I spent many weeks climbing and camping near old mining claims on Chihuahua Mountain above Lake Chelan, at the base of Glacier Peak and north of Cascade Pass. I wondered during those trips whether the joy of prospecting in those enchanting surroundings might have been a major reason for his pursuit of gold. I'm sure he would have denied it.

HORSEBACK TO YELLOWSTONE

Father first learned about Montana from a picture of Old Faithful geyser in one of his school books, so one summer he decided to see Yellowstone National Park for himself. He described to us how he enjoyed that trip across the Continental Divide with his saddle horse and packhorse, exploring parts of the state he had never seen. The trip took a week, and when he reached Mammoth Hot Springs he hired out driving a four-horse team and wagon in the park. He might also have driven some tourist-laden stagecoaches, but Yellowstone had only been a national park for ten years then, so tourist business probably was light.

THE SPANISH-AMERICAN WAR

In 1898 the United States declared war on Spain, and President William McKinley called for 125,000 army volunteers. Always ready for a fight, Father was among the first to arrive at Fort Missoula to sign up.

The avowed reason that the U.S. entered the war was to support Cuba in its fight for independence from Spain, but many in

America were calling for the acquisition of military bases, if not actual colonies, in the Caribbean, the Philippines and even Guam. Father was not aware of those subtleties. His decision to enlist was in accord with his oft-spoken personal tenet, "My country right or wrong – may she ever be right – but right or wrong my country!"

Father was a 32-year-old sawmill owner, and when he lined up with the other recruits he found that most were either in their teens or twenties or were older men who were out of work and whom he probably wouldn't even have hired for one of his logging crews. He stepped out of line, deciding to wait to enlist until the President issued another call.

The Treaty of Paris ended the war with Spain that December, thus also ending Father's brief consideration of a military career.

Ironically, his father, Milton Henderson, had been thirty-four years old and married with five children when the Civil War began so he did not serve in that sorry conflict. Ben's grandfather, Edward Henderson, had been thirty-three and married with four children during the War of 1812 so he too missed military service. When Wymond and I served in World War II, we became the first in our direct lineage since the Revolutionary War to be active wartime combatants.

3   A VISIT HOME

In 1904 Father made his first trip home to Indiana in 20 years.

The brash Hoosier farm boy who in 1885 had fought with his fists to gain the respect of lumberjacks had become a prosperous timber and sawmill owner widely respected among Montana business leaders. As he planned the trip home he realized how much the world had changed in those 20 years! Automobiles had been invented, the Wright Brothers had flown the world's first airplane, and railroads had been built throughout the West. He broadened his travel plans.

One of those new rail lines transited the spectacular Columbia River Gorge so Father began with a train ride through the Gorge.

From the "Largest Log Cabin in the World" in Portland to the clanging cable cars of San Francisco and the brilliant spectacle of the 1904 St. Louis World Fair, the trip was a wondrous experience!

WORLD'S LARGEST LOG CABIN

Portland was the first big city he had seen since leaving Indianapolis, and its citizens were excitedly preparing for the 1905 Lewis and Clark Centennial Exposition. When he

"The Largest Log Cabin in the World" was the centerpiece of the 1905 Lewis and Clark Centennial Exposition in Portland, Oregon.

heard of the great log building that was to be centerpiece of the Centennial, he immediately boarded a streetcar to the 400-acre site at Northwest 28th Ave. and Upshur St.

"Those were the biggest damned logs I'd ever seen," Father told Wymond and me a quarter-century later. True to Paul Bunyan tradition, the "log cabin" would be the largest log building in the world. It was designed in the style of an alpine chalet and covered half a city block – 206 feet long, 102 feet wide and 72 feet high. Father watched as the bottom rows of logs were rolled into place and notched together with adzes and axes so precisely that no nails were needed. The roof would be supported by 52 Douglas fir logs, each 54 feet long and weighing 35 tons. Another 300 logs 6 feet in diameter would form the walls. Those Douglas firs were twice the size of Montana Ponderosa pines.

Truly a world fair, there would be exhibits from every continent, mostly presented in elaborate but temporary buildings grouped around Guild Lake. However, the real purpose of the fair was to dramatize the Pacific Northwest's dominance in forest products and the emergence of its ports as trading and shipping centers for the Pacific Rim.

The log building was intended to be the only part of the exposition not razed when the fair ended, but I learned recently that one other facility survived. The picturesque wooden exhibit hall of the National Cash Register Company was salvaged and barged from Guild Lake across the Willamette River to the village of Saint Johns. A century later, shorn of its decorative cupola, it houses *McMenamins St. Johns Pub* on Ivanhoe Street, where nostalgic visitors may slake their thirsts.

The massive log cabin was renamed The Gallery of Trees and continued to be a major Portland tourist attraction for sixty years until it was destroyed by fire on Aug. 17, 1964.

After a week in Portland, Father boarded a steamer for San Francisco one evening and was surprised when he awoke the next morning to find that the ship was just then passing Astoria. His geography book had shown Portland as a seaport, but where was the ocean?

He learned that before reaching the ocean, ships leaving Portland must follow the Columbia River for ninety miles to Astoria, then take aboard a special pilot to navigate the dangerous entrance bar. The bar crossing was calm that day, and soon he was enjoying his first ocean voyage with occasional glimpses of the rugged Oregon and California coasts.

THE GREAT 1906 SAN FRANCISCO EARTHQUAKE AND FIRE

Two days later the ship entered San Francisco Bay through the spectacular Golden Gate, yet untamed by any bridge, and docked at the Embarcadero among tall sailing ships and steamers from all the world's oceans.

San Francisco was in its heyday. It would be another two years before my future father-in-law, E.Y. Himmelwright, would chauffeur the San Francisco fire chief through the devastation of the 1906 earthquake and fire.

Almost fifty years later, when Jan and I were in San Francisco for our wedding, I heard that story from her father. Ed Himmelwright had been a pioneer automobile salesman in Ardmore, Pennsylvania, where Autocars were built, and in about 1904 he yearned to transfer his sales skills to the company dealership in San Francisco. Driving or hitchhiking weren't options, for probably not even one automobile had yet made that cross country trek, so he "bummed" his way and did indeed become an Autocar salesman in The City.

Soon afterward, he brought fame to the Autocar name by winning the first auto race from San Francisco to Los Angeles. I was delighted to have him show me the engraved gold watch he had received at that event.

Right after the massive 1906 San Francisco earthquake the fire chief conscripted Ed

Himmelwright and his Autocar to drive him for the duration of the fire.

Father was fascinated by the cosmopolitan city with its cable cars, sandy beaches, exotic food, exciting entertainment and anachronistic Chinatown. He had never seen an Oriental before except for the Chinese track-laying crews who were a part of most new railroad construction. Cutting off the pigtails of those unfortunates was considered high sport by many whites. But he was amazed to see that the San Francisco Chinese had their own stores, restaurants, play houses and banks. It was a revelation to an unquestioning WASP!

Father stayed a full week before continuing by train to St. Louis.

A WAYWARD BULLET

There was a near disaster in the St. Louis railway depot. After two almost sleepless nights on the train, Father had fallen asleep on a waiting room bench but awoke with a start as a bullet crashed into the concrete wall.

He saw a policeman rushing toward him with a drawn gun before realizing that the shot had come from his own automatic pistol which now lay on the floor beneath his seat. The gun had slipped out of his hip pocket and was triggered when it hit the floor. The bullet passed under several rows of seats, and only because the station was almost empty at that early hour were there no casualties.

"I'll never own another automatic," he told the police officer. He had bought the new gun for the trip, and he told us that the revolver he had carried for many years could not have fired on impact because he always left the hammer on an empty cylinder. That same day he traded the automatic for a .38 Special Smith & Wesson revolver, which I own today.

The 1904 St. Louis World Fair was unlike any before or since. Its primary purpose was to celebrate the centennial of the 1803 Louisiana Purchase, when the United States acquired

from Emperor Napoleon Bonaparte of France 800,000 square miles of land extending from the Mississippi River to the Rocky Mountains. That had to have been one of the greatest real estate transactions in history.

The new lands were largely unexplored and President Thomas Jefferson shortly authorized the 1805-1806 Lewis and Clark Voyage of Discovery from St. Louis to the Pacific Ocean. The Fair marked that centennial also, as did the 1905 Lewis and Clark Centennial Exposition to be held in Portland the following year.

Also combined with the St. Louis fair was the 1904 World Olympic Games. Father's interest was divided among the athletic events of the games, the fair's technological displays, and the elaborate exhibits of resources and products by many nations and major cities.

Montana's entry also caught his attention. It was the work of a Missoula taxidermist consisting of a mounted buck, doe and fawn deer flanked by four animal hide rugs, a cougar, a wildcat, a black bear and a grizzly bear, their snarling heads realistically mounted.

Father bought the lot! He already was thinking about retiring from lumbering and returning to Indiana, and five years later, those mounted specimens were on display in the parlor of a showplace farm home that he built near Indianapolis.

THE PERIPATETIC GRIZZLY

Those mounted animals were among my earliest memories of life in Indiana, but their future already was in jeopardy. By the time I was 4 years old Mother had relegated them to a storage building where Wymond and I would climb to the dusty attic from time to time to peer at them. Only the two bear rugs finally survived to be returned to their homeland when we moved to Montana.

Forty years later, in 1946, both bear rugs were on the floor of our new ski cabin on Mount Hood. The black bear rug later was stolen, but the snarling, sharp-clawed grizzly remained at the cabin to fascinate two more generations of children. At Christmas 2000 "Big Old Bear," the grizzly, was a gift to Logan Donielson, Father's great-grandchild.

The peripatetic grizzly. Father's 100-year-old Montana grizzly bear rug and its new owner Logan Donielson.

4 INDIANA – 1919

LIFE ON THE FARM

Life on the Indiana farm was a peaceful prelude to the turbulent times ahead for us in western Montana.

To a small boy it seemed that everyone was a relative. There were *Millers, Hornadays, Kises, Rayburns, Varners, McDaniels, Schmidts and Pughs*, all descended from pioneers who had carved homes out of the Indiana wilderness in the early 1800s.

Wymond and I were two of ten cousins, and I remember a time when most of us were together at a birthday party at Grandma's house. Cousin Jack Miller has loaned me a photograph of that birthday party, which appears below.

Uncle Earl's daughter Jemima was the sedate one. She was in college and was the living image of my mother. After graduation and a brief unsuccessful first marriage, she taught high school in Detroit until her happy marriage to Burrows Corporation executive Robert Marsden.

Uncle Chester and Aunt Maeda's two boys, Asher and Jack, were closest in age to Wymond and me. Asher died when he was 14, but Jack was a stalwart 89-year-old living in Indianapolis until his death in 2005.

Duncan, the son of Uncle Carl and Aunt Jennie, was the oldest grandson and a cadet at Culver Military Academy about then. He was killed in a World War II training accident.

Marietta, the delightful tomboy daughter

Cousins at a birthday party at grandmother's house in 1922. From the top:

Harry Miller
Martha Miller
Jack Miller
George Henderson
Wymond Henderson
Marietta McDaniels
Asher Miller

of Aunt Janette and Uncle Mac, was the leader in most of our escapades. Her much-younger brother Carl, the tenth of our cousins, was born in 1930. Carl is now retired from a distinguished academic career and authors a column in *USATODAY.com*. He and his wife Ann live in Blacksburg, Virginia.

Harry and Martha, son and daughter of Uncle Harry and Aunt Carrie, were the youngest grandchildren at the party. Martha passed away in 2001 and Harry died several years earlier.

Another playmate was our second cousin Thomas Henderson, who was my age and who visited us in Montana a few years later. His older brother, Dr. Lawrence Henderson, became our family physician in Missoula and later taught us to ski.

Grandpa Miller was a portly white-mustached man near 80 whose ample lap and warm disposition were perfectly suited to holding grandchildren. Grandma Miller was a small, energetic woman, deferential to Grandpa but usually seeming to call the tune in family matters.

Grandpa and Grandma Miller in 1929

HORSE AND BUGGY

I loved to make trips with Grandpa in his horse and buggy. I would follow him as he pulled the light two-wheeled rig from the barn and led out Old Dan. If Dan hadn't had too much oats that morning he would walk to the buggy by himself and gently back between the shaves for Grandpa to harness him.

Then we would climb into the seat and pull up the warm lap robe, and Grandpa would cluck his tongue to start Old Dan. To my delight he often would hand me the lines and let me drive most of the way to Indianapolis, a snappy one-hour trot.

Uncle Willis Miller was an original environmentalist. When gasoline engines were invented, he railed at the exhaust and noise they created and finally bought a Columbia Electric brougham motor car in self-defense. I believe that Jack Miller was with me one time when we visited him and Aunt Aurelia in suburban Irvington and he treated us to a ride in the electric auto. We watched in awe as he used the single steering arm to guide the silent vehicle smoothly along the paved beech tree-bordered streets.

THE JACKRABBIT APPERSON

Indiana had a fine system of electrified interurban trains, which Mother used when she took us to the city, but when we went with Father, it was in the Jackrabbit Apperson.

When Father moved to Indiana from Montana in 1909 he was anxious to buy his first automobile and to learn to drive. The new Indianapolis Motor Speedway was nearby and being readied for the very first Indianapolis 500 Auto Race, so that was where Father went to find an expert.

Herb Lytle, a top race driver in those 75-mile-an-hour days, was delighted to advise him and to teach him to drive, so he soon was behind the wheel of a right-hand-drive, four-cylinder Jackrabbit Apperson touring car with a fold-down top and acetylene headlights.

Father had run steam-powered mills for years, but a 1909 gasoline car with inflated rubber tires pounding over roads built for wagons was a challenge. Moreover, before the days of electric starters it took a strong arm to crank the engine.

My earliest memory of Sunday afternoons on the farm is of Father laying out his tools on canvas beside the Apperson and lying under the car while he lovingly filled the grease cups, oiled every moving part, and tightened every bolt and nut.

That scene reminds me of my son Randall lovingly inspecting every moving part of the 190-mile-an-hour airplane, which he built by hand in his garage 90 years later.

"Keep it under 40, Ben," Mother would call out as Wymond and I climbed into the Apperson with Father for a trip to Indianapolis. Then as the car vibrated over the rough gravel, we would watch with fascination as the speedometer needle sought the 50-mile-an-hour mark.

Once Father took the family to an Indianapolis 500 race tryout day; we never got to see an actual race but we met one of the driver teams. In those days the driver and the mechanic both rode in the race.

THE WEST WAS CALLING!

It wasn't just the poor corn crop, or the post-World War I farm price collapse either. It was Father. Montana was calling him back.

Mother must have known. When he traveled to Guatemala in the midst of the war to survey a logging opportunity, she had to have sensed that the bonds forged by 25 years in the Bitterroots were stronger than the constraints of family and ancestry in Indiana!

The farm sale was a gala event for Wymond and me. It was better than the county fair, because we were a center of attention. Wagons and autos covered the hillside, and we were welcome at any of a dozen picnics spread among the machinery, tools and household goods by families gathered for the sale.

We were too young to grieve.

Jackrabbit Apperson – 1909. Father and Mother in front seat, Aunt Janette and Nell Hughes in back. Father bought the car in 1909 and kept it until 1920.

Our new home in Pablo Montana was a dramatic contrast with the farm home we left in Indiana. Here Mother and I are sitting on the porch, and Wymond is perched on the roof.

The showplace home Father built on his Indiana farm in 1909. Wymond and George both were born here.

5 MONTANA – 1920

In front of our cabin at the Pablo Mill in 1920. Railroad crossing on the right was where we arrived by train from Indiana. Father's sawmill, log decks and lumberyard are in the foreground with the Mission Range beyond.

INDIANA TO PABLO

Finally it was time to leave for Montana. It was a bitter-cold March day, with wind blowing snow through the corn stubble, and the family was gathered at Grandpa and Grandma Miller's house for good byes.

Wymond and I were bouncing off the walls! Our thoughts were of Indians, mountains and buffalo and we were weary of hugs and kisses.

Father was restless too. He firmly believed that he was about to emancipate his wife and children from the tedium of an Indiana farm and to share with them the joy of turning raw

natural resources into a profitable business.

Mother had no option. It was another step in her family's westward migration, which had commenced in the Scottish Highlands many generations before. Neither then nor later did I hear her complain about the decision.

The excitement began right after we boarded the sleeping car from Indianapolis to Chicago. Our eyes grew wide as we watched the Pullman porter transform our four seats into a double berth, then pull the concealed upper berth down from the ceiling and make up both with starched sheets and blankets. The climax was when he produced a wooden ladder up which Wymond and I scampered to our berth. Somehow we went to sleep.

When we woke up in Chicago the next morning, a blizzard roaring off Lake Michigan had brought city traffic almost to a standstill. To our delight, redcaps took the suitcases from our hands and hurried us through the snow to a Parmalee bus, which bounced its way through rutted streets to the Northern Pacific Railroad Station a mile away.

I was not yet 5 years old, but memories of those two days and nights on the North Coast Limited are vivid still. Mother turned the trip into a geography lesson as the train followed the Mississippi River to St. Paul, crossed the farm country of Minnesota and wheat fields of the Dakotas, and finally joined the course of the Missouri River into Montana. Our noses stayed pressed to the windows as the train climbed the eastern slope of the Rockies, alternately crossing spectacular canyons on high wooden trestles and boring through the mountains in long tunnels.

There was no air conditioning, so passengers often opened car windows for ventilation, and then when the train entered a tunnel they hurried to close them to keep out smoke and cinders. Once Wymond and I started at the same time to close one of the heavy steel sashes, and it came down on my little finger! Boy did I yell! It took months for the nail to grow back.

Meals in the diner were memorable too, as we watched the stewards gracefully maintain their balance in the swaying car while carrying heavy food-laden trays above their heads.

REAL LIVE INDIANS!

"Indian! Indian! Indian!" Wymond shouted, pointing, as we stepped off the North Coast Limited in Missoula. Sure enough, standing on the platform was a group of Flathead Indians dressed in moccasins and blankets and wearing their hair in long braids, waiting to board a train to the reservation.

Mother's hope for a circumspect arrival was shattered, but the Donlan family who was there to greet us had young children too, so they were not fazed by Wymond's outburst. We stayed at their home on Gerald Ave. for two days while Father and his partner Ed Donlan talked business and Mother and we boys were shown the sights of Missoula.

Our odyssey was ending. The next day we boarded a combination freight and passenger train to Pablo 60 miles north on the edge of the Flathead Indian Reservation.

A BLEAK LANDSCAPE

When we stepped off the train at a grade crossing a mile beyond town we had our first view of our future home. An unpainted house and a shed near the tracks were the only signs of habitation among miles of snow covered wheat fields. However when the train pulled out, we saw on the other side of the tracks a sawmill in full operation surrounded by shops, barns and bunkhouses. Beyond the mill was an almost unbroken ponderosa pine forest and, in the background, the snow-clad Mission Range highlighted by a frozen waterfall sparkling in the clear air.

Father had come to Montana earlier to get the new venture under way and then gone back to Indiana for us. He had contracted for timber from the Flathead Indian tribe and already cut and shipped the first lumber before we arrived.

Father knew the business well and the mill would soon show a profit. Stacks of finished lumber were air-drying beside the railroad track, and a supply of logs was in decks ready for the saw. He had lost a small fortune farming in Indiana but he was on his way to becoming a wealthy man again.

Two mill hands carried our bags to the house that was warmed by fires in a big kitchen range and a living room stove. The only indoor plumbing was cold water piped from a spring

Finished lumber air-drying at the Pablo Mill. "Father had already cut and shipped the first lumber before we arrived."

Ponderosa pine logs decked at the Pablo mill. "A supply of logs was in decks ready for the saw."

but limited hot water would come from pipes running through the stove's firebox.

Suddenly we realized that the shed seen from the train was a two-hole unheated privy standing only a few yards from the back door. That and a galvanized washtub would serve our bathroom needs for the next three years. The two rooms already overflowed with our household goods, so Father quickly called in carpenters from the mill to add a bedroom that became "the boys' room."

Father had stocked the cabin with basic food supplies, but that night we ate supper with the loggers in the camp cookhouse before returning to spend the first night in our new home on the Flathead.

BARE BOTTOMS IN THE SNOW

Boy, was that snow cold. Father had just pulled Wymond and me out of our warm bed, opened the cabin door, and tossed us into a snow bank, then he followed and began rolling with us in the fluffy powder. Mother met us at the door with warm Turkish towels which she had rinsed in salt water before they dried, making them sandpaper-rough. They rubbed our skin bright red and warmed us in a hurry. It was one of our first mornings on the Flathead and we found that this would be a regular winter ritual. Father believed in cold baths, and the cabin had no bathroom. I have taken cold showers ever since.

THE ICE HARVEST

"What's an ice harvest?" we wondered one morning in late March as Mother rousted us out of bed early. She said that Father would meet us soon with one of the logging sleighs for a ride to the frozen lake where ice was being cut for the summer. After bacon, eggs and fresh fried potatoes, we bundled into our warmest clothes just as a pair of high-stepping horses pulled an empty logging sleigh up in front of the cabin. The sleigh had been converted to carry ice by adding high wooden sides.

When we reached the lake, horse-drawn road scrapers were clearing off the snow to reveal a crisscross of deep ruts, which had been

George watching horse team and sleigh hauling logs through a field of stumps to Pablo Mill in 1920. On the right is the logging wagon used in the summer.

plowed in the ice during the winter. Then they pulled heavy sharp-toothed ice plows along the ruts, cutting the ice into 300-pound blocks. After being pried loose with picks and long chisels, the blocks were grabbed by huge ice tongs and slid onto the sleighs with block and tackle. A parade of sleighs soon was hauling the blocks to the icehouse, where they were piled to the roof, separated only by thin layers of sawdust.

Later Father showed us the new icehouse near the camp cookhouse. It had double walls filled with six inches of sawdust. He said that the ice would last all summer as we confirmed to our delight the next August on 110-degree days, when we sometimes slipped inside for a contraband respite from the heat.

Mother told us that ice harvesting was a major industry, and that most homes in cities had insulated "ice boxes" with top compartments holding 50-pound blocks of ice replenished from ice wagons on the street.

She said that in Indiana natural ice was cut from frozen rivers and lakes, and it was used to refrigerate railroad cars for carrying perishables. In New York the Hudson River was the source of ice for cold storage plants. Air conditioning for offices, stores, hotels and homes was still in the future.

SUDDENLY IT WAS SPRING

Spring seemed to pounce out of a snow bank in the Flathead. One morning we awoke to hear Father calling, "Boys, we're having a Chinook!" As we stepped outside for our roll in the snow we felt a warm wind blowing from the Mission Range, its searching fingers caressing the snow banks behind our cabin. It was the unseasonably warm Chinook wind, which often is a harbinger of spring in Montana.

The warm weather soon turned roads into muddy morasses. All winter long we had watched high-stepping horses pull steel-runnered log-laden sleighs from woods to sawmill over frozen roads, their harness bells ringing out in the crisp cold air. Now sleighs gave way to wagons whose narrow wheels sank so deep into the mud that the horses didn't have firm enough footing to pull the loads.

NO MORE SLEIGH BELLS

There would be no more morning rolls in the snow, for Father was facing a crisis. Just as the season for home building in the Midwest was peaking and orders for carload lots of lumber were pouring in, the mill was running out of logs. The stacks of lumber along the railroad siding would be shipped out soon, and the decks of logs in the mill yard were dwindling fast. It was our first lesson in economics!

BIG WHEELS AND CATERPILLARS

Always an innovator, Father had bought a gasoline-powered Holt tractor the previous fall. It was among the first track-laying tractors in Montana and was a precursor of the famous Caterpillars. He hired Ed Donlan's oldest son, Arthur, to operate it, and a factory man taught him to maintain it. Although the huge machine had performed pretty well on hard earth the year before, it couldn't cope with the soft sand and mud of spring.

The teamsters guffawed at Arthur and his ponderous pony, but to us boys he was what an astronaut was to a later generation. Arthur basked in our adulation and sometimes allowed us to scramble up and cling to him in his seat for brief forbidden rides through the pines. Nevertheless, the teamsters had the last laugh when the tractor became so badly bogged down one day that Arthur had to call for their help. It took several teams hitched in tandem to extricate him.

Father then turned to another log-hauling system: High Wheels. A pair of giant wheels on a sturdy axle were to be used to lift loads of logs clear of the ground so that they could be pulled to the mill with horses. Wymond and I expected the wheels to be the size of carnival ferris wheels, but when a trial pair arrived, we were disappointed to see that they stood only about twice the height of a man. They straddled the muddy roads all right but they didn't solve the problem of traction for the horses.

WE BECOME RAILROADERS

The Shay Company and others had developed lightweight, geared, all-wheel-drive steam locomotives to haul loads of logs up slopes too steep for regular steam trains. Father decided to apply that same system to the problem of traction in the soft soil of the Flathead. We watched the fallers and buckers continue to add to the supply of logs in the woods, using cant hooks to roll them into decks by hand, but they couldn't get them to the sawmill by hand.

Father had small cant hooks made for Wymond and me to practice with. Mine now hangs on the wall of our Mount Hood cabin.

Even before the powerful little locomotive was delivered, the logging crew had spiked lightweight rails to wooden ties made at the mill, creating a network of tracks leading from the woods right to the millpond. It was an expensive gamble but a real success. Logging crews learned to move the tracks quickly, and before long the inventories of both finished lumber and logs were back to normal. The crisis was over.

LOST ON A RACE TRACK

Many roads had been impassable until late May, and we hadn't yet seen much of the countryside, so on a sunny spring day Father took us on a sightseeing trip. He folded down the top of the Buick touring car and drove south through Ronan and St. Ignatius to Missoula and then up the Clark Fork River through Hellgate Canyon and along the Big

Blackfoot River to the Bonner mill, where Father had gotten his first job when he came to Montana 35 years before.

Then just at dusk as we started home, a thunderstorm struck with heavy winds and rain; I remember the confusion as Wymond and I tried to help Father and Mother fight the wind and put up the car's ungainly top and snap in the isinglass rain curtains.

"I thought we just passed that grandstand," Mother remarked an hour later, looking back at rain-drenched benches beside the road. Father was watching ahead through the mud-splattered windshield, steering with one hand and sweeping the single wiper blade to and fro with the other. Wymond and I were peering at the road through the fogged-up curtains.

"There's another grandstand," Wymond shouted shortly. Father braked and climbed out in the rain and mud for a look. Then he realized that he had taken a wrong turn leaving the last town and we were driving around and around on the racetrack at the county fairgrounds! He had to chain up and make one more round of the track before finding the right road on thru Ronan to Pablo.

FLATHEAD LAKE

Pablo is in the heart of the spectacular Flathead Valley, 150 miles south of Glacier National Park and near the Canadian border, and Flathead Lake would be our next sightseeing destination.

Polson at the south end of the lake was only five miles from our sawmill, but the road was steep and crooked, so we hadn't gone there during the winter. It was Mother's first trip over a mountain road, and she would never forget it. Whipping around the narrow switchbacks with no guardrails and with deep valleys on either side was exciting to us boys but it frightened Mother almost to tears. Father's attempt to calm her by pointing out the beauties of the lake with one hand while casually steering the car with the other just made it worse.

Perhaps it was part of his nature as a fighting man, but Father never seemed to have empathy for emotions of fear or pain in others. Mother never did lose her fear of mountain driving, although I always thought that riding at a gallop across fields and over fences in a sidesaddle as she had done would have been even more frightening.

There was no road around the east side of Flathead Lake. However after a calming stop for huckleberry pie and ice cream in the Polson cafe, we followed a good gravel road on the lake's west side. We drove through lush farms and cherry orchards to Kalispell near the north end of the lake and then on to Whitefish near the British Columbia border.

Mother hadn't learned to drive the 1909 Apperson in Indiana, but on the return trip to Polson in the Buick she received her first driving lesson. Wymond would start school in Pablo that fall and driving would be essential. However Father did not include the stretch from Polson to Pablo in her first lesson.

THE BUFFALO NICKEL

Like a buffalo nickel, Pablo had a buffalo on one side of it and an Indian on the other. Five-cent coins then carried beautiful engravings of a bull buffalo on one side and of an Indian chief on the other, while on one side of the town of Pablo was the American Bison Reserve and on the other side was the Flathead Indian Reservation.

One morning when Mother handed each of us his weekend allowance of a buffalo nickel, Wymond studied the engravings on his for a few moments then looked up to complain, "We've been in Montana for months now, so why haven't we seen a buffalo or even an Indian teepee?"

Father spoke up. "We can remedy that today," he said with a laugh, adding that the Flathead Valley might be the only place in the world where buffalo and Indians could be seen on the same day's drive. It was Saturday and, Mother began filling her picnic basket.

She had been studying Montana history, and during the drive to the Flathead Valley she told us some of the sad story of American buffalo and American Indians. Almost all of the millions of buffalo that once roamed the West had been killed by hunters, she said, and white settlers had taken much of the Indians' ancestral land, so all but a few remaining buffalo and many of the Flathead Indians now were protected in government reservations right here on the Flathead.

Years earlier when the buffalo had been nearing extinction, the United States had established a National Bison Range at Moiese, Montana, between Missoula and Pablo, so by 1920 several hundred of the great beasts roamed its 18,000 acres.

Nevertheless, when we reached the strong steel fence that enclosed the reserve, we saw nary a buffalo. Mother spread out our picnic lunch on a blanket so that we could eat while keeping watch for our quarry.

"Like a buffalo nickel, Pablo had a buffalo on one side of it and an Indian on the other."

Finally we saw our first buffalo!

Father was using Mother's bird-watching field glasses and spotted a lone buffalo far across the miles of grass-covered rangeland. Excitedly passing the glasses back and forth, each of us caught sight of what Father said was a buffalo, although I wasn't sure that I could have told a Montana buffalo and an Indiana milk cow apart at that distance.

Fortunately we made many trips to Missoula that summer, and if we watched carefully we usually were rewarded with buffalo sightings. On one lucky day, a big buffalo bull came right up to the fence, and Mother was able to take a close-up picture of the shaggy-coated, humpbacked beast.

HUNTING FOR INDIANS

"Now let's go hunt Indians!" Father said smiling, and to our delight, he drove us right to the summer encampment of the Flatheads, with its acres of brightly decorated teepees. He knew the tribal leaders because he was buying reservation timber for our sawmill under contract with the tribe. Many of the Indians were dressed in beaded buckskins, moccasins and colorful blankets and wore their hair in waist-long braids.

The Flatheads were artistic craftsmen, and because it was a weekend there was a sizable assortment of beaded baskets, bowls covered with delicately woven maidenhair fern stems, beaded gloves and soft buckskin clothing displayed in front of many teepees.

One wrinkled Indian brave was wearing an elaborate headdress made of eagle feathers, beaded buckskin clothing and knee-high moccasins and was smoking an elaborately decorated pipe. When Mother asked if she might take a picture of him in front of his teepee his squaws carefully blocked her view until Father explained what payment likely was expected. Mother was thrilled and that day began her rare collection of Flathead artifacts,

which she acquired over the next several years.

YELLOWSTONE PARK

By July the roads were dry and dusty. Remembering his first trip to Yellowstone National Park years before, Father was as anxious to see it again as he was to show its volcanic wonders to the family. We all helped pack the Buick with food, tents, bedding, tools, spare tires and extra repair parts for the 300-mile drive across the Continental Divide.

There were no hard-surfaced highways in Montana outside of cities then, but most roads were graveled. A few intersections had directional signs, but finding the right route depended mostly on a telephone pole code that Wymond and I learned how to follow. It was sort of like a treasure hunt. Phone lines paralleled most roads, and rings of various colors were painted around some of the poles. Father had a map that decoded the scheme. The transcontinental highway we followed had red, white and blue rings on its poles. At main intersections Father sometimes made several false starts before selecting the right route. It took most of a week to drive from Missoula to Old Faithful Inn.

Yellowstone park, with the world's largest geyser field, frightened me. When a geyser would erupt without warning nearby, I would flee, and as we watched the colorful bubbling "paint pots" suck down tourists' handkerchiefs and spew them back out, I pictured myself being sucked into that scalding cauldron.

I admired the grandeur of Yellowstone Falls and enjoyed watching the yellow open-topped sightseeing buses filled with gaily dressed tourists. Father described to us how different the park had been when he had driven four-horse teams there 30 years earlier.

Wymond was fearless and would have hand-fed the grizzly bears at the garbage dump if our parents had let him, but I had heard too many stories of people being mauled by

Grizzlies so observed the garbage pit feeding frenzy from afar.

HUNTERS HOT SPRINGS

Highlights of the Yellowstone trip for me were the many stops we made along the way. Best of all was Hunters Hot Springs. It was a resort near West Yellowstone that boasted the largest mineral water swimming pool in Montana and had a water slide that began near the rafters. We hadn't learned to swim yet, but while Mother watched fearfully, Father allowed us to climb to the top for breathless slides into the water, where he waited at the bottom to retrieve us.

I am reminded of a natural water slide among the cliffs of Kauai in Hawaii, where a half-century later, 5-year-old Darcy made similar slides, to her Mother's horror, and was retrieved from the pool at the bottom by her siblings and me.

Mineral baths were highly recommended for rheumatism so we stopped a few days at the hot springs both coming and going.

On the trip back to Missoula, Mother's fear of mountain roads was proved to have been justified. As we crossed a high ridge and were driving down a steep grade there came

Uncle Carl visited Pablo in 1920 and was the principal player in the ticktack caper.

a sudden bump and the car lurched to a stop. Mother was looking into the deep valley on her right when a wheel rolled quietly past between the car and the road's edge, then toppled over in the road. It was our right rear tire and rim that had come off, dropping the wheel itself onto the ground! The repair was simple, but we had been lucky. Happily that was the only car problem I remember on the entire trip.

THE TICKTACK CAPER

Our cabin on the Flathead had no spare room so when Uncle Carl came for a visit that summer and Father settled him in another cabin near the mill, Wymond and I saw an opportunity for some fun. We figured that an easterner such as Uncle Carl might be scared on his first night alone in the West, so we decided to help that scare along.

Father had told us that when he was a boy, neighborhood kids used to bedevil newlyweds by "ticktacking" their bedroom walls. By fastening a string tautly to a nail in the side of a frame house and rubbing the string with rosin, the whole house could be made to vibrate with a loud, spooky hum.

Father became our co-conspirator. He helped us drive a large nail into the thin outside wall of the guest cabin and run several feet of strong twine to a hiding spot behind some nearby rocks. We tested the scheme and were delighted with the result. Our ticktack was ready!

After supper, we boys walked in the dark across the tracks with Father and Uncle Carl and waited while they discussed stoking the wood stove for the night, bolting the door from the inside and turning off the gasoline lantern. Finally we all said good night and as the cabin door closed Father held his lantern high so that Wymond and I could run to our hideout among the rocks.

Father walked away with the lantern, and it became pitch dark in our redoubt except for the faint light from the cabin window. As we huddled together shivering from the night air and from our keyed-up nerves, it seemed that Uncle Carl would never go to bed. Finally his light faded out and we could wait no longer.

I pulled the string as taut as I could and Wymond began to rub it with the rosin. Sure enough, the cabin began to moan. The sound seemed spookier and louder in the dark, sending chills up our spines.

Then things happened fast. There was a roar from Uncle Carl as he burst through the door in his nightshirt, rattling a big logging chain and starting to circle the cabin while stumbling in the dark. We were a couple of scared kids and rushed over to the road where we knew Father would be waiting. He quietly smuggled us back to our own cabin where we excitedly reported our adventure to Mother, then piled into bed smug with our success.

Long after midnight, we were awakened by a commotion in the next room. We peered in and saw Uncle Carl seated beside a washbasin, while Mother applied iodine and bandages to cuts and bruises over much of his head and shoulders.

Then we learned the aftermath of our night's mischief. Mother had known that her brother was subject to nightmares and sleep walking, so she had forewarned him of our planned ticktack trick. Thus he had been ready with the satisfying response to our deviltry, but later that night he had suffered a real nightmare, jumped out of bed and dived headfirst through the cabin's only window.

His injuries weren't permanent, and after a lengthy visit he was able to return to his thriving farm machinery business in Iowa. A few years later, when I was 12, Mother and I visited Uncle Carl and Aunt Jennie in Des Moines, and I learned to drive a Model T Ford. He became my favorite uncle.

Another time, when Wymond and I were in high school, Aunt Jennie visited us in Portland and we guided her and Father on a climb to the summit of Mount Hood. See Chapter 17 for the story of that climb.

SECTION SEVEN

Walking along an unused logging road east of Pablo, you could smell Section Seven before you reached it. A pungent odor wafted from the swamp, and you knew it was from the lush, green leaves of the bright, yellow-hooded blossomed Lysichitum americanum (some call it skunk cabbage) that grew in the pond.

You might hear frogs too, if they didn't hear you first. Then through a screen of hellebore you could see the ebony surface of the great swamp reflecting the dark, overhanging forest, its surface tension broken only by the fleeting tracks of skippers scuttling about searching for whatever skippers search for.

As you stepped barefoot into the soft mud, you could feel it squishing up between your toes. That was the fourth of the senses that created the magic of Section Seven.

At the edge of the bog were delicate white bog orchids and in the moist earth and moss were Indian pipes and pink lady's-slippers. A field of blue camas interspersed with white arrowhead Wapato flowers stretched beyond.

At first it seemed dead still, but as you sat on the bank and unwrapped your sandwich, you were aware of insect noises, birdcalls, the sound of a frog plunking into the pool and, soon, the rustle of a chipmunk that had picked up the scent of the sandwich.

Mother had known most of the native flowers and plants of Indiana, and it delighted her to identify many of them in Montana and to find others that she had never seen. We learned to recognize the yellow monkey flowers, purple shooting stars, white petaled marsh marigolds, yellow pond lilies, fringed water plantain and, farther back from the bank, brilliant blue gentians.

The *chweeee* trill of a Spotted Towhee turned your attention upward, and you saw a crossbill warbler among the branches busily harvesting pine nuts with its specialized beak. A brown creeper clung to a trunk, probing the bark for insects. Mother showed us how the larvae of some flying insects secreted a sticky substance that collected an armor of tiny gravel around their cocoons to protect them while they lay on the bottom of the pool or creek waiting to hatch out.

Although the name Section Seven was just a surveyor's designation of a certain square mile of land near the Mission Range, it evokes magical memories for me, for it was where Mother introduced Wymond and me to wilderness botany.

THE ELUSIVE WATERFALL

High above Section Seven was the glittering waterfall that we had first sighted when we stepped off the train from Indiana. On freezing winter days it appeared as a shimmering sheet of sheer crystal covering a fancied window into the heart of the Mission Range, but on warm summer evenings its unleashed waters reflected the blended gold and purple hues that line Montana's sunset clouds.

Seen from our cabin far below, it nestled like a jewel in a setting of dark green forests. I decided that one day I would climb to its top. Mother compared the unnamed waterfall with Yellowstone Falls, and I said that ours was probably as big. Of course Wymond disagreed, declaring that it would only take us an hour to hike up and find out – if I wasn't afraid to try!

Father agreed to help settle the argument, so one Sunday Mother packed lunches and we began the trek. Father shouldered a knapsack and led us past the sawmill, through the lumber camp and along one of the new railroad tracks that led to the base of the mountain.

AN UNLIKELY CLIMBING TEAM

It was as unlikely a climbing team as I have ever been a part of. I was a chubby 5-year-old, Wymond was a self-important 6 and Mother was a carefully attired lady wearing riding breeches, high laced boots and a fashionable wide-brimmed hat. Father strode in front dressed in his usual work clothes.

If the logging crew lounging beside the bunkhouse was amused as the boss and his Midwestern family passed by, Father certainly didn't give a damn.

I am certain that Father realized from the beginning that the climb was beyond our ability, but he didn't let on. There was no trail, so before starting he pointed out the contours and his proposed route. The waterfall was at the head of a deep gulch with narrow ridges called hogbacks on either side. He explained that when we entered the timber we would not be able to see our goal again until we got to the bare top of a hogback, so we should watch our back trail so that we could find our way home.

It was my first mountain climb, and that briefing and the sight of our disparate little party remain clear in my mind today.

I was the first to wear out, and after Father carried me for a while, Wymond's bragging rights were secure so he, too, gave up. Mother's rheumatism was paining her so she was ready to turn back.

The climb ended halfway to the top of the hogback with a picnic of lemonade, sandwiches, deviled eggs and huckleberry pie. We never made a second assault on the elusive waterfall.

SNOWSHOE RABBITS

We learned about sex from a snowshoe rabbit! All winter we had watched the snow-white, long eared rabbits leap lightly along on the soft snow as we struggled knee-deep trying to catch them. As the snow melted we saw their fur slowly lose its camouflage of white and turn a brownish gray to match the summer sagebrush. In summer they were called jackrabbits.

We wanted to catch one, so Father showed us how. First we learned to track them. They left only three footprints: one for each of the large back feet, which propelled their long leaps, and another one where their two front feet landed tight together. Then we followed the tracks until we found one of their haunts: an opening in a small thicket with overhanging branches. There we set our first box trap.

The trap was simple. It had three parts: a wooden apple box, a figure-four trigger carved with a pocketknife from three wooden sticks, and a carrot for bait. We caught a rabbit the first day.

When we saw that the trap was tripped, we ran and got Father to come and remove our quarry. Reaching into the box he pulled out a plump rabbit by his long ears and held him up so we could see his feet. The large hind feet each had four toes spread widely to create snowshoes that allowed him to move easily over the snow.

Wymond and I took turns holding the agitated animal, while Father fashioned a cage of chickenwire behind our cabin and Mother put some sacking and a supply of vegetables on the floor. However our rabbit wouldn't stay on the makeshift bed and kept jumping against the fence, frantic to get out. Finally we tired of teasing him and went to bed.

The next morning when we peered into the cage we learned about sex! There were eight furry baby rabbits nestled in the sacking, their eyes wide open and their little mouths competing for the mother's milk.

Our "he" was a "she," and her agitation had been to try to get out of the cage and find a place in the woods to bear her litter!

Mother was perplexed. She had raised rabbits in Indiana for years, but those were born blind and naked. She learned later that our rabbits were not true rabbits but snowshoe hares common to Canada and the Arctic and found in the U.S. only in small areas near the Rocky Mountains and the Appalachians.

Our "snowshoe rabbit" at Pablo, 1920. The correct name is snowshoe hare.

We quickly improved the makeshift hutch with more bedding, sunshades and a steady supply of vegetables and green pine twigs.

Within a few months the rabbits were tame and the cage was left open. At Christmas we even put a special Christmas tree in the yard for the rabbits and decorated it with rabbit food hung from the limbs.

To us they always were rabbits. We never got around to calling them hares.

SCHOOL DAYS

Mother might have schooled us at home – after all, she had taught primary grades in Clermont for 10 years before she married Father – but he believed that experience in the schoolyard was as important to a boy's education as was the schoolroom itself.

So Mother would watch us through field glasses most mornings as we walked the railroad ties from our sawmill to Pablo. It was only a bit more than a mile, but on our left

Pablo Montana public schools, 1920. Grade school on left and the high school on right. This is where the Indian boys pretended to scalp Wymond and me.

was unbroken forest rising to the white-clad summit of the Mission Range, and on our right was "the Swede's wheatfield."

Sure the forest was home to bears, cougars, wildcats, lynxes and wolves, but in the quarter-century that Father had lived in the mountains he had not heard of a child ever being attacked by a wild beast, and the rattlesnakes in the Swede's wheatfield only crawled onto the railroad track to sun themselves and were easily evaded – weren't they?

Sixty years later on a backpacking trip into the Mission Range wilderness, I watched a gray wolf trot ahead of me across a snowfield above Gray Wolf Lake and wondered if one of his ancestors might have been watching Wymond and me while Mother was watching us walk to school those mornings.

Wymond had turned 6 in March so he began school that fall of 1920. I wouldn't be ready until 1921, but as brave as he usually was, when Mother took him to school the first morning Wymond wouldn't allow her to leave unless I stayed with him. So for several weeks we attended first grade together.

We were among the few white children in the class, and that resulted in some memorable moments. One morning during recess, a group of Indian boys took us behind the outhouse and holding us by the hair drew the cold steel of their knives around our heads. They said they were going to cut off our scalps and hang them on their saddles when they rode home from school that night.

Our teacher came to the rescue and assured us the Indians were using the backs of their knives to scare us, but that scene is still my clearest memory of school days in Pablo.

THE MOONSHINER'S SON

I also remember Pete. Pete was a strapping half-breed who was enrolled in first grade for the second or third time. Reservation Indians attended good schools run by the U.S. Bureau of Indian Affairs, but other Indian and white children in Pablo went to public school.

During the two years that Wymond and I were there, the average teacher's tenure probably was less than two months, and some days no teacher showed up at all. Then Mother or another parent might fill in. Of course students with special needs such as Pete simply took the same grade repeatedly.

Prohibition became the law in 1919, creating a completely new industry of bootlegging and moonshining, and Pete's father was in the forefront. Homemade whisky sometimes caused blindness or even death, so of course Father had no thought of buying any. However one day Pete's father came by our cabin hoping to sell some to Father. Afterward Father reported the conversation.

"How do you know it won't kill people who drink it?" Father asked, and Pete's father replied, "You know my boy Pete? Well, when I make a new batch I always give Pete all he can drink. If it don't kill Pete, it won't kill you!"

Between teacher shortage, illness and blizzards we missed many days of school each year. When we stayed at home Mother taught us and kept us well ahead of our grade levels.

SCALPS AND SCALPELS

It began with a bellyache that wouldn't quit! Mother applied the usual remedies and it got worse. I had just started first grade and was still worrying that the Indian kids might scalp me as they had threatened to do the year before. Mightn't that give a bellyache even to a grownup? But Wymond had been in school for a year already and he still had his hair!

Country doctors made house calls in those days, but Dr. Hobson in Polson could not come to Pablo that time. Father's distrust of doctors was outweighed by his love for his family, and at Mother's urging, he bundled us into the Buick for a snowy drive over the mountain.

Dr. Hobson's diagnosis was quick: "Acute appendicitis; we should operate tonight." Neither Father nor Mother was willing to approve such sudden and drastic action. They knew that Thornton Brothers Hospital in Missoula was highly regarded, so Dr. Hobson agreed to accompany the family to Missoula to consult with Dr. Owens, a prominent surgeon there. (I do not remember the first name of either of those doctors.)

Dr. Hobson provided hot packs to lessen the ache in my belly on our trip back across the mountain – perhaps the only practical treatment available before antibiotics.

The next day Dr. Hobson was aboard the morning freight train from Polson when it stopped for us at the sawmill, and he rode with us to Missoula.

Dr. Owens was waiting at the hospital. He confirmed the need for immediate surgery, and our parents agreed, but Father told me later that even then he was not fully convinced that I should "go under the knife," as he put it. He described vividly how he had stood with the two doctors during the operation. When the appendix was removed he had thrust out his hand saying, "Give me that!" and kept it in his hand until the operation was over.

I didn't die, and afterward the doctors showed him that the offending organ had been "as thin as tissue paper and ready to burst." He said, too, that there was a piece of string inside the appendix.

Of course my memory of the experience is so intertwined with what I was told later that I can't separate the two, but I do remember the aftermath clearly: adhesions!

I was kept in bed for more than a week and not allowed even to turn over or to "strain my insides." Mother stayed in my hospital room

The family picking huckleberries during Grandpa and Grandma Miller's Montana visit. Left to right: Verlinda Miller Henderson, Grandma Miller, unknown, Ben Henderson, George Henderson, unknown, Grandpa Miller, and Wymond Henderson.

day and night and enforced the orders, but when I finally was allowed to move I found that the inactivity had permitted many things inside me to stick themselves together, and as they pulled apart, they hurt like knife thrusts.

They were called adhesions and lasted for many years. Even in high school when I started gymnastics I frequently had similar sharp pains, which I blamed on the adhesions, but I had no other after-effects.

During World War II when I sailed for many months at a time on ships with no medic aboard, the adhesions were gone, and I was thankful that I need not worry about a possible emergency appendectomy.

SEVENTY-FIVE CANDLES

Mother wasn't one to brag, but when it came to angel food cakes she wore her pride on her sleeve. Her cakes won blue ribbons for texture and flavor at county fairs, and the family just didn't feel that a birthday was complete without one of "Linnie's angel foods."

That skill was about to be tested by Grandpa Miller's 75th birthday celebration. He and Grandma had come west in August for a visit, and although his birthday wasn't until December, Mother wanted to celebrate it with him so she promised him an angel food cake with 75 candles.

That took some planning. Mother used 11 egg whites in her angel foods and they always rose above the top of a standard cake pan. The problem was that if the oven temperature wasn't constant or there was any vibration while the cake was rising, it would fall and be ruined.

It was too hot to fire up the big kitchen range, so she would have to coax the light metal coal oil summer stove to hold a steady heat. We boys had long known to stay away from the house when Mother had a cake in the

Yellow Beach at Flathead Lake, Montana. Wymond and I are standing in the water.

oven, but when trains came by the cabin the whole building would shake, and the freight trains had no regular schedule.

Her careful planning was rewarded. While the family waited in the back yard among the jackrabbits, she slipped the cake pan into the sheet metal oven and sat quietly until the cake had risen and she could invert it in its extra tall pan to cool. It was a beauty!

What was the secret of Mother's success with angel food cakes? Maybe it was her disdain for cream of tarter. Often when she tasted someone else's prized cake she would sniff and say, "Do you taste that cream of tarter?" Or perhaps it was that she used 11 egg whites while most recipes call for ten. More likely, it was just her skill in blending the ingredients and controlling the baking process.

Grandpa was so proud! During his party the next day he drew in a big breath and blew out all 75 candles at once. He did not know that two small but playful boys surreptitiously blew from either side, and we never told him.

PICKING HUCKLEBERRIES

One sunny August morning soon after my sixth birthday, we all walked over to the grade crossing with Mother to wait for the train to Missoula. We knew that the pain in her joints was much worse and that she was going to the doctor for several days of treatment, leaving Father and us boys to bach for ourselves.

As the train pulled away Father said, "Come on boys, let's go huckleberry picking while she's gone!" We hurried to the cabin, and Father began loading pots, pans, food and blankets into the Buick and telling us what to put into our own small packs. It all went so smoothly that we should have realized that Mother had planned the whole affair, but Father made us think that it was a secret.

The road to Polson at the south end of Flathead Lake was familiar, but our adventure would begin after Father turned onto the single-lane dirt road, which clung precariously to the Mission Range on the lake's mountain-flanked east side. Father said that because the road ended just beyond Yellow Bay, he expected no oncoming traffic, but after an hour here came a big White truck of the kind used to haul troops in the recent war. The two cars stopped head-to-head and we listened with trepidation as Father and the truck's driver conferred in the middle of the road. There was no room to pass, so someone would have to back up. Finally, they decided that the nearest wide place in the road behind us was closer than a similar passing spot behind the truck, so it was up to Father to do the backing.

He told Wymond and me to follow the Buick on foot with the truck following on our heels as he backed our car carefully along the twisting road. After a quarter-mile he found a wide spot and pulled close beside the cliff, while the truck crept gingerly by above the lake. The driver said there were no other cars between us and the end of the road, so we started on.

At Yellow Bay a stream rushing down from the mountain had created a gentle sand beach, and when Father stopped the car all three of us ran for the clear cold water, rolling up our pants on the way.

At moments like this, we were shocked to see how badly Father's back was scarred. Some of the injuries may have been from rough-and-tumble fights, but he said that most were from accidents in the woods or in sawmills.

He told us about a time when a circular saw had exploded, sending a piece of steel through his cheek and jaw and taking two teeth with it. While the filer replaced the saw, Father staunched the blood and went on to finish the day's work. Then he walked three miles to the railroad and caught a ride on a freight train to the nearest town where there was a doctor to sew up the wound.

The next morning he boarded the return freight train and after another three-mile walk was only a little late for work. That scar was almost hidden by his full mustache.

We reached the end of the road by mid-afternoon, but the trip was far from over. Father loaded most of the supplies into his pack and assigned some lightweight items to us, and we started up through the trees.

We learned that huckleberries grow well in old burns where they are open to sunlight, and we were headed for such a spot about two miles above. There was not much undergrowth in the yellow pine forest, so it was good footing, but the way was steep. Father would not tolerate many rests and told us instead to slow almost to a stop when we got tired but to keep going. However when we reached the huckleberry patch, our fatigue left us as we stuffed ourselves with the glossy black fruit.

We gathered firewood from the forest floor, and soon Father had a campfire going and served a supper of pork chops, sourdough biscuits and gravy. We topped that off by roasting marshmallows for as long as we could keep our eyes open.

UNDER THE STARS

Father didn't carry a tent but spread blankets over a soft bed of fragrant evergreen boughs and kept a slicker handy in case of rain. There was ample room for the three of us, and because I was the smallest, I got to sleep in the middle, protected from bears by Wymond on one side and Father on the other.

That was our first night sleeping under the stars, and none of the many hundred since has seemed to me to be its equal.

When we awoke in the morning Father already was picking berries, but he had sourdough batter ready for hotcakes, which we devoured along with bacon and eggs and syrup out of a classic tin Log Cabin can.

We picked berries by the bucketfuls that day, and Wymond tried hard to pick the most, but when we got home it was reported that my little one-quart bucket seemed never to have gotten full. I was either the slowest picker or the fastest eater!

Supper that evening was fried chicken, which Mother had cooked ahead along with sourdough biscuits and honey. We fell asleep listening to Father tell stories of summers 30 years earlier when he had camped like this in the North Cascades of Washington while prospecting for gold.

The next morning, after eggs and pancakes smothered in huckleberries, we broke camp early in order to get the berries home to be canned right away.

If there was oncoming traffic on the one-lane road that morning, we must have met at places where there was room to pass, for we arrived at the sawmill in time for the cook to put up the berries in Mason jars that same day. It was a favor he had promised to Mother.

6 MISSOULA

Launching my balsa wood airplane in front of our new home at 315 Daly Ave., Missoula, Montana.

A BRICK HOUSE

Nineteen twenty-two had been a banner year. Father's skills as a lumberman were paying off, and the new sawmill was making money. There were thousands of feet of air-dried pine lumber stacked ready to ship and a year's supply of logs in decks waiting for the saw; however, Mother was suffering.

Two years of blistering summers and snowbound winters in our tiny cabin on the fringe of the Indian reservation had taken their toll. Not only had her formerly robust health given way to crippling arthritis, but her active intellect was being dulled by isolation from other adults.

A year earlier doctors had decided that infected teeth caused the rheumatism, so one day she took the train to Missoula and had them all pulled. That hadn't helped either.

Father did not understand or even sense her needs, but at last he realized that the family he adored was in crisis and that a partial solution might be for Mother and us boys to move to Missoula before the next school year began.

He took fast action, and soon we owned a new three-bedroom brick house a few blocks from the University of Montana, near the new Paxson grade school and close to the palatial home of the Donlans on Gerald Ave.. It had indoor plumbing, central heating, electric lights and even a dial telephone.

NEW KIDS ON THE BLOCK

Neighbors gaped from their porches in late August as we and our belongings arrived at sedate 315 Daly Ave. atop two horse-drawn lumber wagons, with Wymond seated beside one teamster and I beside the other. We jumped to the ground and headed for the nearest tree, then learned that the entire outdoors no longer would be our bathroom.

Now that we were to become city dwellers we were bound to miss the freedom to run our trap lines in the Mission Range but we still could look forward to spending summers at the cabin on the Flathead.

After visiting Missoula Mercantile to replace our logging camp clothes with school outfits, the Donlans' high school-age son Morris showed us around our new environs.

Radio and television broadcasting hadn't been invented, but there were silent black-and-white movies with live piano music at the Bluebird Theater, and on Saturdays we could watch Tom Mix westerns and Charlie Chaplin and Harold Lloyd comedies for 10 cents.

The University of Montana campus and athletic fields became our playground, but on rainy days our favorite haunts were the University museum and the science and journalism buildings.

Just inside the entrance to the museum hung the 6-by-9-foot oil painting "Custer's Last Stand," the masterpiece of Montana artist Edgar S. Paxson, which pictured the famous Battle of the Little Bighorn. In it the artist painted in almost portrait detail each of some 200 Sioux and Cheyenne Indians and the soldiers of the U.S. 7th Cavalry.

As we sat studying that dramatic scene, we must have looked not unlike a couple of kids staring at a television screen today. That Paxson masterpiece now hangs in the Buffalo Bill Historical Center in Cody, Wyoming.

History and artifacts from the Lewis and Clark Expedition attracted us to the museum, and in the journalism building we were allowed to peruse years of back issues of *Daily Missoulian* colored comic pages.

SPREADING OUR WINGS

When we left our house on a non-school day and Mother would ask where we were going, "To the university" would be our dissembling response, not adding that from there it was an easy bicycle ride to Kelly Island where the Bitterroot River flows into the Clark Fork. There we could hunt for Indian arrowheads, stone knives and petrified deer antlers without Mother knowing to worry about the whirlpools created by the confluence of the two rivers.

Another favorite goal for exploring was

Hellgate Canyon, where the Clark Fork runs below steep rock walls pocked with caves. Always the fearless one, Wymond would inch along narrow ledges above the rushing river and wriggle into dark caves while I stood watch, concerned both about his safety and about the possibility that Mother might learn of these exploits.

Many fall Saturdays brought football games hosted by the University of Montana Grizzlies, and it wasn't long until we learned to slip through the team entrance as easily as could the ball boys.

As I remember those games, most of the team played both offense and defense, and we would wait excitedly for the red-headed quarterback, I think his name was Bill Kelly, to suddenly lose his temper, throw off his leather helmet and take charge of the game. He was Wymond's role model a few years later when Wymond turned out for high school football in Klamath Falls.

"BEND ZEE KNEEZ – TWO DOLLARS PLEEZ"

"Bend zee kneez, two dollars pleez!" Austrian ski instructors did not begin to populate the American ski school scene until late in the 1920s, but by 1923 Wymond and I already were learning the Hannes Schneider Arlberg ski technique.

Father's nephew Dr. Lawrence Henderson, who had been on the staff of the Mission Hospital at St. Ignatius, Montana, for two years doctoring Flathead Indians, decided to specialize in eye surgery, so in 1922 he sailed to Vienna for graduate study. Life in sophisticated Vienna proved a bit much for the Indiana farm boy, so on holidays he would board a train for St. Anton in the Austrian Alps.

Hannes Schneider was a crusty mountaineer who had spent World War I teaching Austrian army recruits to ski. When the war ended and the new sport of skiing blossomed in Europe,

The central portion of Edgar S. Paxson's masterpiece, "Custer's Last Stand." As we sat in the University of Montana Museum studying that dramatic scene, we must have looked not unlike a couple of kids staring at a television screen today.

Mount Sentinel, Montana, where we learned to ski in 1923. The University of Montana is in foreground, and the whitewashed "M" is at the top of photo.

Schneider found that his wartime teaching methods worked well with Britons and Americans who began flocking to the Alps. Thus was born the world famous Arlberg ski technique, and Lawrence was an early pupil.

EIGHT-FOOT-LONG SKIS

When he returned to Montana Lawrence brought his skis with him, and that Christmas he bought skis in Missoula for us boys. Those skis would have daunted Hannes Schneider. They combined features of both jumping and cross-country skis with the anomaly of double grooves in the bottoms of one pair. For bindings there were wide leather straps threaded through flat slots in the skis and then buckled across the soft toes of our logging boots.

Father solved part of the problem by having the blacksmith make copies of the bindings on Lawrence's Austrian skis and installing them on ours. However Wymond's 8-foot pine skis and my seven-and-a-half-foot ash skis were more than twice as long as we were tall.

OUR FIRST SKI LESSON – 1923

It came time for Lawrence to give us our first ski lesson, and he chose Mount Sentinel. The peak thrusts abruptly 2,000 feet above the Bitterroot flats, providing a green backdrop for the University of Montana campus in summer and a snow sports mecca in winter.

As we started up the mountain, skis bundled in our arms, our goal was the large "M" whitewashed on a rock outcropping several hundred feet above. We did not make it nearly that far, and our enthusiasm for skiing waned as we struggled up to where Lawrence waited.

Then as Lawrence swept back to the bottom, carving a smooth "S" in the unbroken snow, our enthusiasm returned. When we tried to duplicate his feat we soon emerged laughing from an explosion of powder snow. Finally we concluded that skiing might be fun after all!

Lawrence was a patient mentor and soon was introducing us to stems and stem turns. By the end of another winter we could climb to the "M" and sometimes ride those awkward skis all the way down without a fall. But like most kids we preferred schussing to stemming!

The Arlberg technique was much maligned in later years, but I still depended a bit on its three-point security when I last competed in a slalom race 75 years later!

THE CHAUTAUQUA

The chautauqua was our first exposure to culture. After we moved to Missoula, Mother realized that because Wymond and I had lived all our lives on the farm and in lumber camps, we never had attended a live orchestra performance or even a stage play, so when it was announced that a circuit chautauqua was coming to town, she signed us up.

Dozens of those traveling tent shows brought to residents of small cities and towns educational and entertainment events including plays, opera, and speakers on current affairs, travel, and social and political issues. They were an important cultural medium in the era before radio and television broadcasting.

Mother told us that in Indiana she had looked forward to the annual chautauqua, where a large tent covered several hundred seats and a stage. A live band would play the latest fox trots during intermissions. Wymond and I thought that it would be fun, until we learned that attending chautauqua would shorten our summer vacation at the Pablo mill by a week.

I remember that chautauqua well, and it did provide many new experiences, but there were only a few that we really enjoyed. The band concerts were fun, but the speakers were as boring to us as Sunday church service. Vaudeville acts laced into the programs provided blessed relief, but Shakespeare was the worst of all. Fortunately my next encounter with the Bard was in high school, where a dedicated and talented teacher stripped away most of my prejudices.

I believe we were too young for chautauqua, and when the week of culture was over, we were mighty happy to head back to our cabin on the Flathead and our long-eared rabbits.

ELEPHANTS AND NAKED LADIES

The Ringling Brothers and Barnum and Bailey Circus brought sparkle to our lives. We had never seen an elephant or a giraffe, much less a naked lady, a wolf-boy or a three-headed calf, all of which the handbills said would be exhibited in the circus' carnival.

Touted as "The Greatest Show on Earth," the original Barnum and Bailey Circus had begun touring the nation by train in 1888, and Father remembered attending one of its first appearances in Missoula. He was anxious to see it again, especially "The World's Strongest Man" and the performances by trapeze artists.

Father drove us from Pablo to Missoula a day ahead of the circus and woke us at dawn the next morning so that we could ride our bikes out to the railroad siding south of town to watch the circus train unload. The speed and precision with which the cars of animals, equipment, musicians, performers and roustabouts were unloaded and the huge tent erected were breathtaking.

P.T. Barnum had said "Every crowd has a silver lining," and his meaning was apparent that morning. Rather than being pushed back out of the way, our crowd of onlookers was welcomed by costumed performers who strolled among us. I am sure that P.T. Barnum would have considered even us kids on bikes to be part of the crowd's *silver lining*.

At nine o'clock, the circus parade started into town, led by a uniformed marching band belting out John Philip Sousa music and followed by a towering elephant that seemed to be keeping step with the booming bass drum. Spectators gathered along the route, and by the time the parade crossed the Higgins Ave. Bridge, the sidewalks were overflowing.

We had raced ahead on our bikes and found seats on the curb in front of the Wilma Theater, where we had the best view of the horse-drawn animal cages, the acrobats performing on bareback horses, and the tumblers, jugglers and sleight-of-hand artists who mingled with the watchers.

Bringing up the rear of the parade, to the delight of children, was a tiny full-grown mare only 3-feet high, followed by her frisky colt, which was less than half as tall as its mother.

THE MONKEY BOY

The next day Mother joined us in front row seats that Father had bought for the spectacular show. The gymnastics and high trapeze acts were our favorites. A few years later Wymond and I became expert gymnasts ourselves and even performed in the Portland Rose Festival.

When the circus ended, Father took us into the sideshow tent while Mother rested. That was my downfall. I had been born with a "red wine stain" birthmark on my right leg. Such a birthmark can be disfiguring when it occurs on a person's face, but on my leg it would have been of little notice had it not been covered with long dark hair like that on my head.

The birthmark was a source of embarrassment to Mother and therefore of shame to me. I was not allowed to wear short pants or shorts until I started high school and learned to use smelly hair removal cream. Neither was I allowed to learn to swim.

Not much had been made of my "hairy leg" within the family until that day. But in the sideshow's "freak house," along with the bearded lady, the three-headed calf and the wolf boy was the monkey boy, whose body was covered with hair. He probably was a very small, very hairy man passing off as a boy.

We were barely out of Father's hearing when Wymond gleefully pulled up my pants leg and said, "Hi there, monkey boy," and began calling me that or "freak of nature" whenever he wanted to rag me. Of course, others picked up the words in the cruel world of children.

I didn't dare complain to Mother, and Father would only have been chagrined that I didn't simply give the offenders a licking. I realize now that my birthmark became a source of childhood withdrawal and loneliness. Perhaps it was a reason why I became so driven to succeed.

CRUISING WITH CRISSY

Cruising through downtown on Saturday nights is not a recent phenomenon. It was already a regular routine of young people in Missoula in the twenties, and the Donlan's daughter Crissy, in her classy new two door Hudson coach, was a regular in the parade. Home from college for the summer, she was one of the city's very eligible young women and seldom was without an escort. However when she was alone, she sometimes let Wymond and me scramble into the front seat beside her.

The cruisers focused on Higgins Ave., which was Missoula's main drag, and shuttled between the University of Montana campus, spread below Mount Sentinel, and Greenough Park, which enfolds Rattlesnake Creek in the shadow of Mount Jumbo. It was a scenic drive that traversed most of the city, but few in the entourage of carefully groomed cars would have been looking at the scenery.

When Lawrence returned from Vienna and became attentive to Crissy, the two of them would join the parade in his sporty Stutz Bearcat roadster with no doors, the top down and bronze headlamps glowing.

Lawrence had not seen his family since he came to Montana to practice medicine on the Flathead reservation four years before, and he was awaiting a visit from them.

NO MORE GUNFIGHTS

Later that summer "Uncle" Ward Henderson was peering through the mud-splattered windshield of his new Buick, trying

The Ed Donlan home in Missoula. The Donlan children – Chrissy, Arthur and Morris – were George and Wymon's closest friends.

to avoid the worst chuckholes, as he and "Aunt" Daisy and 10-year-old Thomas neared the end of 2,000 miles of gravel road that linked Brownsberg, Indiana, with Missoula.

Ward still dreamed of Montana as it had been a generation earlier, and the reunion with son, Lawrence, and Cousin Ben in Missoula, just 10 miles further down the Bitterroot River, would bring reality to those dreams. He sped up a little.

Word of the accident reached Mother first, and she hurried Wymond and me into the car and headed up the Bitterroot. It was a memorable scene. Two white chickens were perched on the overturned car, complaining loudly, while Aunt Daisy and Thomas retrieved jars of home-canned fruit and vegetables scattered along the road among suitcases, bedding and camping gear. Still strapped to the running boards were an open chicken cage and another that still held a placid red capon.

There was only one injury. The usually voluble Ward was holding his jaw with both hands, silently enduring the excited report from his normally quiet wife, saying, "I told him to slow down for that curve."

Lawrence had been away from the hospital when the accident was reported, but soon his Stutz roadster skidded to a stop beside us.

Since Aunt Daisy and Thomas were unhurt, Lawrence hurried to the hospital with his father, leaving the rest of us to wait for a tow.

"Now we'll see some fun," was Father's comment when Mother reached him by phone at the mill. She had learned that Ward's jaw was broken and would be wired shut for weeks. This was a severe handicap, since he loved to argue and could out-talk most adversaries. But Ward had the last word after all. Mumbling through clenched teeth and waving hands for emphasis, he gave no quarter in verbal combat. He had one missing tooth so thrived on a liquid diet fed through a glass straw.

FULFILLING WARD'S DREAM

Buffalo roaming the open range, gunfights in the streets and steely-eyed sheriffs hanging desperados in the courthouse yard: That is how it had been in the Wild West in the late 1860s when Ward and his cousin Ben were boys together in Indiana. But only Father had heeded the call to adventure and gone to Montana. Ward stayed in Indiana, married gentle Daisy, took over the family farm, raised two sturdy boys, and grew prize-winning hogs and fields of corn.

Now in 1924 Ben set out to fulfill some of

his cousin's dreams, starting with a trip for the family to see the buffalo in the National Bison Range and then showing them his extensive logging and saw milling operations at Pablo.

Because Lawrence had commenced his medical practice at the mission hospital in St. Ignatius, he knew the Flathead Indian Reservation well, and the family was invited into the teepees of some of Lawrence's Indian friends there.

Ward's hope to see a gunfight in the streets and to watch an Indian hanging faded as he traveled Missoula's paved avenues, but he got to relive a bit of history when Lawrence took him to Lolo where the Lewis and Clark Expedition had camped on their crossings of the Bitterroot Range in 1805 and 1806.

THE HANGING

Then one morning near the end of their visit Ward rushed into breakfast holding the *Daily Missoulian*. The paper reported that an Indian convicted of murder would be hanged in the county courthouse yard the next day. Would Father go with him to the hanging?

Wymond wanted to go too, but not I. Of course, Mother said no for both of us, but Father and Ward went together, thus satisfying the third of Ward's long-held dreams of the Wild West.

In late August to celebrate the unwiring of Ward's teeth, there remained enough of the food Aunt Daisy and Thomas had salvaged from the car wreck, including the red capon, for Mother to cook a farewell Hoosier supper of fried chicken, fluffy mashed potatoes, gravy, sweet potatoes and persimmon pudding. The restored jaw survived the test with ease.

The supper also turned out to be a farewell to Lawrence. The year in Vienna had prepared him to specialize in eye surgery, and he had found an opportunity to join an ophthalmology clinic in Watertown, New York.

Wymond and I had hoped that Lawrence and Crissy might have married, but our parents told us that mixed marriages between an Irish Catholic family and one rooted in Masonic Protestantism were rare in those days.

LAWRENCE THIRTY YEARS HENCE

I visited Lawrence 30 years later in upstate New York. I found he had ample opportunities for outdoor sports with a boat on Lake Ontario and New England ski resorts on all sides. I had with me a color motion picture of skiing on Mount Hood, so I showed it to him, and he confided that he had never lost his love for the West. We enjoyed reminiscing about the Flathead Valley and his times teaching Wymond and me to ski on Mount Sentinel.

7 THE PABLO FIRE

Mother took this photo of the catastrophic fire that destroyed the Pablo sawmill in 1925.

The sawmill's shrill steam whistle pierced the hot, still air echoing from the green forest back across the wheat fields toward Pablo. Then a thin wisp of gray smoke twisted upward.

A long moment later came cries of "Fire! Fire! Fire!" and timber fallers dropped their saws, teamsters unhitched their loads and every member of the crew rushed to join the sawmill hands in fighting the flames.

A half-hour earlier the freight train from Polson to Missoula had passed through, with its fireman shoveling coal to build up steam for the pull over Evaro Hill and its oversized spark arrestor filtering the smoke belching from its stack. But one tiny, red-hot clinker had slipped through the mesh and dropped between the tall stacks of dry lumber lining the rail siding.

We boys were on the Flathead with Father for the summer, and Mother had just arrived by train from Missoula. Our frame cabin was across the railroad grade from the mill and safe from direct flames, but Father sent a crew to wet down the roof and watch for sparks.

Wymond and I stood on the railroad, transfixed, while Mother used her new Kodak postcard camera to capture dramatic pictures of the inferno and the billowing smoke that soon darkened the sky.

Fear of fire never is far from a sawmill man's mind. Father had insisted on regular fire drills and on keeping emergency equipment ready. The bright red fire buckets stacked at strategic spots in the mill had intrigued me, all of them cone-shaped with pointed bottoms to discourage use as regular buckets. Now we watched lines of men fill them at the millpond and pass them from hand to hand in a bucket brigade to throw water onto the flames.

A SINGLE SPARK

The usually stolid teams of draft horses now pulled water tankers along at a fast trot, their harnesses clanging. A few men who at first had climbed on top of the lumber piles had to make hazardous jumps to safety as the flames licked closer. Arthur Donlan hitched a plow to the Holt crawler tractor, which finally proved its worth in rapidly clearing firebreaks between the mill and the forest.

Some of the camp buildings were saved, and the fire didn't spread to the forest, but the sawmill, lumber and most of the log decks were a total loss. In late afternoon the steam boilers failed, and the whistle finally fell silent, but the decks of logs continued to burn, and the sawdust pile would smolder into the winter.

Insurers for the Northern Pacific Railroad and those for Donlan and Henderson escaped liability. Father's fortune was wiped out, and without insurance compensation he was liable for massive loans that had been made against security of the mill, equipment, and log and lumber inventories.

We could keep the house in Missoula for the time being, and Father undertook a small logging and sawmill contract on the Coeur d'Alene River below Missoula, while he and Ed Donlan looked for another worthwhile business opportunity.

ALONE!

I learned about bravery at Henderson, Montana. Two miles can be a mighty long way when you are walking down a dark trail in the forest alone and you are very frightened and 8 years old!

It had been an exciting morning as Mother added a lunch to my packsack and drove me to the depot in Missoula for my first train ride all by myself. I was going to visit Father at the new sawmill near Henderson, 50 miles down the Coeur d'Alene.

The daily freight train usually carried a combination baggage and passenger car, but that day it did not, so I got to ride in the red caboose with the conductor. After Frenchtown and Donlan, the train stopped at a siding where the sign read "Henderson," and I climbed down onto the tracks.

Then as the caboose pulled out of sight around a bend, I realized that I hadn't seen Father. There wasn't a station or even a work shack – just a short section of double track and a rough wagon road leading into the timber. I hadn't been to Henderson before, but Father had said that he would meet me, and we would walk to the mill site together, so I sat down on a stack of railroad ties and ate lunch while watching hopefully down the road.

Then I began to get scared. Father always had told us that we were brave little boys, and I was sure that nothing ever frightened him, but he wasn't here, and there were real mountain lions in those woods, and the next train wouldn't come until tomorrow. I was truly *alone!*

I started walking down the wagon road and soon broke into a run, running not just from mountain lions but running from *alone!* The pure panic couldn't go on forever, but when I ran out of breath and out of tears I stayed scared and kept on sobbing, walking ahead and looking backward. Then suddenly there was Father striding toward me, and *alone* disappeared!

That was when I learned about bravery. Father gave me a huge hug and told me how proud he was of me for being so brave. Later when we were having supper in the camp cookhouse, he bragged to the men that when an accident at the mill kept him from meeting me, his brave little boy had walked all the way from the railroad to the mill by himself.

I never told anyone how scared I had been. That would be a secret between *alone* and me.

8 HAYES CREEK

George and Wymond flanking the log chute Father built in Hayes Creek.

WINTER CHUTE LOGGING IN THE BITTERROOTS

The portable sawmill at Henderson on the Coeur d'Alene River provided family income that winter, but Father needed to get a logging contract soon in order to begin recouping the money he had lost in the Pablo mill disaster.

Late in the spring the Anaconda Copper Mining Company called for bids to log a large stand of its privately owned timber in the Hayes Creek watershed of the Bitterroot Valley. With Ed Donlan's backing he put in a desperately low bid and won the contract. To make a profit he would have to complete the job within a year, which meant cutting the timber that summer and getting the logs to the railroad during the winter.

Father had a bold plan. He would build a network of wooden chutes like bobsled runs, and when winter came logs would be rolled into the chutes and sent racing like 2,000-pound bobsleds down the canyons to the Bitterroot River far below.

It was an innovative logging technique. He told us that sometimes in summer chutes slicked with grease had been used, but he knew of no large-scale logging having been done in winter using snow chutes. Time was short. The trees had to be felled, bucked into logs and decked along the chute alignments while the chutes themselves were being built.

Jobs in the woods were hard to get that year, so it wasn't long until there was a line of loggers, blacksmiths, carpenters and cooks carrying their blankets up the trail from the railroad siding to the camp. Adze and broad axe men supplemented the usual crews of

Wymond and George in the Hayes Creek logging camp, horse barn in back.

fallers and buckers. Some were shipbuilders from Puget Sound who were expert with the tools used in building wooden ships.

THE POLIO EPIDEMIC

It was an exciting summer for two exuberant boys.

An epidemic of highly contagious infantile paralysis (polio) was crippling dozens of Montana kids and many adults that year. Suspected sources of infection included swimming pools, playgrounds and other places where children gathered, so to our delight we were to spend the summer at Hayes Creek.

In June when the end-of-day bell on Missoula's Paxson school rang, Father and Mother were waiting to pick up Wymond and me in the family's big Reo Speedwagon truck loaded with supplies for the summer. Father headed the truck out across the Bitterroot flats where the Flathead Indians had put up their colorful tepees, ready to gather the medicinal roots of the brilliant bitterroot flowers. In a few more miles, we sped across the Bitterroot River Bridge, passed the parade grounds of Fort Missoula then headed toward the town of

Lolo near where Lewis and Clark had camped little more than a century before.

At the Hayes Creek rail siding we helped put tire chains on the Reo and then clung inside the stake-body as Father turned up the Creek following the newly built wagon road. Although he had worked one summer 40 years before driving four-horse freight wagons in Yellowstone National Park, this barely passable road proved too much for him in a 1923 gasoline-powered truck. Halfway up the four-mile grade a team of horses had to be hitched to the Reo to pull us into camp, much to the delight of a dozen or so teamsters just bringing their horses to the barn.

Usually no families lived at logging camps, but Father always tried to have our family with him. Very soon we were helping him build a snug log cabin, which would be our home for much of the next two years.

We watched as the pristine forest trail into the canyon was overrun by the wagon road and heard the valley reverberate with the thunder of falling timber, the clatter of horses and harness, and the sound of hammers and saws. A bustling logging camp seemed to spring right out of the ground.

ADZES AND BROADAXES

Part of the crew built bunkhouses, a cookhouse, barns and offices, while others commenced felling the towering yellow pines. The log chutes were made of pairs of pine logs that were flattened on one side with adzes, then finished mirror-smooth with broadaxes. Laid side by side a few inches apart, they formed a wide V-shaped trough. The pairs then were joined end to end, and by October the entire network was ready for the first heavy snowfall.

Wymond and I were a rapt audience as one of the shipbuilders who had been a seaman in sailing ships in his youth filled our heads with scenes of tall clipper ships tacking into the trade winds. They carried cargoes of wheat and "Oregon Pine" across the Pacific to Australia and returned with cargoes of wool, silks and other exotic products of the Far East. (Oregon Pine was the trade name applied to Douglas fir lumber overseas.)

Treasure Island was a favorite book. It brought Long John Silver and Jim Hawkins to life for us. Silver and Hawkins widened our horizons beyond the mountains and valleys of Montana and may have been a factor in our decisions to spend World War II in the Merchant Marine rather than the ski troops.

MISCHIEF

For Wymond and me the summer was a mixture of fun and learning along with a bit of mischief. One of the teamsters – crippled Bob Peet, who once had been a cowboy – taught us how to braid smooth, round horsehair lariats. He had second thoughts when he realized that we were eyeing the flowing tails of his prized team of draft horses as a source of raw material. By the time we each had finished braiding a twenty-foot-long horse-hair lasso we had deftly dodged the hind feet of most of the 20 horses in the new barn. Later I blamed that barn for breaking my arm!

TWO LITTLE SAVAGES

That summer Grandma Miller had sent us the book *Two Little Savages* by naturalist Ernest Thompson Seton. Seton told how to make Indian war bonnets using feathers from turkeys instead of from eagles and how to make real breechclouts from tanned deerskin. Right then we decided to play Indian. When the camp cook baked turkeys for the Fourth of July dinner, we asked him to save the feathers for us. Father provided buckskin from a recent deer hunt, and with Mother's help, we were soon decked out like little Indians ready for the warpath.

But as we were about to start out half-naked to skulk through the forest looking for enemies, we realized that our shining white skins didn't fit the part! Seton's woodcraft book provided the answer. We boiled up strips of alder bark that produced a dark stain to rub on our skin, turning us as brown as Indians. Father thought we looked fine, but Mother was so furious, she would not allow us to go down to the cookhouse to eat until we "looked like little gentlemen." This took two successive Saturday night baths; meanwhile we had to eat in the cabin for two weeks.

After a few days of fruitless skulking and a night in a cold leaky fir-bough shelter, the fun of playing Indian faded faster than our browned bodies.

BOOTLEGGERS

The bootlegging was Wymond's idea!

He remembered our pot of reddish brown alder bark juice hidden in the woods. "That sure looks like whiskey," he said, "Why don't we put it in bottles and sell it down at the bunkhouse?" Bootlegging was a familiar subject, because Prohibition was just 4 years old. The only source of liquor was bootleggers who either made it themselves or smuggled it across the Montana-Canada border.

We waited until most of the crew had gone into the woods the next morning, then quietly collected a half-dozen empty whiskey bottles and filled them with the alder bark juice. It really did look like whiskey! After supper we each put a full pint bottle under our coats and walked to the bunkhouse. There a couple of loggers noticed that we were hiding bottles and quickly paid us a dollar each for the contraband. Wymond and I raced back to the cabin, proud of our easy earnings. A dollar was a lot more than we made in a week selling the *Women's Home Companion* and *Ladies Home Journal* door-to-door in Missoula.

Our excitement was short-lived. Mother was shocked, and although Father was quietly proud of our undertaking, both parents joined in using the opportunity to carefully explain the moral, ethical and legal factors which were at play. I have always remembered that lesson. Our punishment was to go back to the bunkhouse and return the money with apologies. Of course everyone in camp soon had the story, much to the chagrin of the victims.

TICK FEVER

"He's hiding in my belly button," I cried out one evening in the midst of our daily family wood tick inspection. Wymond giggled, but Mother wasn't amused. Sure enough she saw a tiny black tick head almost buried in my soft belly button. Logging accidents were not the only deadly hazards in the Bitterroot Valley. Rocky Mountain spotted fever carried by wood ticks was fatal to 80 percent of its victims in those years, and there were no effective repellents or vaccines.

Ticks from deer and sheep often end up on people. Our only prevention was to wear long-sleeved shirts, tuck trousers into shoe tops and splash kerosene onto our clothes every morning. If we saw or felt a tick during the day, we would ask for help in getting it off. The bedtime full body search was critical.

Bitterroot Valley wood ticks were even more virulent than those in other parts of the Rockies. That was why in 1921 Montana established the Rocky Mountain Laboratory in Hamilton to research the deadly fever. In a few years an effective vaccine was developed. Mother knew how to pluck the tiny tick out of my belly with tweezers. Only female ticks carry the poison, and some of them do not. Fortunately I suffered no ill effects.

QUARANTINE

Our summer vacation ended on Labor Day, and it was back to school, but then it seemed as if our house had a quarantine sign on it throughout the fall. When there was a communicable disease in a home, the home was placed under quarantine, and no one except the doctor was allowed to enter or leave. Deliveries were left on the porch. Measles, mumps and chicken pox all qualified, and Wymond and I each had each of them but never at the same time. Of course when one of us was quarantined, neither could go to school.

The workweek in those days before strong unions was six 10-hour days, so Father usually came home for Sunday. On Saturday nights when the house was quarantined, we would turn out the lights, close the blinds and wait in the dark until he quietly slipped in the back door. Then on Monday he would be gone before dawn.

SCARLET FEVER

Wymond and I survived measles, mumps and chicken pox without aftereffects, but scarlet fever was a different matter. It was epidemic in Missoula that year and sometimes caused lifelong damage. Wymond didn't come down with it, but it hit me hard.

After a week of sore throat, red rash, high temperature and frequent delirium, I developed numbing earaches. Lawrence was our doctor, and told Mother that he would have to pierce both eardrums to reduce the inner ear swelling. However the cries of protest from the same little boy he had just taught to ski dissuaded him, and he decided to wait another day, hoping that the swelling would decrease by itself.

It was a bad decision. My left ear recovered without surgery, but that night the right eardrum ruptured, causing temporary loss of hearing and a tear that took weeks to heal. Lawrence told us that he hoped never again to be faced with such a decision involving a loved one. The high fever damaged my heart, but I outgrew the damage by the time I enlisted in the military 20 years later.

FAST SLEDS AND BROKEN ARMS

We were healthy again by December, and on the first day of the Christmas vacation Mother and we boys headed back to Hayes Creek. Father met us at the railroad siding with horses and a sleigh. The temperature was well below zero with only a skiff of snow on the ground.

We saw that Father was worried. It was past the time to send the logs down the chutes, and that called for lots more snow!

When we arrived at the cabin, we found that winter had transformed it into a tiny ice palace. The happy gurgle of the creek was stilled, for it was frozen solid. In place of the colorful maple, alder and birch leaves there were bare branches rimed with sparkling frost. The roadway from camp to the cabin was like a sheet of ice.

We spent Christmas Eve day selecting a bushy balsam fir Christmas tree from among the tall pines, and that evening we fashioned strings of popcorn, cranberries and paper angels to drape around the tree. Then, to the end of each limb, Mother tied a streamer of bright tinsel, that sparkled in reflected light from the Coleman gasoline lantern.

When we crawled out of our warm bed on Christmas morning, our spines tingled with excitement as we spotted two shiny Flexible Flyer sleds under the tree. We hardly took time to bundle up against the sub-zero cold before trying out the sleds on a test run down to camp. The sleds lived up to their name, for their steel runners encountered little friction on the icy road.

Ignoring Mother's caution pleas, in a few days we each had learned to navigate the quarter-mile track at breakneck speed, turning sharply to miss the barn, then coasting to a stop 50 yards beyond. Wymond's sled was longer than mine and had some steering capacity. I could steer only by dragging a foot. He always beat me to the finish, but sometimes I could coax my sled to coast farther than his across the flat. Then I would claim a victory of sorts.

THE PURLOINED SLED

Of course Wymond wouldn't allow me to touch his sled, but the temptation was overwhelming. One day I slipped out alone and piled onto the big sled. An Olympic racer on a new luge couldn't have been more thrilled. But unlike a luge course, our road didn't have banked turns.

Soon I was headed full speed for the center of the barn. I didn't know how to steer the sled and was too frightened to roll off so I panicked and froze to the handlebars. If it had been my own sled with handlebars at the front, my hands and head would have hit the barn together, but the handlebars of Wymond's longer sled were set back a foot, protecting hands from being crushed and absorbing some of the impact.

That was when the barn broke my arm!

The next thing I knew, I was looking up into Bob Peet's face as he dragged the sled and me from a pile of broken boards. He checked me over with experience born of years as a rodeo rider and concluded that the only serious injury was to my left arm, which hung askew.

Bob Peet met Mother and Wymond

Bob Peet in front of the horse barn where George crashed Wymond's sled.

halfway up the hill, dragging the sled and carrying me in his arms. Mother's concern was for me, and Wymond's was for his sled.

Both bones in my left arm were broken and took six weeks in a splint to mend, but the cuts and bruises healed quickly, and in a couple of months I was back sliding gingerly down the road again – on my own sled.

LEARNING TO DRIVE

"Give her hell, George," Father shouted at me one day as we approached the turn-off from the graveled highway onto the Hayes Creek Road. He had taught us each to drive on country roads when we were 9, for drivers' licenses were not required in Montana except in town. I was 10 years old and was at the wheel of our Reo truck, half-standing and half leaning against him as I had learned to do out on the highway. But neither Wymond nor I had ever driven the four miles up the rough wagon road to the logging camp.

Most cars had stick shifts on the floor in the '20s, but there were four different shifting patterns among them. Since our Buick touring car and the Reo truck shared the same non-standard pattern, we could drive either one, but the truck was much harder to downshift.

Excited but hardly believing, I quickly shifted into second, jammed down the throttle and swung into the turn with good speed to begin the 1,000-foot climb. If I allowed the truck to stall we would have to back all the way to the bottom of the narrow track, and even though I adjusted the speed and steering to avoid skidding or wheel spins on the corners, it was all I could do to keep us on the badly rutted road.

Then came the real test. As the grade steepened the Reo slowed and almost stalled. Father quickly reached around me and executed the complicated double-clutching maneuver to put the truck into low gear. It wasn't a perfect shift, and the gears complained loudly, but the teeth took hold and the Reo slowly crawled up the last mile to the crest of the hill.

Father shared my pleasure, but Wymond sulked, for he was 11 and had not yet conquered the Big Hill to Hayes Creek. It was one of those small victories that can loom large in a youngster's memory. It still does in mine!

A WARM WINTER

Father always had been an optimist. He had gambled willingly on his ability to do the logging in record time, but he hadn't reckoned with the weather. In his 25 years in Montana, he had not known a winter like this one. Disaster threatened.

We boys had hoped to see the chutes in action before school started, but instead we were back at Paxson school, and I was in Miss Rennick's Montana history class reading about the Lewis and Clark Expedition.

Father had told us how in 1805-06 Lewis and Clark had crossed the Bitterroots through Lolo Pass not far from Hayes Creek, and once he took Mother, Wymond and me on horseback to where we could see the pass. Now we wondered how much snow the explorers had encountered in those same mountains a century earlier.

THE LEWIS AND CLARK JOURNALS

My friend Keith McCoy of White Salmon, Washington, is a renowned historian and student of the Voyage of Discovery, so I asked him what the journals said about snow depth during their crossing of the Bitterroots. Keith loaned me copies of some pertinent excerpts from the hand-written journal entries made by Captains Meriwether Lewis and William Clark that describe that crossing.

[Clark] *Tuesday September 16 1805...began to snow about 3 hours before day and continued all day and by night we found it from 6 to 8 inches deep...the snow had entirely filled up the track...I was fearful at one time that my feet would freeze in the thin mockersons which I wore...Wednesday September 18...to describe the road of this day would be a repitition of yesterday except the snow which made it much wors to proceed...*

On the return in 1806 the journals state, [Lewis] *Monday June 16 1806...the dog tooth violet is just in blume, the honeysuckle and a small species of white maple are beginning to put forth their leaves, where they are clear of the snow, those appearances in the comparatively low region augers but unfavourably with respect to the practibility of passing the mountains...The snow has increased in quantity So much that the great part of our rout this evening was over snow... we found ourselves invelloped in snow from 12 to 15 feet deep even on the south sides of the hills: here was winter with all it's rigors...*

Those journals made it clear that in the winter of 1805-06 the weather would have permitted chute logging at least from November until late spring.

FINALLY IT SNOWED

The deep freeze had continued without snow for another month, then in late January the temperature shot up overnight, and storm clouds rolled in from the west, dropping three feet of fluffy snow in the Bitterroot Valley.

The snow blanketed Missoula too, so Mother declared a school holiday for us, and soon we were perched on a ridge above Hayes Creek looking down on the canyons alive with loggers struggling waist-deep to reach their places along the chutes. Most carried cant hooks, but some had picks and shovels.

It was a spectacular scene as the loggers began using their cant hooks to roll log after log into the chutes. The logs quickly gathered speed, and when they neared a bend, "sand monkeys" would shovel sand into the chute to slow them down. then pile in more snow to renew the momentum. When a log jam occurred, loggers in caulked boots would run down on top of the logs and set chokers to which teamsters could hitch their horses and start the logs on their way again.

We boys were also wearing caulked boots. Wymond wanted to climb onto one of the logs for a ride, eliciting an emphatic *no* and strict orders to stay well clear of the trails beside the chutes from then on.

Father expanded the crew so that chuting could continue seven days a week from dawn to dusk, praying that the favorable weather would hold long enough for all the logs to be sent to the railroad that winter.

THE CHINOOK

But in early March a warm Chinook wind blew down from the Rockies across the Bitterroot Range, turning the log chutes into leaky flumes. It would be another winter before the contract could be completed.

In our naiveté, we were pleased with the news, for it meant that we would spend another summer at Hayes Creek, but it meant financial disaster for Father.

For the proud, prosperous lumberman who had retired in 1909 with a fortune, which he believed would assure lifetime financial security, it was the last of a series of blows that left him with neither funds nor credit to undertake another business venture. The Pablo fire with no insurance payment had cost

perhaps a million dollars in lost assets and new debt, and he now would be faced with more debts for failing to complete the Hayes Creek contract within the contract's one-year terms.

I don't recall much about that year, except that Father kept a small crew hand-logging the lower slopes at Hayes Creek during the summer, and when the next winter brought heavy snows in early November, he was able to chute the remainder of the logs down to the railroad in less than two months, minimizing the loss a little. In early spring Father made a trip to Idaho and Washington looking for a job, while we stayed in Missoula with Mother.

BARNSTORMERS

The wing walker had the best view.

When the World War I biplane flew down through Hellgate Canyon and turned toward the Bitterroot flats, it seemed as though every kid in Missoula jumped on his bike and tried to be first to watch the plane land. Wymond was near the front, riding his new red Ranger

A Curtiss JN4-D Jenny, World War I fighter plane like the one in which we made our first flight at Missoula

with 26-inch wheels, while I struggled to keep up on Wymond's old 24-inch bike.

The pilot flew low over our phalanx of cycles, made a pass to check the landing area and then headed back toward town. We saw the flyer in the front cockpit climb onto the wing, his white scarf streaming in the wind.

Flying low across the Higgins Avenue Bridge, the wing walker waved to the upturned faces of shoppers at the Missoula Mercantile store. Then the plane climbed high above the University of Montana campus and Mount Sentinel. When it was back above the landing area, the wing walker scrambled from the wing then suddenly let go and leaped off. A few seconds later a parachute blossomed, and we reached the field just as the daredevil touched the ground and began folding the chute.

The aerial exhibition had attracted a sizable crowd, and the barnstormers were busy taking people for plane rides at $5 apiece.

We did not have any money, so we sat beside a drum of gasoline and watched in envy as two kids who had been driven from town by their parents got rides. That evening Wymond and I made a decision. There was a carved leather fireplace bellows for sale for $5 at McKay's art store, and we had saved up money to buy it for Mother for Christmas. It was now only August, so wasn't there still time to earn another $5 by Christmas? Maybe the barnstormers would take both of us up for $5.

TWO KIDS IN A JENNY

We were waiting by the plane when the fliers woke the next morning. But they told us that there was a rule against carrying two passengers in the front cockpit of a *JN4-D Jenny*, so why didn't we flip a coin to see who would go? We said it had to be both or neither. There was no one else waiting to pay for a ride, and we were holding out $5, so the pilot pocketed the money, picked us up to estimate our weight, and stuffed the two of us into the front cockpit. There were only two helmets, so he put one on each of us and flew bareheaded.

It was 1925, and in only two years Charles A. Lindbergh would make the first nonstop flight across the Atlantic. Lindbergh had barnstormed in Montana that summer of 1925, flying aerobatics and putting on wing walking and parachute jumping exhibitions with a similar *JN4-D Jenny*. Later as I watched newsreels of Lindbergh's landing in Paris and saw crowds carrying him bareheaded away from the *Spirit of St. Louis*, I wondered if he might have been the same bareheaded pilot who took Wymond and me on our first flight that Montana morning.

FIRST FLIGHT

The raw joy of that first takeoff is bright in my memory. As the pilot opened the throttle, the plane bounced over the uneven prairie grass and then seemed to be sucked from the earth toward the unbounded blue sky.

Turning past Mount Sentinel with the right wing almost brushing the whitewashed "M," the plane leveled off to provide a wing walker's view of most of our familiar world.

Rattlesnake Creek, where we waded on hot afternoons; the business district, where we spotted McKay's art store; the Wilma Theater, from whose stage Will Rogers had delighted us with stories and rope tricks, and the railroad depot, where we soon would gaze in awe at Queen Marie of Romania as she stood on the platform of a special transcontinental train taking her to dedicate Maryhill Castle in the Columbia Gorge.

Finally headed back toward the landing field, we saw the great tent that housed the circuit chautauqua and the rail siding where we had watched the Barnum and Bailey Circus unload and begin its elephant-led parade through downtown Missoula. Then with the morning sun lighting the nearby Bitterroots, the plane glided over our home at 315 Daly

Ave. to land just beyond Paxson school.

After we climbed unsteadily from the cockpit, I must have suffered a memory block, for I simply cannot recall reporting our flight to Mother. She would have been mighty interested! I am sure that we didn't discuss it that next Christmas either, when we presented her with the leather fireplace bellows which she knew we had bought with money earned from our door-to-door magazine sales. That bellows still calls up warm memories for me as it hangs beside my fireplace in Oregon.

9 ACROSS THE BITTERROOTS

Our future lay on the other side of the Bitterroot Range.

The Clearwater River and its tributaries, including the Selway and Lochsa, drain the vast lands from the summit of the Bitterroots at the Montana-Idaho border to Lewiston at the Washington-Idaho border where the Clearwater pours into the Snake. Most of that land is in national forests, Indian reservations and other federal and state uses, but over the years timber claims, homesteads and federal grants had created large tracts in private ownership.

In early 1926 Father heard that the Weyerhaeuser Company had acquired from the Diamond Match Company a large stand of virgin white pine timber between the Clearwater and the North Fork and soon would begin logging it to supply a new sawmill and paper mill at Lewiston. He hoped that the company would let contracts for the logging, so he took the stage to Lewiston to see if he could put in a bid. It turned out to be too early for a decision, so while he waited he got a job as a carpenter building warehouses in Orofino, 60 miles up the Clearwater.

For several cold months, the proud 60-year-old drove nails and hand-sawed lumber, working side-by-side with men one-third his age. He wrote to us at home every night and sent back his wages to pay the family's living expenses. I would walk down Higgins Ave. with Mother as she paid bills by hand to save postage and would watch her write monthly checks for $42.50 to the building and loan association to keep the mortgage payments on our house current.

In one of his first letters, Father related that after several days of steady hammering, his right arm gave out, but he managed to stay on the job by changing the hammer to his left hand for a while. He was a switch-hitter at baseball and was ambidextrous with hammer, axe and saw.

TO BUILD A TOWN

Finally late that spring, the company told him that they planned no contract logging but offered to hire him to build their new headquarters on the site of the Clearwater Timber Protective Association's barns and corrals. It was a significant responsibility, and he relished it. The Weyerhaeuser Company must have been checking his qualifications during the cold winter months while he was driving nails in Orofino.

We were delighted. Mother told us that we wouldn't have to sell the Missoula house right away, and when school ended we might get to join Father in Idaho for the summer.

Weyerhaeuser's new timberlands were a true wilderness. From Orofino an automobile road climbed torturously out of the Clearwater Canyon and threaded through 40 miles of forest to the little town of Pierce. Pierce had been the center of Idaho's gold mining boom in the 1860s and its population had soared to 3,000, but for the last half century it had become a virtual ghost town. Now a logging boom was to give it new life.

Beyond the end of the automobile road at Pierce was 13 miles of rough wagon road leading to the Clearwater Timber Protective Association's headquarters, and from there to the Montana border there were only trails.

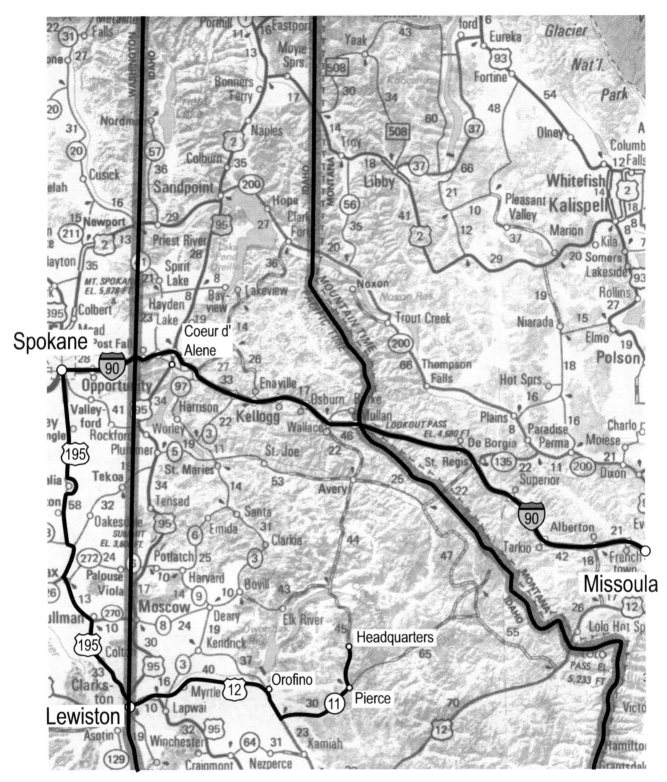

The northern panhandle of Idaho between Montana and Washington. My family had to travel through Spokane and Lewiston to reach Headquarters from Missoula because Highway 12 through Lolo Pass did not exist in 1927.

Since 1905 the Clearwater Timber Portective Association, created by four private timber owners, had maintained a network of fire lookouts supplied by packhorse and mule trains over more than 100 miles of trail.

The Weyerhaeuser Company had chosen the strategic CTPA location as a base from which to begin harvesting the timber under its enlightened sustained forestry program.

The CTPA would move to a new site nearby, and Father's first task was to build a sawmill. Then he was to manage construction of what eventually would become Headquarters, Idaho. No one could have been better suited for that daunting assignment. He began by riding horseback over the still-snowbound wagon road from Pierce to the CTPA headquarters and selecting a sawmill site. Then he returned to Lewiston, bought a steam boiler and sawmill machinery, ordered basic supplies for the new camps and had the lot hauled to the site by horse drawn freight wagons.

MISSOULA TO LEWISTON

By July 1 he was ready for Mother, Wymond and me to join him, and we were eager to go. Paxson School had been out for two weeks, so Mother closed the house in Missoula for the summer, and we boarded a stage with a half-dozen suitcases strapped to the top and our little fox terrier Tippy on our laps.

The straight-line distance from Missoula to Headquarters is just 80 miles. In later years, after a road was built through Lolo Pass, the distance by car would be only 160 miles, but in 1927 the trip covered 350 miles by stage, rail and saddle horse.

The first 165 miles was through the mountainous Idaho panhandle to Spokane, where we changed stages and gave Tippy a run. Then we headed across 200 miles of fertile wheat fields in eastern Washington's Palouse country. Suddenly a great gorge appeared, and the road dropped precipitously down hundreds

of feet to the great confluence of waters at Lewiston where the Clearwater River surges down from the Bitterroots to join the Snake as it emerges from Hell's Canyon. After a dawn-to-dusk drive on dusty gravel roads in 100-degree heat, the classic Lewis and Clark Hotel in Lewiston was a welcome oasis.

The next day was July 3, and we rode the Brill car (a gasoline engine-propelled rail car) to Orofino, transferred with Tippy and the baggage to yet another stage, and finally pulled into Pierce's dusty street in late afternoon to be greeted by Father waiting at the very end of the auto road. It had been a tiring trip for Mother, but we boys were wide-eyed with wonder at the little town whose false front buildings and wooden sidewalks looked like a street scene in a Tom Mix Western movie.

The resemblance grew as we climbed the hotel's creaking stairs to our rooms, each with a sagging double bed, a table and chair, a washbowl and pitcher, and a colorful china chamber pot with clanging lid. Father showed us how to brace the back of the chair under the doorknob to provide a degree of security often unmatched even by modern locks.

FIRECRACKERS AND DYNAMITE

Dinner was meat and potatoes, gravy, cole slaw and apple pie served family style on a long oilcloth-covered table. We devoured it. Mother went back to the room after dinner, while Father took Wymond and me for a walk along the wooden sidewalks, and described to us the various methods used for mining gold.

"You'll be panning gold yourselves in a few days!" Father declared, sending chills of excitement up our spines.

He had assembled an arsenal of fireworks for the Fourth of July and had as much fun exploding them as we did. He had been a powder monkey at various times in his career, using black powder and dynamite for blasting mine shafts in rock cliffs and blowing stumps for road building, and he helped us devise ways to use the "cannon crackers" to fashion mortars for lobbing rocks at distant targets.

Mother was distraught by the obvious danger, but Father had schooled us with proper safety precautions. He spread out both of his big hands and responded, "See, I still have all my fingers!" However he would not allow skyrockets, declaring them forest fire hazards.

HORSEBACK TO HEADQUARTERS

Mother missed her sidesaddle.

We had been rousted out early the next morning to be sure we would be ahead of the freight wagons on the dusty 13-mile horseback ride from Pierce to Headquarters. At first it had been fun for all of us, but after a few jolting miles Mother realized that sitting astride a hard Western saddle was a far cry from galloping smoothly over her Indiana farm sidesaddle.

Wymond and I knew little more about horseback riding than what we had seen in Western movies, and we were quick to complain. Soon we were arguing over whose turn it was to carry Tippy, for the little fellow would not have survived long among the horses' hoofs. Mother suffered most but said little, subscribing to her Victorian creed, "A lady doesn't complain about something which she either cannot or does not intend to do anything about."

Finally about noon, the dark road through the timber opened into a lovely green meadow with a beaver dam in its center and surrounded by a half-dozen sturdy log cabins, barns and a log corral. It had been the Clearwater Timber Protective Association's home base and now was to be the headquarters of Weyerhaeuser's Idaho timber operations.

After gently lifting Mother from her painful saddle and casting a wicked grin at us boys as we slid off our horses and collapsed onto the ground, Father led us into the comfortable three-room log cabin overlooking the broad valley. He knew that we would learn to ride horses in a hurry, but he couldn't have anticipated that in two years he would hire Wymond and me as teamsters to drive four-horse teams hitched to heavy freight wagons.

GOLD FEVER

We panned our first gold on the next Sunday. Father still had the gold pan that he had used as a prospector in Montana 40 years before. Its bright steel inside shone like a mirror and we fought for turns carrying it while he hefted a spade and mattock over his shoulder. With Tippy in the lead, we trudged past the beaver dam to its inlet and followed the rushing creek on up to a place where it spread out over a series of riffles.

"That's where the gold is boys; all you have to do is dip it out," Father said as he cleared the larger rocks and shoveled a spade full of gravel into the gold pan. As he talked, he began to swirl the gravel and water rapidly round and round in the pan, allowing the surface of the mixture to continually spill out over the edges.

"Millions of dollars worth of gold were mined from these streams during the Pierce gold rush in the 1860s, so there must be a large deposit of gold sandwiched among layers of rock in the mountains above," he speculated. "It would have been there since the mountains were formed millions of years ago."

We listened impatiently as we watched the gravel keep sluicing out until only a small bit of black sand remained.

"Is that gold?" Wymond shouted as we realized that there were shiny yellow particles sparkling among the sand. With a few final delicate swirls, Father washed out the last of the black sand leaving only tiny specks of gold to greet our delighted eyes.

"The first prospector to discover gold in this part of Idaho would have hurriedly set out stakes to mark his strike and then rushed to the nearest Government Land Office to register the claim," Father said. "And that would have triggered the Pierce gold rush, which brought thousands of other prospectors to pan the creeks for more placer gold and blast tunnels into the hard rock seeking the mother lode. In a few years, miners found the most accessible gold in the area, but he told us that prospectors still panned the creeks and drilled the rocks, hoping to make another major strike.

We spent the rest of the day taking turns with the gold pan, hardly stopping even to eat the lunch Mother had sent along. Soon we realized that we would need a lot of practice before we could match Father's skill, but like all gold miners, we were undaunted.

SLUICE BOXES AND FLUMES

Father explained that prospectors called our first pan of gold with its small yield "finding colors." Colors indicated that further exploration of that creek might be worthwhile. Once a meaningful deposit was located, sluice boxes were used to speed up the process. Often the uneven bed of a stream will develop riffles with deep pockets under them. As gold bearing sand and gravel sweep across the riffles, the heavier black sand lodges in those holes. After countless centuries, the holes sometimes become rich deposits of placer gold.

That is when the hard work begins. The miner builds a series of sluice boxes several feet long and perhaps a foot wide with shallow cleats nailed across their bottoms. The boxes are placed beside the stream, and a fast flow of water is diverted into them. Then the miner excavates a section of streambed, throwing the gravel and sand into the sluice.

Streambeds often change course, so sluicing often was done at some distance from the existing waterway or deep below the existing ground level. The sluices usually needed more water than the stream could supply, so the canyons above Headquarters were threaded with abandoned earthen flumes that had been dug to carry water to the sluicing sites. Wymond,

Tippy and I spent many days roaming deeper into the mountains, following the flumes to their sources, taking turns panning the creeks and dreaming of making a strike of our own.

Wymond was more patient than I was at panning gold, just as he had been more patient at picking huckleberries. When we left Headquarters in the fall, we excitedly brought our small bottles of gold dust and nuggets to the Pierce hardware store where the proprietor weighed it on a tiny gold scale and handed us each several dollars. Wymond got twice as many dollars as I did but I surely don't remember how many that was.

PADDY THE BEAVER

"I expect that Paddy the Beaver is at work at the upper end of the meadow," Mother told us one morning soon after we arrived at Headquarters. She had heard a tree crash to the ground where there were no loggers at work. "Why don't you go up there and see what he's doing?" she suggested. This was exciting news. The children's book *Paddy the Beaver* written by naturalist Thornton W. Burgess was a bedtime story that our parents read to us before we could read ourselves, and we practically knew it by heart. Now we finally would get to see a real live beaver!

We hurried through the grassy meadow with Tippy hopping along at our heels. Just before we sighted the beaver dam, we heard a loud boom followed by total silence. By the time we reached the pond, the water was calm and there wasn't a sound – not even a chattering chipmunk. Then we recalled from the storybook that when Paddy the Beaver sensed danger he would use his big flat tail to slap the water as a warning. At the loud noise the beavers would dive into the underwater entrances to their houses. We saw no beavers that day, but later by leaving Tippy and his happy barking at the cabin, we learned to creep like little Indians to the very edge of the pond. There we watched the beavers with their chisel-sharp teeth fall trees to strengthen their dam and to provide tender twigs to store for a winter food supply.

MOTHER'S BEAVER FANTASY

"This whole meadow might have been created by beavers," Mother told us one day. To our delight, she began spinning a romantic tale to explain how that could have come about. It was like a prequel to Burgess' story, and I recall it so clearly that I will paraphrase it here.

"As Ice Age glaciers receded from the continent millennia ago," Mother speculated, "streams of crystal clear water would have cascaded down the glacier-scoured canyons, germinating windblown seeds and others long dormant and creating a lush mantle of flower-flecked green forests to cover the barren land."

She fantasized that the scent of tasty willow bark traveling down the stream might have enticed a pair of adventurous young beavers to work their way upriver until their instinctive engineering genius halted them at a place where a dam could block the water's flow. Then they would gnaw down trees and bushes, weave them together and pack them with mud to create a pool where they could build a half-submerged home for their expected family.

"As the pond filled with silt, the beavers cut more trees to raise the dam, and in turn still other trees would die as they were submerged by the rising water, and if that cycle had been repeated over thousands of years, it could have created our lovely meadow," she concluded.

It was a delightful story, and I came to believe that it was more fact than fiction.

BEAVER PELTS AND BEAVER HATS

A century before we arrived at Headquarters, the beaver colony had faced certain extinction when a wave of beaver-hungry trappers crested the Rockies and found their way into the heart of what would become Idaho.

Tall felt hats made from beaver pelts had been *de rigueur* among fashionable Europeans for 300 years, and by 1600 Western Europe's beavers had been trapped almost to extinction. By 1700 Russia no longer could supply the demand, and the hat making industry had turned to North America for pelts.

Eventually competition between the United States and Great Britain to lay claim to western America became more than just a quest for sovereignty. In fact the lucrative new fur trade was largely responsible for the rapid exploration of the Rocky Mountains.

THE MOUNTAIN MEN

America's legendary "mountain men," Canada's Hudson's Bay Company and the French North West Company out of Quebec led the way. President Thomas Jefferson recognized its significance and negotiated purchase of the Louisiana Territory from Emperor Napoleon of France, then sent Lewis and Clark to explore it.

The trappers found what seemed to be an endless supply of beavers. In the eighteenth and early nineteenth centuries almost a half-million beavers were trapped in the United States and Canada every year, and their pelts shipped to Europe, mostly for making hats.

Then a happy quirk in the fickle fashion world saved North America's beavers from extinction. Almost overnight the trendsetters of Europe doffed their beaver hats, donned silk top hats and decreed that henceforth silk would be *de rigueu*r. Suddenly a prime beaver pelt that once could have been traded for a barrel of whisky might only pay for a couple of drinks. Fur trapping of other species continued to flourish, but beaver pelts no longer were the common medium of exchange in the West.

THE 1860 IDAHO GOLD RUSH

Another crisis threatened the beaver colony

in the 1860s with the discovery of gold in the upper reaches of the Clearwater. Gold-crazed miners arrived by horse and on foot, swelling the population of tiny Pierce to 3,000 in just a few weeks. The prospectors spread out over the creeks and mountains between the Clearwater River and the North Fork and soon the land was laced with long flumes laboriously hand-dug to carry river water to sluice boxes on the mining claims.

When we arrived at Headquarters 50 years after the gold strike, Wymond and I spent many hours following the flumes back to their sources and recreating in our minds the scene when hundreds of miners were furiously working the streams for gold. We could see where water from the beaver pond had been diverted to flumes, and we wondered how the beavers had survived before rebuilding the neat dam and pond at the head of the meadow.

"YOU CAN'T DROWN A BEAVER"

"Come along and I'll show you the new reservoir we're building to supply water for the camp," Father said one morning as he left the cabin. As we arrived with him at the construction site, we saw teamsters using horses and Fresno scrapers to build a high earthen dam across the entire meadow.

"You'll drown all the beavers!" we shouted almost in unison.

"You can't drown a beaver," he responded. "They'll just move up the creek and build another pond." We were not consoled. They were "our" beavers, and after the centuries they had survived in this pristine place, Father was about to destroy their home.

That evening Mother talked to us about the often-heartbreaking choices that must be made when civilization comes hard up against the creations of nature.

It was a difficult lesson, and it flashed back to me a decade later when Father was working on construction of Bonneville Dam and

Wymond and I watched its reservoir drown out forever the spectacular flow of the river through the Cascades of the Columbia.

TIPPY

Tippy's death was the first personal tragedy of my life, and it remains a sad scene in my memory. He had been our canine companion in Missoula, Hayes Creek and during our first summer at Headquarters.

When we moved from Pablo to Missoula we missed our yard full of pet rabbits, so Father bought us the frisky fox terrier to help fill the void. We named him Tippy for the way he seemed to dance about on his tiptoes. We survived having his wiggly tail bobbed to proper terrier length and emptied our piggy banks to buy him the best collar in the pet store.

He was a sturdy little dog until he was almost a year old, but then he was stricken by the dreaded distemper for which there was no vaccine then. After weeks of tender care Tippy survived, but the disease left him with one hind leg paralyzed. We loved the game little cripple even more as he raced to keep pace with our bicycles on his three good legs.

An early project for Wymond and me at Headquarters had been to build a tree house in pine trees near the cabin. It wasn't an architectural gem, but it had the only elevator that side of Orofino. That was a cloth-lined wooden apple box for Tippy suspended from the tree house on a rope, and we could pull it up and down with a crank arrangement.

But one day as Tippy was just starting a ride downward, the contraption got out of balance and he was catapulted out and fell a full 15 feet to the ground. The fall did what the distemper had failed to do: Tippy never recovered. For days we ministered to him, but the injuries were internal, and the veterinarian who took care of the horses and the CTPA pack mules finally advised us to "put him out of his misery."

After supper we tied Tippy to one of the trees under the tree house and walked a few yards away with Father, who sighted his .30-.06 rifle as Tippy watched, wanly wagging his tail, until the rifle cracked and he was gone, his little collar still hanging from the leash.

For a few moments I stared stunned as the terrible scene engraved itself in my memory. Then I ran sobbing into the cabin while Wymond rushed to the tree and helped Father arrange Tippy's remains for burial.

THE GOLD MINE

"That sonuvabitch Sears has staked a gold mining claim right in the middle of camp!" Father exploded as he burst into the cabin one Monday morning. He had left early to help load a freight wagon for a two-day trip to the new camp on the North Fork, and as he crossed the bridge to the barn he noticed a series of stakes extending far up on either side of the creek.

He sized up the situation quickly, and from his own experience as a prospector he realized that his mild-mannered carpenter foreman had gotten gold fever and now probably was forsaking all else.

He walked down to where Sears was standing in the creek assembling a series of sluice boxes and preparing for cleanup in the lower one. "You're fired," he called. "Come to the office for your time, and clear out of camp with your belongings before dark."

But it wasn't that easy. When Father stormed into our cabin, he went straight to the telephone on the wall and rang up the sheriff in Pierce. It turned out that Sears had planned his move carefully. He had shown Father that his mining claim was properly filed, and he said that mining laws allowed him to live on the claim and have access to it even though the land was privately owned. He had even quietly moved his bedroll and a few supplies to a small tent on the claim.

The sheriff said that there was no need for him to come to Headquarters now, because he wouldn't be able to evict Sears without a court order anyway.

Father called the Weyerhaeuser office in Lewiston, and they referred the matter to the corporate attorneys in Tacoma. Superintendent Kinney decided to come up from Lewiston for his own inspection. That wasn't easy, for although trucks could get over the road from Pierce that summer, the road wasn't passable for passenger cars, and construction of the new railroad was far behind schedule.

Father's work was disrupted, and Mother shared his frustration, so life at our cabin was pretty edgy. Then one afternoon as Wymond and I were skinny dipping in the new reservoir, the same thought came to us both. What would happen to Mr. Sears' sluices if the dam sprang a leak?

That evening after supper we went to the tool house, carried a pick and a crowbar up to the dam and stashed them behind a log. The next morning we stood on the bank watching Sears dig into the creek bottom. When he reached bedrock he started to shovel fine gravel into the sluices. We casually wandered up to the

Ben Henderson at Headquarters, Idaho.

dam. The floodgate was made of short pieces of heavy planking held against buttresses by the water pressure. We set about to pry a crack at the bottom of the top plank, intending to release a couple of inches of water.

THE FLOOD

Wymond pried open a small crack with the crowbar, and I worked one end of the pick into the crack and pulled back on the handle with all my weight. As soon as a little water got under the edge of the plank the pent-up pressure threw the plank upward like a matchstick and the entire top 6 inches of water in the reservoir began rushing through the opening.

We started running headlong down the creek, watching for the expected devastation, but to our surprise we found that we were keeping ahead of the flood. We slowed to a walk and with an eye on the creek, we reached the sluice boxes and began talking to Sears. Soon he must have heard a sound for he glanced upstream and saw a wall of water starting to fill the narrow creek bed from bank to bank.

The frightened miner dropped his shovel and scrambled up the opposite bank. The torrent scattered sluice boxes and tools in all directions, finally floating them downstream.

Father sent a crew to repair the floodgate, but before they finished the torrent of water had scoured the stream to bedrock for miles.

By the time the excitement died down, Frank Sears had gathered his bedroll and headed down the road to Pierce.

The flood was blamed on faulty construction. We never tried to retrieve our pick and crowbar, and no one was known to have been near the dam when it "broke." Of course Wymond and I had a perfect alibi, we were watching Sears at work when the flood occurred!

It was too good a story to keep secret long. Father had suspected us from the start but of course he preferred "not to know."

BIG ISLAND

I hauled back fruitlessly on the hand brake while Wymond urged the four straining horses to pull harder as our heavily loaded freight wagon careened down the side of Dead Man's Gulch close behind Big Island Sam's similarly laden wagon.

"Keep 'em pulling," Sam shouted back at us as his team reached the bottom of the bank and came to a stop in the loose gravel.

I was mighty glad that Wymond was driving on this roughest stretch of the 24-mile wagon road from Headquarters to Big Island. After all, Wymond was 12 years old and I was just 11, but of course I didn't let him know.

Big Island Sam and Sam Riggs were freighters who had been hauling supplies to Father's new camp at Big Island in the North Fork of the Clearwater all summer. That morning Sam Riggs hadn't gotten back from a two-day trip to Orofino to "have his teeth fixed," and the wagon he usually drove was loaded and waiting in front of the barn.

It was our second summer at Headquarters, and like many youngsters, Wymond and I had become "horsy," doing chores for the teamsters and riding with the Clearwater Timber Protective Association's pack strings on supply trips to surrounding fire lookouts. Big Island Sam and Sam Riggs had taught us to drive their four-horse teams around camp loading lumber and supplies.

Handling four horses is a special skill. The driver must hold four leather lines between the fingers of each hand, eight lines in all, and we were proud when we learned to do that with our small hands.

We stood with Father as he and Big Island Sam discussed what to do about the absent teamster. Sam was upset with the prospect of unharnessing both teams and spending the day in camp. Besides, the delay would slow important work at Big Island.

THE BEESECHERS

Wymond and I glaced at each other, then the words tumbled from us together. "Let us drive Sam Riggs' wagon, Father. Can we please?" Father ignored us at first, until Big Island Sam put in, "Why not, Ben? They've driven these teams quite a bit, and not much can go wrong on that narrow road with them following right behind me."

Father was impressed, not only with Sam's confidence in us but because the three-day trip would mean extra work for Sam even with our help harnessing and unharnessing the horses and feeding and corralling them at night.

He gave us a long, hard look, then said, "Are you sure you're up to it? You'd each have to do a grown man's work, and once you began you couldn't slack off or quit until you got home!" Of course, we expressed no second thoughts. He hesitated, and then said, "Well, let's go up and talk to your mother."

Mother's reaction was predictable. "Let those two little boys drive a freight wagon over the pass to Big Island and spend a night in the woods on the way? You can't be serious!" she exploded when Father broached the subject.

"But they're growing up, Linnie," Father replied. "We can't stop that, and this is a chance to give them more responsibility. Why, I was earning four bits a day driving a team of oxen clearing land in Indiana when I was 12 years old." We sensed that the discussion was going our way and began stuffing things we'd need into a pack sack.

Mother was holding back tears a short while later as she watched while we climbed over the wagon tongue and onto the seat of the second wagon and Wymond untied the lines and fitted them between his fingers. A powerful Belgian Sorrel named Blackjack was our team leader, and as Wymond slapped the lines, Blackjack leaned into the traces and the team surged forward while Big Island Sam's wagon led the way.

THE NORTH FORK

The Idaho sky was a cloudless blue, the white pine forest a blanket of green covering the mountains east to the Montana border, and our suntanned bodies were spots of brown reflecting the early morning sun. It was a moment of sheer ecstasy that sparkles in my memory.

For several miles the road climbed gradually through open timber toward a divide between the Clearwater and the smaller but swifter North Fork where it circled under 7,200-foot-high Pat Mountain. Soon the rolling dust from the first wagon turned us gray from head to foot, and we had to tie our red bandanas around our faces in order to breathe.

At the first stop Sam told us that the regular teamsters usually took turns in the lead and the second wagon stayed far enough behind to allow the worst of the dust to settle. However we couldn't bring ourselves to lose sight of the tailgate of Sam's wagon, so we endured the dust all that day.

We soon learned one big difference between driving freight wagon and riding in the back seat of the family Buick. It had been agreed that Wymond and I would take turns driving, but when it came time for the first change, our usual sibling bickering erupted. As our voices grew louder, Big Island Sam pulled his wagon to a stop, tied up the lines and walked back to see what was wrong. When he realized it was just a childish argument, he reached up with his big hands, lifted the two of us out of the wagon and deposited us on the ground.

"I'll only say this once," he said, glowering down at us. "I'm the boss of this outfit, and from now on I'll tell you when to change drivers. I expect you to act like grownups, not kids, and if there's any more grousing like this, the one who isn't driving will walk behind the wagon until the next change. Now climb back on your wagon. We're almost to Dead Man's Gulch, and we'll have work to do there."

DEAD MAN'S GULCH

An hour later we halted the wagons at the narrow gulch and peered over the edge. There was no sign of a road either to the bottom or up the other side. "Are we going to drive right over this bank?" Wymond asked, and Georgie almost wet his pants.

"Oh, we'll get across all right," Sam replied. "First help me rough-lock the wheels, then we'll drive down to the creek and water the horses while we have our noon meal."

Pulling two logging chains out of his wagon, he showed us how to fasten them around each back wheel and clamp them to the wagon bed so that the wheels couldn't turn. We then located chains in our wagon, and with Sam's help rough-locked its wheels the same way.

He said that if we tried to drive down the steep slope without rough-locks, the heavy wagons would roll so fast that they would overrun the horses, but this way the teams could easily keep ahead of the wagons as the rough-locked wheels skidded through the dirt.

We watched as Sam drove his team to the bottom and signaled for us to follow. That was when I silently thanked goodness that it was Wymond's turn to drive. Not only was he a year-and-a-half older than I was, but he was more like Father in daring and disregard of danger. He slapped the reins and Blackjack had the horses almost at a trot by the time we safely pulled up at the creek.

Boy were we hungry. Mother had packed a basket with cold fried chicken, corn on the cob, potato salad and a whole apple pie. The three of us devoured it quickly, and it seemed to mellow Big Island Sam a bit after the dressing-down he had given us earlier.

When the horses were watered Sam hitched his team in front of ours, and we rode in the wagon seat while he straddled the wheel horse of his team and rode it bareback as the eight horses pulled our wagon up the steep bank out of Dead Man's Gulch.

Leaving our wagon at the top, we helped him unhitch the two teams and drive them back to the creek so the eight horses could bring up Sam's wagon the same way.

WILD STRAWBERRY MEADOW

We had changed drivers twice since noon (on Big Island Sam's orders). I was driving when the road suddenly opened into a large clearing with a sturdy log cabin in the center, a relic of gold rush days with wild strawberries carpeting the ground and the sod roof. Wymond and I named it Strawberry Meadow.

"There's our home for the night, boys," Sam announced, smiling, as he pointed to the cabin. "The roof doesn't leak, so we'll cache our food there in case of a thunderstorm, but I'd rather sleep outside myself." A piece of sheet steel lay across some large rocks in front of the cabin with a rough wooden table beside it. Sam didn't elaborate, but we figured this was the regular overnight stopping place for him and Sam Riggs on their trips to the North Fork.

Sam assigned us camp duties and told us to unharness our horses, take them to the nearby creek to drink, and then to hitch them to a long rope that was stretched in the shade of nearby trees in lieu of a hitching rail. Soon he brought his horses and a sack of grain. We put a feedbag on each horse then returned to the wagons to unload our blanket roll and the utensils and food for supper.

As Wymond gathered wood and began building a fire under the sheet steel stove, and I carried water from the creek and started my assignment as camp cook, I thought about the very few chores that we were given to do each evening back at Headquarters before Mother called us to supper.

By the time the coffee came to a boil, Big Island Sam had laid out the harness for morning and joined us around the fire. Father had taught us how to settle coffee grounds by dropping eggshells into the pot before pouring.

Sam liked the coffee but I got mixed reviews on the meal.

While boiled potatoes and onions were no problem, I could not pretend that my lumpy mixture of flour and hot water was really gravy. Sam helped me mash the potatoes, and served with salt and big dollops of butter the potatoes tasted pretty good. Wymond's hot fire brought the sheet steel to a good temperature for grilling the inch-thick T-bone steaks, and there were canned peaches for dessert. Sam grunted grudging approval overall.

We boys unrolled our bedrolls among the wild strawberries. To discourage snakes, we looped the horsehair lariats we had braided at Hayes Creek around the beds and were asleep before dark.

Sam had the fire going when Wymond and I awoke. He cut thick slices from a side of bacon, and I put them on the grate to cook slowly as the steel heated up. I made toast on the grate by first scattering salt on it to keep the bread from burning as I had seen the camp cooks do. Mother had taught us how to fry eggs in a heavy iron skillet by pouring water into the pan and putting on a tight lid so the eggs would poach in the steam. That avoided trying to turn them over without breaking them. Buttered toast slathered with strawberry preserves capped the meal.

THE NORTH FORK SAWMILL

It was late afternoon by the time we reached the North Fork, and we heard the whine of a saw and smelled fresh-cut lumber before we sighted the river. It ran in a deep canyon, and we saw that a road with switchbacks had been roughed out on the side hill so there was no need to rough-lock our wagons.

Earlier that summer the freighters had hauled in a steam boiler and machinery for a small portable sawmill that was cutting lumber and timbers for the new camp. We were told that this was a base camp for cutting logs that would be floated down the North Fork to Lewiston in spectacular river drives.

We put our bedroll in the bunkhouse, helped Sam care for the horses then stripped off our clothes and jumped into a quiet cove of the cold river for a bath and shampoo. Mother would have approved of us when we answered the supper gong, our faces shining, our hair combed and wearing clean clothes.

A TRIUMPHAL RETURN

With nearly empty wagons, the trip back to Headquarters was made in one day. Although the wheels had to be rough-locked to go into Dead Man's Gulch, we didn't have to double up the teams for the pull out.

It was a triumphal return. I expect that Mother had been anxiously watching the road all afternoon and Father "just happened" to be working near the barn when we drove in. Big Island Sam had managed for it to be my turn to drive on the last stretch, and to our delight he made a glowing report on our performance. Sam Riggs was back on the job and took over our team, so we were free to talk about the trip right through supper. We didn't wind down until we were too sleepy to say more.

10 LEWISTON IDAHO – 1927

THE ROARING TWENTIES

The exuberant, free-spending culture of the Roaring Twenties passed our family by.

After Father completed the camps at Big Island and Headquarters in 1927, he had been confident that he would get a logging contract from Weyerhaeuser. His hopes were dashed when the company's own crews began felling the timber and floating logs down the North Fork to Lewiston. He soon was out of work.

Those years which preceded the stock market crash of October 1929 and the Great Depression of the Thirties became hardscrabble times indeed for our family.

Wymond and I were ready for junior high school, and because we no longer had a home in Missoula it was decided to move to Lewiston where we could start school while Father looked for a new business opportunity.

We had to take placement exams before entering the Idaho school system, and Mother probably was more gratified than we that we tested above our grade levels. I was 12 and Wymond 13 so I became a freshman and he a sophomore in junior high, then after one term I was transferred to an avant-garde program for practice teaching at the Lewiston State Normal School (later Lewis-Clark State College) and moved a half-grade ahead. It was the fifth different school I attended in six years!

LEWIS AND CLARK CAMPED HERE

Lewiston was an attractive, culturally advanced college town at the confluence of the Snake and Clearwater Rivers where Idaho and Washington adjoin. Lewis and Clark had camped there on their way to the Pacific in 1805 and again on their return trip in 1806. It was a natural center for trade and transportation, and its traditional resources of orchards, farms and wheat ranches were being supplemented by new sawmills and paper mills.

Housing costs were high, so the best that the family could afford to rent was a second floor walk-up, one-bedroom apartment with a Murphy bed that pulled down from the living room wall at night where Wymond and I slept. We did most of the shopping because Mother couldn't climb up and down the stairs without help. We even learned to do the laundry using a washboard and hand wringer in tubs in the basement and hanging the wash to dry on lines under the building – a slow process in winter weather. I never did learn to iron.

FATHER WAS UNDAUNTED

Mother must have been mighty discouraged that winter, but she didn't share her concern with us, and Father's self-confidence never flagged! The lumber business was booming, and he was sure that he soon would be back in business for himself.

More private timber was coming on the market as railroad companies sold land they had received from the government in the 19th century to subsidize opening of the West, and the U.S. Forest Service and Bureau of Land Management had begun to depart from their traditional policies of lock-up conservation and were encouraging sustained yield forestry.

Father felt that he had a good record with the Weyerhaeuser Company, which was building new mills in Idaho, Washington and

Oregon, so he began his search for contracts at their home office in Tacoma. When that failed he went south to Kelso where the Long Bell Lumber Company was building a new mill and a company town named Longview. There, too, he was unsuccessful, so he went up the Columbia River to Portland where half a dozen other timber companies were headquartered, again to no avail.

THE KING'S OFFICER

During his travel we looked forward to the often lengthy and always lighthearted letters that he wrote home almost every night, many of them in rhyme, relating his observations of the country and the people he met. They were especially timely because I was then studying Chaucer's *Canterbury Tales* in school.

When Father ran out of money for bus fare, the determined 62-year-old hitchhiked another 300 miles from Portland to the sawmill city of Bend, then on to Klamath Falls where Weyerhaeuser's newest sawmill was under construction. There he finally gave up the quest for a contract and hired on as a millwright helping to install machinery as he had done when building sawmills of his own in the past.

By the time he could send money home our only income was what Wymond and I earned picking fruits and vegetables. Wymond was a faster picker than I, but I made up for that some with the 15 cents an hour I earned in my first after-school job sweeping out Mrs. Cunning's stationery store each evening and the 25 cents an hour that I was paid for making occasional deliveries for the drug store next door. Those pennies really counted at a time when 10 cents would buy a pound of hamburger.

The ignominy of pleading with the apartment house manager every week to delay the rent payment no doubt exacerbated Mother's declining health. There then was no unemployment insurance or medical insurance, no food stamps or school lunch programs nor any other welfare plans, and at no time since the Pablo fire had there been an opportunity for Father to put aside savings. Neither had it ever entered his mind that there might come a time when he would not be able to earn a good living for his family, so his letters continued to be optimistic and buoyed our spirits a little.

A BOY SCOUT AT LAST

Despite that hand-to-mouth existence, I have happy memories of the year we lived in Lewiston. When we moved from Headquarters I had just turned 12 so I was old enough to join the Boy Scouts. Wymond joined too, but he didn't last long. He had a brilliant mind and natural artistic and physical skills but he quickly sensed that scouting involved a degree of both self-discipline and team discipline that he was unwilling to accept in exchange for unfettered freedom of action.

That was one circumstance in which Father's indomitable will was inherited by both of us boys – but with opposite effect. Father was a devoted Mason and had told us how diligently he had studied at night in the logging camps as a young man to rise through the fraternity's ranks and become a Knights Templar and a Shriner. Unlike Wymond, I approached Scouting with a positive zeal equal to Father's. I still have my 1927 Boy Scout Handbook, which records that I became a Tenderfoot that October and a Second Class Scout the next March – but I almost died trying to become a First Class Scout in record time!

WITH BYRD TO THE SOUTH POLE?

It was an era when adventurers and scientists were in worldwide competition to establish dramatic world records. Charles A. Lindbergh had just made the first non-stop flight across the Atlantic Ocean, barely beating out Navy Rear Admiral Richard E. Byrd for

Admiral Richard E. Byrd.

that record. Then Byrd, who had been credited previously with the first flight over the North Pole, announced plans to become the first to fly over the South Pole.

That two-year expedition would require some 100 men, three ships, three airplanes and a half-dozen dog teams at an estimated cost of a million dollars in private financing, so the famous admiral undertook a massive fund-raising drive.

A real attention-getter was his announcement that he would select a Boy Scout to be a member of the expedition. The competition was heralded in "Boys' Life," the official monthly magazine of the Boy Scouts of America, and I was an avid reader.

It was escapism that allowed me to fantasize that I could be the Boy Scout selected for that unparalleled opportunity, but I set out to qualify as purposefully as Father had pursued his rankings in the Masons. I thought that my experience in the mountains and logging camps would give me a leg-up over the city scouts I knew, but I also believed that it was important that a candidate be a First Class Scout.

Poring over the First Class requirements in the scout handbook with my fellow scout Richard Anderson, we found that we both had the required time-in-grade as Second Class, but we hadn't met the hiking requirement. We overcame that hurdle one Saturday with a 14-mile round-trip trek to Asotin, Washington. In those years Mother was concerned about my health, because the hard case of scarlet fever I had suffered earlier might have damaged my heart, so to avoid worrying her further I didn't tell her about that hike.

The requirements also stipulated that a First Class Scout must swim 50 yards. That brought me up short! Richard had learned to swim in summer camp, but Father wasn't a swimmer and Mother had a fear of water, so neither Wymond nor I had learned.

NEAR DISASTER IN THE SNAKE

Richard said that swimming was easy and that he would teach me – but I almost died trying. On a warm June evening the two of us scrambled down the east bank of the Snake River to a quiet pool where we had seen people swimming before. We laid our clothes on a rock and began my lesson. Richard told me to wade in to where the water was shoulder high and then duck under with my eyes open to get the feel of being under water. He stayed above me and I took a tight grip on his hand.

The "quiet pool" must have been a whirlpool for before I was hip-deep an undercurrent swept my legs from under me. Fortunately Richard was only knee-deep, and as I frantically flailed the water, he managed to drag me sputtering to shore before the current could take me the short distance downstream to where the Clearwater joined the Snake.

By the time we were dressed our clothes were almost as wet as our hair, and because we didn't want to worry Mother about swimming, we ran through several lawn sprinklers on the Normal School campus on our way home to account for our drenching. It was another two years before I finally did learn to swim.

SIXTY MERIT BADGES SHORT

My carefully hand-printed application to Admiral Byrd, attractively illustrated with pen and ink drawings made by Wymond, brought a courteous hand signed note from the Admiral explaining that Paul Siple, an 18-year-old Eagle Scout and Sea Scout with sixty merit badges and credentials as a budding scientist, had been selected to join the expedition. I was disappointed but not really surprised, and I treasured the Admiral's note for many years.

We kept abreast of the expedition through Byrd's pioneering weekly short-wave radio broadcasts from "ten thousand miles away in Little America," as he named his base in Antarctica, and I followed Paul Siple vicariously as he became one of the expedition's best dog sled drivers. I was sorry that he wasn't among the crew of the Ford Tri-Motor airplane when Admiral Byrd successfully made history's first flight over the South Pole in November 1929.

TROUPING THE WEST

Traveling companies of actors and musicians had begun to troupe the mining camps and early settlements of Idaho when it still was part of Montana Territory, and the successors to those pioneer thespians were enlivening Lewiston's cultural life when we arrived 75 years later. They performed on the same Main Street theater stages that were used for silent movies on other nights. Their repertoires ranged from drama to vaudeville and slapstick comedy.

My first exposure to serious poetry was when an actor read from the stage a dramatic poetic saga of the Modoc Indian Wars written by the controversial poet Joaquin Miller, who lived for a time in Canyon City, Oregon. A devout Quaker and a Civil War pacifist, he had been part-owner and editorial writer for the short-lived *Eugene City Democratic Register* in Eugene, Oregon. In the 1860s he participated in the Idaho gold rush with uncertain success.

Mother encouraged our interest in theater, but stage plays or fiction were not of interest to Father. He much preferred Fatty Arbuckle's slapstick comedy and Scotsman Harry Lauder's rollicking renditions of "When I Was Twenty-One" and "Roamin' in the Gloamin.'" Regarding fiction he would say, "I can dream my own dreams. I don't need to have someone dream them for me."

WHEN FRIENDSHIPS COUNT

When school let out in the spring of 1928, the family was anxious to join Father in Klamath Falls, and under Mother's direction Wymond and I began packing for the move. Then we became aware of how much our neighbors had admired Mother's fortitude in coping with that stark fall and winter. Mr. and Mrs. Prine, who owned the grocery store, Mrs. Cunning, who had hired me at her stationery store, her son Tom, Richard Anderson's family, who owned the hardware store on Main Street, and others simply took over the tasks of cleaning out the apartment and packing our belongings. Then they arranged for tickets and bundled us on board the early morning motor stage to Oregon.

11 KLAMATH FALLS – 1928

BACK TO THE WILD WEST

The Old West was slow to die in Klamath Falls.

When Father met us as we climbed off the stage into the clamor of Main Street on Saturday evening, the dissonance contrasted tangibly with the staid Main Street of Lewiston that we had left early that morning. Music was blaring from the Rialto Cafe, shiny new Model A Fords were crowded among spud-laden farm trucks, and a topless Cadillac touring car packed with rodeo cowboys from Lakeview was using its musical horn to claim the center of the street.

It had been a wearying 500-mile ride over gravel roads down the Snake and Columbia Rivers and south on Highway 97 almost to the California line, but Wymond and I had napped part of the way, so we were wide awake to the new sounds and sights. Father told us that it was the day when Indians on the Klamath Reservation received their government checks, and although prohibition had been the law since 1919, it seemed as if the Volstead Act hardly applied to Klamath and Lake counties. No sooner would the Indians leave the reservation at Chiloquin and cash their checks than they, along with much of the rest of the population, would find a source of whisky, and the jails would begin to fill.

We carried our bags the few blocks to the Peyton Apartments where Father showed us our new home. It was a second floor walk-up, the same as we had in Lewiston, but instead of a Murphy bed there was a separate room for us boys. The central fire station was just around the corner, the county courthouse was a couple of blocks away, and our bedroom window was directly across the alley from the Elks Club ballroom, where the Saturday night dance with live music was just getting under way.

Mother must have reflected sadly on the tranquility of our log cabins at Hayes Creek and Headquarters, but the tradeoffs were that we would be close to the new Klamath Union High School, Fremont grade school and Carnegie Library and handy to markets and medical facilities. We made our beds quickly, and fortunately the fire department didn't get a call that night!

STRAFED BY A PELICAN

A wonderful bird is the pelican,
His bill will hold more than his belican.
He can take in his beak
Food enough for a week,
But I'm damned if I see how the helican.
Dixon Lanier Merritt

A shadow fell across us, and we instinctively ducked our heads as a large white bird sailed silently above, flapping its 9-foot wings slowly, then settled onto a nearby nest in a swirl of cattails.

It was our first morning in Klamath Falls, and Wymond and I had crossed the Link River Bridge near our apartment to explore along the edge of Lake Ewauna. Standing knee-deep in marsh grass, we watched as the bird opened its huge beak and saw that it was filled with small fish it had scooped from Upper Klamath Lake a mile away. The bird was delivering the bounty to a nest full of chirping chicks that noisily crowded to reach their squirming meal. To our

An American white pelican on Tule Lake near Klamath Falls. Tim Boyer photo.

relief it soon flew off, either not knowing or not caring about our presence.

It was the first pelican we had ever seen, but we soon learned that the birds are icons of Klamath Falls, with restaurants, hotels and even sports teams named for them. Mother was fascinated by our story and said that few amateur ornithologists ever had such an opportunity to watch a pelican's feeding ritual close up.

JOB HUNTING

We wouldn't do much exploring that summer, for it was time to seek summer jobs to pay for clothes and school supplies in the fall.

Although Wymond was only 14, he was tall and sturdy and looked older, so he got a job at the Ewauna Box Company handling heavy bundles of boards as they were milled and stacked for shipment and assembly into crates and boxes. In a few more years wooden boxes would be replaced by the cardboard containers common today.

Wymond was delighted, but job opportunities for a 12-year-old such as I were slim. There was a "help wanted" sign on the Shell service station, and I pictured myself pumping gasoline from the big glass tanks out in front, but it turned out that the job was to wash the glass in hundreds of foot-square steel windows that were the trademark of Shell stations. The Bon Ami cleaner left a white residue on any spot not carefully polished, and after a week the manager and I agreed that my future didn't lie in "doing windows."

One day Father offered to help me find a job, so we went out on Main Street together to begin the search. Before long he had convinced a wholesale grocery truck operator that I could be very helpful to him as he made deliveries along his county wide route, commenting that it would be good experience for me too. By the end of the first week I was doing most of the work while the owner drank Green River sodas in the shade of the truck. When I asked about being paid, he said he had understood from Father that I would work "for the experience." He must have thought that the cookies and sodas that we took from inventory for lunches were enough pay for a 12-year-old apprentice, but since cookies wouldn't pay for school clothes I renewed my job search.

MAGILL'S DRUG STORE

"Grand Opening Saturday – Free Gifts!" read a sign hanging above an open storefront on Main Street. Remembering the drug store job I'd had in Lewiston, I stepped through remodeling debris to look for the manager. A tall, middle-aged man wearing a white coat was carrying several boxes full of bottles. As he passed me, two of them were about to fall to the floor, so I reached out and grabbed them. "Thank you boy," he said, "but what are you doing in here?"

"I've worked in drug stores before and I thought you might need help and I need a job!" I blurted.

It turned out that he was chief pharmacist Richard Morton who would manage the new store. The timing was right. After giving me a long speculative look he called to another white-coated man, "We're not going to be ready to open by Saturday unless we have more help," he said. "See if this boy can help you with unpacking those boxes and stocking the shelves." The younger man, who also was a pharmacist, lost no time in telling me what to do, but neither did he stop his work to teach me how. I must have caught on quickly, for when lunchtime came Morton told me that the owner, Lloyd Magill, would be there after lunch, and we could talk to him about a job.

It was several blocks to the apartment but I ran most of the way, taking the stairs two at a time, and reported my news to Mother. She quickly fixed me a sandwich, and I ran back to the store. Lloyd Magill was there, and Morton had told him about me. I learned later that Magill owned a thriving drug store in Bend and had a son about my age who was in Hill Military Academy in Portland, so he may have had doubts about the competence of a

12-year-old boy working in his new store. He asked how much the Lewiston drug store had paid me, and when I told him 25 cents an hour, he hesitated, then said, "Well, it will be worth that if you can help us get the store opened by Saturday, so get to work."

A FOUR-BIT HAIRCUT

The store was ready by Friday night, and after Morton paid me the $12 I had earned, Mr. Magill casually flipped me another coin, saying, "Take this four bits and get a haircut and come back tomorrow in clean clothes ready to help with the opening." I had my summer job, but since haircuts cost a dollar, I had to provide four bits out of my wages.

The younger pharmacist, Cruikshank, was my boss, and I quickly learned the difference between a schoolteacher and a boss. When Cruikshank told me to do something, he expected me to finish that assignment without asking questions before starting another. I tried to learn by watching others, but after he had shown me once how to do a job, I'd better not ask him how the next time.

I still shudder when I recall an incident with a Coca Cola keg. Soft drinks were made by squirting flavored syrup from a jar behind the counter into a glass, then filling the glass with ice and soda water under pressure – thus the name "soda fountain." The half-gallon jars of syrup were replenished from larger containers in the basement. Once after I had learned the procedure, I took an empty Coca Cola jar from the fountain to the basement, set it under the spout of a keg of Coca Cola syrup and turned on the spigot. When it appeared that the slowly flowing liquid would take several minutes to fill the jar I didn't want my boss to think I was loafing in the basement so I left the syrup running and ran upstairs to finish another task.

Soon I was preoccupied, and then Cruikshank spotted me. "Didn't I tell you to fill the syrup jars for the soda fountain?" he called out. I scrambled to my feet and made for the basement with the boss on my heels. The syrup jar was just ready to overflow onto the merchandise-crowded floor when I closed the spigot.

Cruikshank had a short temper and took me straightaway to Morton, expecting to see me fired on the spot. But Morton, who had a son of his own, was more tolerant and gave me a second chance. Sometimes today when faced with a choice between expediency and good judgment, that experience comes to mind.

Me in my starched white shirt, trousers and red bow tie, ready to stop traffic as a 12-year old disc jockey for Magill's.

A 12-YEAR-OLD DISC JOCKEY

On opening day the free samples of cigarettes and perfume slowed down foot traffic on Main Street a little, but the big Wurlitzer really made the difference.

When Pharmacist Cruikshank rolled the store's new high fidelity electric phonograph out onto the street and a small boy in starched white shirt and trousers and wearing a red bow tie began playing cowboy ballads by Vernon Dalhart and jazz music by Gus Arnhiem's orchestra, featuring a young crooner named Bing Crosby, even automobile traffic slowed to listen. Soon a wedge of onlookers stretched from the front door to beyond the curbing, and the crowd began to call out requests.

The Wurlitzer didn't have a record-changer, so I was kept busy changing disks. Top-of-the-line Victor Red Seal 78 rpm records cost 75 cents and a secondary brand were 68 cents, and by closing time on the first night the most popular numbers on both labels were sold out.

Pharmacist Cruikshank was in charge of the record department, so our relationship warmed up in a hurry.

KOAC in Corvallis and KGW in Portland were the nearest radio stations. Their reception in Klamath Falls was poor, so phonograph records were a popular source of home entertainment. My Saturday night record show became a regular part of the Main Street scene on several nights a week all that summer.

Lloyd Magill was so pleased that when he built a new store in Medford the following summer, he had Richard Morton take me to the opening, commenting, "George brought us good luck in Klamath Falls, and I want him to help with the Medford opening too."

12   CRATER LAKE 1928 – 2002

Standing on the rim of Crater Lake, 1928.

TOO BLUE TO BE BELIEVED

Crater Lake reflecting a Parish Blue sky in its 2,000-foot-deep pool of pristine water is a sight of unsurpassed grandeur. A neighbor invited our family on a drive to the renowned national park soon after we came to Klamath Falls. Wymond and I were anxious to go but were skeptical too. We didn't think it possible for Crater Lake to compare to Flathead Lake or Glacier or Yellowstone national parks, which we had known in Montana.

We were so very wrong! After climbing for several miles from Highway 97 the road had leveled off, the sky brightened, and as we peered out the car windows, we no longer could see a mountaintop ahead but suddenly were gazing down into the crater of legendary Mount Mazama, filled with water too blue to be believed.

Our host stopped first at Crater Lake Lodge, but we were anxious to get to the water, so he drove several miles around Rim Drive to the only trailhead. While Mother waited at the car I grabbed a clear glass bottle that I'd brought from the drug store, and Wymond and I raced down the mile-long trail to the dock, followed at a brisk walk by Father.

A boat filled with tourists had just returned from an excursion to Wizard Island, so it was a few minutes before we could fill our bottle with blue lake water to take up to Mother. By the time Father arrived, wearing a broad grin, we had filled and emptied the bottle several times, then we turned to him with disappointed and wondering faces – the water in the bottle wasn't blue at all.

As we climbed dejectedly back up the trail, Father explained the simple science involved and assured us that on an overcast day the lake wouldn't appear blue either. Our naturalist Mother wasn't surprised but thanked us as she drank the cool, clear water.

DEJA VU – CRATER LAKE – 1938

It was ten years before I visited Crater Lake again, and that time we made a precarious ski run from the crater rim down to the lake and then dove into the icy blue water.

On Memorial Day 1938 five of us who worked together on the Mount Hood National Forest decided to spend the holiday skiing on Mount Lassen in Northern California. We ironed paraffin, beeswax and graphite onto our ski bottoms so they would slide in the warm spring snow, strapped them to the homemade roof rack on my well-worn red Dodge sedan, pooled our funds to pay for gasoline and headed south on Highway 97. That night we rolled out our blankets beside the highway, picking up several wood ticks in the process, and drove on to Fort Klamath for breakfast.

I remembered that when we lived in Klamath Falls there had been an annual Fort Klamath-to-Crater Lake Ski Race. "Let's drive up and see if there's still snow at the rim," I suggested. "Maybe we could ski down, swim in the lake and wash off some wood ticks too."

By the time we were halfway to the rim there were high snow banks on each side of the car, for snowplows had just opened the road. When we stopped in the plowed-out parking area at the top, few words were exchanged as we hurriedly put on our skis and began poling along the rim looking for a way down the 1,000-foot-high crater wall. We finally selected a frightfully steep gully that appeared to be snow-filled all the way to the bottom.

EXTREME SKIING

We all raced for Cascade Ski Club, but Boyd French Jr. was best at running slaloms. He started first, making connected turns all the way down, but some of us resorted to side slipping in the narrowest parts of the gulch.

No one fell, and when we reached the bottom we threw off our clothes and dived into the ice-cold water. I had become a good swimmer since my near-fatal lesson in the Snake River 10 years before, but on this day none of us swam more than enough to get back to shore and scramble shuddering onto the snow bank.

It was a hard climb back up the steep snow chute. Our slick-soled ski boots were not practical for climbing so we put on our skis and side stepped and traversed all the way.

AMBUSHED

Waiting for us when we reached the rim was a grim-faced official in a campaign hat, snappy gray uniform and shiny riding boots standing in the melting snow.

"Who is in charge of this party?" he demanded. All eyes turned to me for a response. It turned out that our greeter was the chief ranger of Crater Lake National Park. I remember that his name was Frost, and since he was holding the Dodge's registration certificate and the name of the owner matched the name on my driver's license I hardly could deny the assignation.

When he learned that we all worked for the U.S. Forest Service I began to feel uneasy. The two federal agencies were bitter bureaucratic rivals, and five Forest Service smoke-chasers would not rate very high with this National Park Service executive. I decided that it might improve our position if he knew my role as a newspaper writer and ski columnist for the *Oregon Journal.* When he asked who had given us permission to ski down the crater wall, I avoided the question by telling him that I was gathering information for my column and asked him about the Park Service's policy toward organized skiing. It was a loaded question because right then I was part of a campaign by Oregon outdoor clubs to block an effort to make Mount Hood a national park.

Soon we realized that while we might not have broken any specific rule, we could at least face a charge of trespassing. Ranger Frost was a reasonable man and was anxious that our adventure not tempt others to undertake similar transgressions. Finally he and I struck a highly informal agreement. As long as I discouraged skiing inside the crater rim, the Park Service would not file charges against us. I fulfilled my end of the bargain in my *Oregon Journal* "Ski Scout" column that November with the following information: "…skiing must henceforth be confined to snow fields sloping away from the lake on penalty of ejection from the park, so we can't recommend the shoreline schuss, but it was fun!"

Breathing a collective sigh of relief, we headed for Mount Lassen, not thinking that it, too, might be under the same jurisdiction as Crater Lake. Fortunately by the time we reached Redding, California, the temperature was 110 degrees and the wax on our skis was melting and running down the hot steel sides of the Dodge. We changed plans and finished the holiday with a drive west through the Trinity Alps to the picturesque old mining town of Weaverville and on to the cool Pacific Coast.

DEJA VU – CRATER LAKE – 1949

It was an eerie feeling 11 years later to be the only soul in that awesome crater with no succor possible should my tiny aircraft cease to fly. Suppressing a shudder, I carefully advanced the throttle on the 65-horsepower Aeronca and felt a surge of relief as the engine responded smoothly and the propeller bit harder into the thin air, taking me back above Wizard Island

I was a bank officer and had been flying the two-place Aeronca on a business trip from Portland to Medford. Crater Lake wasn't in the flight plan, but after a stop in Roseburg to make a call on the Douglas County Bank I had topped off the gas tank and taken off for Medford, climbing to 8,000 feet in order to watch the parade of snow-clad Cascade peaks thrusting into the blue sky on the left. Suddenly the karma felt right!

The air was smooth, the sky was CAVU (ceiling and visibility unlimited), and the engine was throbbing confidently in the cold dry air. Making a quixotic decision, I zipped up my parka against the late winter chill and pointed the Aeronca east, climbing slowly for an hour until the plane crested Crater Lake's west rim and Wizard Island appeared under the high-wing monoplane's left wing. Crater Lake in winter grandeur sparkled like a brilliant blue gem nestled in a rumpled ermine robe.

It took another five minutes to fly the five miles across to the east rim, then I circled and returned over the north rim and let down into the crater itself to scan the 1,000-foot-high encircling walls, hoping to spot the snow-filled gully we had skied down 11 years before.

From the air the slope looked nearly vertical, and it proved futile to try to locate one narrow gully along the 18-mile perimeter. Then the thought struck me that I was skimming over the waters of America's deepest lake. I hastened to climb back to 8,000 feet and followed snowbound Rim Drive until Rim Village and Crater Lake Lodge appeared below.

The highway to the lake wouldn't be open for another three months, and until then this majestic spectacle of Crater Lake in pristine winter garb would be shared only by an occasional visitor on skis or snowshoes. It was unlikely that Ranger Frost, who had been our nemesis in 1939, still held that post, and the chances were slim, too, that anyone would make a note of the Aeronca's registration number as I set a course to Medford. (I recently checked my pilot log book for 1949 and did not find an entry for that flight.)

DEJA VU – CRATER LAKE – 2002

The saga of our family's adventures at Crater Lake culminated in July 2002 when *Sunset Magazine* carried a six-page tribute to the park's centennial written by daughter Bonnie Henderson after she and her sisters Donna and Darcy had made an eleven-day backpack trip over the Pacific Crest Trail from Crater Lake to McKenzie Pass. They invited me along but I didn't think I could keep up their pace.

13 KLAMATH FALLS: FOUR JOBS A DAY

Pharmacist Cruikshank was my immediate boss at Magill's and had a huge influence on my early life.

Our trip to Crater Lake was about the only family recreation we had during the year-and-a-half we lived in Klamath Falls. Father worked six days a week at the sawmill, but his wages paid for little more than food, rent and Mother's doctor bills, while Wymond and I earned most of our own expenses.

When Wymond started Klamath Union High School in the fall he decided not to try out for freshman football, but instead got an after-school job at the Ewauna Box Company where he had worked during the summer.

I vowed not to be the only man in our family who wasn't fully employed. I would turn 13 in August and would begin mid-eighth grade in Fremont School. I was small for my age and my voice hadn't changed yet, so prospects for getting a real "grown-up" job seemed dim.

I was in line to get a much-sought-after newspaper route as a *Morning Oregonian* carrier in the spring, and that would require a bicycle. Also I hadn't had a new overcoat since we left Missoula, and I wanted a camera and some radio equipment so that I could qualify for Boy Scout merit badges in those fields.

Boy, did I need a job!

Mother had a suggestion. "You've made lots of friends working at Magill's, and some of them might be glad to have you ask for help," she said, "but rather than asking for a job just ask for their advice and see what happens."

I spoke to Pharmacist Cruikshank, who told me that the manager of the Willard Hotel where he lived was having difficulty getting someone to mop out the lobby early every morning. "It's easy work, but he needs a person he can depend on," Cruikshank said. My eyes widened when he said that the hotel paid four bits a day for the chore. Cruikshank took me to see the manager and he hired me.

The owner of our apartment house also owned the nearby Peyton Fuel Company and when Mr. Peyton heard of my early morning job he asked if I would stop at his office in the mornings on my way to the Willard and build a fire in the wood stove so that it would be warm when his employees arrived. I agreed, and since the Willard had established a price he agreed also to pay four bits a day.

I dreaded those mornings when Mother hustled me out of bed before six to trudge in the dark through snow-covered streets to Peyton's office. After I had the fire burning I'd close the damper, lock the office and hurry across Main Street to the Willard where I mopped the entrance and lobby so they would be sparkling when the manger unlocked the hotel for the day. As I trotted home for breakfast, I'd remind myself that for those two morning jobs I was earning a dollar every day even before school started. Mother sometimes had to write excuses for me for being tardy for eighth grade.

A RED-AND-GREEN BIKE

The Saturday disc jockey job at Magill's continued until cold weather forced Cruikshank to roll the Wurlitzer inside, but I continued to work as a delivery and stock boy on Saturdays and some week days.

That led to a fourth job. One afternoon the circulation manager of the *Klamath Evening Herald* phoned for a bottle of Bromo Seltzer and a sandwich to be sent over from the drug store. When I made the delivery I saw why he needed the Seltzer – the person who ran the mailing machine hadn't shown up for work, so the manager was having to perform that tedious job along with his own just when the paper was coming off the press. It was near the end of my shift at Magill's, so I called Cruikshank, who agreed to let me fill in at the paper for the rest of the day. It turned into a permanent after-

school job until the *Oregonian* carrier route opened up in June.

To my delight I earned as much that winter from my four part-time jobs as Wymond did at the box factory, so in the spring I bought a shining new green-and-white Ranger bicycle and a warm overcoat.

Those earnings also launched two hobbies that eventually led to careers: photography and ham radio. For $5 I bought a new Kodak Folding Brownie camera that I used in 1935 to snap a picture on Mount Hood of the climbing dog Ranger. That image won the *Oregon Journal's* photo contest. I also bought parts to build a radio spark transmitter and crystal receiver, leading to my World War II service as a radio operator in the Merchant Marine.

THE KLAMATH TAJ MAHAL

To Wymond and me it resembled pictures of the Taj Mahal in our schoolbooks, but Klamath Falls' new monument to the opulent Twenties predictably was named the Pelican Theater. We had watched as workmen built the walls of what looked like Italian marble and sculpted a large white pelican on its facade. Then they installed rich maroon carpeting and hung colorful curtains and a large silver screen behind the proscenium. Soft leather seats were widely spaced and star-like lights twinkled in the vast ceiling.

THE PELICAN SPEAKS!

On opening night the restless shafts of two revolving Hollywood spotlights searched the sky from Keno to Bonanza and from Merrill to Algoma, enticing people to patronize Southern Oregon's first sound motion picture house. The striking structure may not have rivaled the Taj Mahal but the advance promotion crew from Hollywood could hardly have done better for the original.

Lloyd Magill had been among the Main

Street businessmen given opening night passes, and Wymond and I were tightly gripping a pair of them as we worked our way to the front of the crowd that night. Colored lights above the entrance spelled out the playbill:

WARNER BAXTER IN "THE ARIZONA KID" IN LIFELIKE SOUND AND LIVING COLOR

It would be our first "talking picture."

After the crowd settled and the lights dimmed, we almost jumped out of our seats as we felt the floor begin to vibrate and heard a low rumble from the front of the theater. Then a section of floor near the stage slid open and the console of the great Wurlitzer pipe organ rose slowly while the organist's hands and feet flew among the pedals and keys to perform a booming opening overture.

Decades later as I listened to a recital in Notre Dame Cathedral in Paris, I felt the vibrations from its pipe organ and thought back to that moment in Klamath Falls.

Oh yes, *The Arizona Kid* was a great success! The crackling-sharp acoustics of the new theater made it seem that Warner Baxter was riding his horse right down the main aisle.

SIGHT WITHOUT SOUND

Imagine what it had been like in the past to attend a sound movie shown in a theater that didn't have sound projection equipment. Dialog was provided by subtitles and background music by a live piano, but watching musical films in silent theaters could be bizarre.

One time in Plainfield, Indiana, Cousin Jack Miller and I saw a silent version of a film in which the female star sang My Wild Irish Rose. While she was silently mouthing the Irish melody, a young boy walked onto the stage and sang the words in his childish soprano – with a Hoosier accent!

The Jazz Singer with Al Jolson, the most

On my way to Bend wearing the new overcoat I bought with pay from my job at Magill's drug store.

popular singer of the time, was the first sound movie ever produced. I first saw it in a silent movie theater in Bend. Jolson's voice was strong and deep but as we watched him belt out his songs that night, a Bend boy stepped from the wings and sang along with Jolson, in a youthful tenor!

Later Mother took us to the Pelican Theater to finally see and hear Al Jolson perform his classic songs "Mammy" and "Sonny Boy."

14 KLAMATH FALLS TO PORTLAND – 1929

UPROOTED

"George, report to the principal," my high school teacher announced one morning in the fall of 1929. Twenty pairs of 14-year-old eyes swung up from schoolbooks and fastened on me. I almost bolted for the boys' room!

But the news was good. Mother was in the office explaining to the principal that she planned to take me out of school to help her on a trip to visit her family in Indiana, and I would need school records so that I could finish the semester in Indianapolis.

OUR WORLD WAS OVERTURNING!

Father exploded the bombshell at dinner: He had sold the family farm in Indiana to Mother's brother Carl at a handsome price!

Uncle Carl knew that Father had lost half his fortune 20 years earlier trying to raise corn on that lovely hilltop farm, which he learned later was underlain with gravel. However Uncle Carl had decided that it would be a fine site for an upscale horse ranch, located as it was just five miles from the Indianapolis Speedway and adjacent to the Indianapolis Country Club. His farm machinery business in Iowa was riding the crest of the 1920s boom, and his decision might also have been influenced by our family's financial straits and his concern over Mother's health.

Father wasn't one to dwell on problems of the past, and he didn't appear to have much concern about the future, either. His only thought was that now he could return our family to the lifestyle we had enjoyed before the Pablo fire plunged us into poverty.

"There's no place for a small operator in the lumber business anymore," he concluded, "so we're going to move to Portland, and I'll go into the real estate business."

Mother was to visit her family in Indiana for the first time in years, but because she wasn't well enough to travel alone, I was to accompany her. Wymond would continue at Klamath Union High School until the Christmas break, then be rewarded with a trip to San Francisco with Father. We all would then meet in Portla and on New Year's Eve.

PULLING UP ROOTS

I was the only one who really had put down roots in Klamath Falls, and now in just a few days I was to leave with no plan to return.

Father and Wymond were happy to quit their heavy sawmill jobs, so I got little sympathy. I turned my *Oregonian* route over to an anxious successor, bid farewell to Lloyd Magill, Richard Morton, Pharmacist Cruikshank, Mr. Peyton, the *Evening Herald*, the Willard Hotel and the firemen at the firehouse next door who used to let me slide down the fire pole and sometimes sound the siren on fire calls. I wouldn't see Klamath Falls again for 20 years!

When Mother and I boarded the train for Indiana, I realized just how much she needed me. Her swollen ankles would barely support her, and her gnarled fingers could hardly hold a cup. When there was money to pay for treatment, she had spent hours with chiropractors and non-medical healers armed with diathermy machines, magnetic devices and bottled remedies without success. Her illness went through cycles of remission, but although specialists agreed on a diagnosis of rheumatism, none had provided lasting relief.

From the moment we boarded a luxurious Pullman car in the Klamath Falls depot until Aunt Janette and Cousin Marietta met us at the Indianapolis station, the trip was for me an explosion of new experiences tumbling one over another. Our railroad car soon was coupled into the Union Pacific's crack *City of San Francisco* headed for Chicago.

I used my new camera to take pictures from the train as the tracks crossed Great Salt Lake, which then was lined with beaches and bathing resorts. Mother told me that except for the Great Lakes it was the largest lake in America, and from its center the shores were out of sight beyond the horizon.

Snow already covered the mountains, and soon a second powerful steam locomotive was coupled to the train as a "helper" to pull it slowly up the Continental Divide to Promontory Point, where just 60 years earlier, a golden spike had been driven to celebrate completion of the first transcontinental railroad across North America. The train then wound down the Eastern Slope of the Rockies to the prairies of Nebraska and on to Des Moines, Iowa, where we stopped for two days to visit Uncle Carl and Aunt Jennie.

MYSTERIES OF A MODEL T FORD

To my delight Uncle Carl's secretary took me for a tour of the city in her Model T Ford, then asked, "Can you drive?" When I said that I could, she handed me the key and suggested that I go for a drive while she went into the office to open the morning mail. I didn't volunteer that I had never driven a Model T with its unique planetary transmission and three pedals on the floor, but I was undaunted.

Many Model Ts had to be hand-cranked but hers had a self-starter, so I managed to get it under way before I learned that when you push in the "brake" pedal the engine would die unless you pushed the "low" pedal halfway in at the same time. By the time I delivered the Ford's keys back to its owner, I had mastered the art of using both feet on pedals while handling the throttle with one hand and steering with the other. It was a timely lesson, because in a few years I would buy a Model T of my own.

We spent an evening reliving with the Millers the visits they had made to Montana, including the one in 1922 when Uncle Carl jumped through the cabin window.

MILLERS AND HENDERSONS GALORE

We continued by train to Clermont, where we spent a month with Grandma and Grandpa Miller in the same farmhouse where Mother and her brothers and sisters had been born. Cousin Marietta McDaniels and Aunt Janette and Uncle Mac were living with the grandparents too, but Cousin Carl wasn't born until a year later. I learned to enjoy Uncle Mac's dry wit as I rode with him on sales trips around Marion County.

I didn't have to go to school in Indianapolis after all. Mother decided that she needed my continuing help, and since I already was a semester ahead of grade level I could wait until we reached Portland to enter a new high school. Father had asked that I visit as many of his family members as I could, so after showing us their own farm in Brown County, Uncle Chester, Aunt Maeda and Cousin Jack, who lived in nearby Plainfield, took us to see the Ward Henderson family in Brownsburg and Father's sister Anna Pickett in Indianapolis.

Later we called on Uncle George Dallas Henderson, Father's younger brother, after whom I was named, and met Aunt Rissa and our cousins Verna, Bertha and Lorella Jean who was only 5 at the time. Uncle Dallas had just been made manager of the Ripley County Farm Bureau, and while Mother visited with Aunt Rissa, he took me to see the Henderson homestead on Laughery Creek near the Ohio River and to the schoolhouse near Versailles where Father had once taught school.

Father's businesses in Montana were named "Donlan and Henderson" and were partnerships with prominent Montana business and political leader Ed Donlan. The Northern Pacific railroad stations bearing their names were sites of two of their early sawmills, and Dallas Henderson likely was in charge of the sawmill at Henderson in 1904 when Father made his first trip home to Indiana.

Later Dallas also visited their parents in Indiana, where he met Rissa. After a two-week courtship they were married and returned to Henderson where Rissa was postmaster for several years.

FATHER AND THE INTERNET – 2002

One day in June 2002 as I was writing this memoir and wracking my brain to recall what Father had told me some 80 years before about the Montana towns of Henderson and Donlan, I typed "Ben W. Henderson" on the keyboard of my Macintosh computer, and to my astonishment, Father's smiling countenance appeared in the monitor. I unknowingly had opened a Web site devoted to Henderson family ancestry. The site is maintained by Bryce Stevens. He is a grandson of Uncle Dallas and very knowledgeable of our family genealogy.

Thus through what my son Randall refers to as "the black magic of the Internet," two first cousins, Lorella Jean Stevens and I, the only living members of our generation in our branch of the Henderson family tree, now are exchanging Montana lore of a century ago.

A COUNTRY BOY IN DETROIT

Before returning to Montana, Mother and I went by train to Detroit to visit Mother's oldest brother, Dr. Earl Miller and his wife, Margaret. Uncle Earl had been head of the Department of Experimental Medicine at Park Davis Company in Detroit but at the time of our visit was quite ill. Aunt Margaret was with him constantly, so Cousin Jemima and her fiancé really showed me the city.

In 1929 Detroit claimed to be the world's fastest-growing city and was the center of the automobile industry, so it was exciting indeed to a boy who had seen little more of the world than lumber camps and small western towns.

I watched Buick automobiles being built on an assembly line in nearby Flint and saw Ford Tri-Motor airplanes being assembled in Dearborn. I toured Greenfield Village, Henry Ford's newly opened replica of an early American settlement, and rode to the top of Detroit's Golden Tower, the Fisher Building skyscraper, where pioneer radio station WJR was broadcasting a live program. Finally I saw Groucho Marx and the Four Marx Brothers live on the Cass Theater stage.

I remember Uncle Earl's warm smile as he waved us goodbye from his bed while holding the fringed Pendleton Chief Joseph shawl that Mother had brought him from Oregon.

In late December we headed back to Oregon, but before leaving Detroit I spent a memorable evening ice skating in starlight on the seemingly endless frozen channels of Belle Isle Park in the Detroit River, which separates the city from Windsor, Canada.

ROSES FOR NEW YEARS

After a final week of farewells in Clermont, we began our return trip to Oregon on a brittle cold day much like the chill day 10 years before when we had boarded the train to leave Indiana for a new life in the West. The wind whistled through the snowy corn stubble as it had in 1920, and a blizzard blowing off Lake Michigan greeted us in Chicago the next morning as we transferred by Parmilee bus to the North Coast Limited.

Three days later when Father and Wymond met us at the depot in Portland, the sun was warm, the grass green and there were roses blooming outside. That sight of roses on New Years Eve captured Mother's heart. For 10 years she had endured raw winters in Montana, survived blazing summers in Lewiston and suffered the Klamath Falls climate, which only a fond Mother Nature could love. From that morning on she was a devoted Portlander.

SAN FRANCISCO'S TENDERLOIN

Wymond's Christmas holiday had been shorter but even more exciting than mine. He and Father had shared expenses with one of Wymond's teachers on a drive from Klamath Falls to San Francisco in the teacher's Model T Ford. Wymond was bursting to tell me about the sights of The City and especially about Father bootlegging him into a bawdy "adults only" show at the Little Green Street Theater in the Tenderloin district. After all, he was almost 16 and I was 14. Wasn't it time for both of us to learn some things?

They ended their vacation with a two-day steamship trip along the California and Oregon coasts and up the Columbia and Willamette Rivers, arriving in Portland on Dec. 30, a day ahead of us.

HALCYON YEARS

"Let's get a red Stutz with four speeds ahead like the one Cousin Lawrence had in Missoula," I urged as the family left the stately old Portland Hotel on New Years Day 1930 to begin shopping for a new automobile. Wymond would probably have opted for a Stutz, too, if I had not mentioned it first but now he spoke for one of the new low-slung Cord L-29 straight eights with front wheel drive. Mother favored a Buick like the one she had learned to drive near the Flathead in Montana, but Father was intrigued by a powerful 133-horsepower Hupmobile straight eight and by a 16-cylinder Cadillac, both on display at dealerships on West Burnside Street.

Father was enjoying being prosperous again, and when he had money in his pocket he didn't hesitate to spend it. Before the year was a week old he had bought the sleek black Hupmobile, rented an attractive home at 612 East 45th St. North in the Alameda district, outfitted us boys in new clothes, and to our embarrassment, driven us right to the front entrance of Grant High School on the day that we enrolled as new students.

The Great Depression was imminent, but the full impact of the 1929 stock market crash hadn't yet trickled down to the average consumer, and Father had no doubt that he soon would be earning fine commissions as a realtor. To him the dour days of Klamath Falls were a vague memory, and ahead lay halcyon years for the family.

Soon our household goods, which had been in storage in Missoula since 1927, arrived at our new home by truck. Right on top of the load were our long unused skis and poles. Of course Wymond and I immediately started agitating for a trip to Mount Hood, whose snowy peak beckoned from the nearby horizon. It was an easy sell, for it gave Father a reason to give the Hupmobile a highway tryout.

15 GOVERNMENT CAMP – 1930

"At first the winter crowds were almost overwhelming, but the village had responded quickly by morphing itself into a ski resort." Cars at Government Camp during a ski tournament, Jan. 6, 1929. Ralph Eddy photo.

The exciting scene that greeted our arrival at Government Camp a week later surprised us all. Nestled on Mount Hood's sunny south slope, the village had been a popular summer resort. And when Oregon began keeping highways across the Cascades open year-round, winter sports fans had responded by heading for the formerly snowbound passes in droves. At first the winter crowds were almost overwhelming, but the village had responded quickly by morphing itself into a ski resort.

In 1926 two dozen hardy Norwegian and Swedish immigrants had formed what later became Cascade Ski Club, and its members excavated tons of earth by hand to build a ski jump on the east side of Multorpor Mountain. (The name is a combination of the first syllables of Multnomah, Oregon and Portland.) In 1929 the club replaced the original ski jump with a fine new one nearer the village, and almost overnight ski jumping became a popular spectator sport. That November ski clubs in Oregon, Washington, Idaho and Alaska joined to create the Pacific Northwestern Ski

The Government Camp area had three toboggan slides: one at Battle Axe Inn, one on Multorpor Mountain and the one pictured here at Summit on Jan. 15, 1928. Gary Desiata photo.

Association. The PNSA promptly sanctioned its first jumping championship to be held on Multorpor in 1931.

TOBOGGAN RUNS

As we drove into town in our shiny new Hupmobile that day, we were startled to see a toboggan loaded with shouting youngsters racing down a course beside the highway. They came to a stop in front of a massive log-and-stone lodge whose sign read "Battle Axe Inn."

There was a second toboggan run starting on a scaffold near Summit and another on Multorpor Mountain. It was said that these toboggans could reach speeds of almost 60 miles an hour, but after a few years soaring insurance rates brought their demise.

BATTLE AXE INN

We learned that it had been built in 1925 and had more than 30 guest rooms and a fine dining room warmed by a great stone fireplace. The lobby was so crammed with antique furnishings and curios that it was a museum in itself. A few years earlier on a visit from Missoula to Yellowstone National Park we had stayed at Old Faithful Inn, and when we saw Battle Axe Inn we agreed that although it was much smaller, it could be compared favorably with Yellowstone's Old Faithful.

I have many happy memories of Battle Axe Inn, including the week in 1945 when Father, Sandy Sandberg, Sandy's black Labrador dog Rochester and I stayed there while we were building our own cabin a half-mile to the east. Dogs were not allowed in the inn, so Sandy took great delight in bootlegging Rochester in and out of our room through a back widow.

"Pa" and "Ma" Villiger operated Battle Axe competently and firmly, to the satisfaction of paying guests, though often to the frustration of rowdy weekend crowds and ski bums. Ma Villiger was famous for her homemade huckleberry pies as well as for her bulky hearing aid with wires leading to a microphone nestled in her ample bosom. Father's hearing was failing, too, but he refused to get a hearing aid and always referred to Ma Villiger as "that old lady with a bug in her ear."

HOT SPRINGS, HOTELS, AIRPORTS

Battle Axe Inn shared the mountain side of the highway with a Texaco station and several stores and cabins. There was also a large two-story hotel called the Mount Hood Hut. Originally the building had belonged to Mrs. Little, the wife of one of the three original Government Camp homesteaders. It had been moved from further up the mountain to the edge of the highway in the 1920s.

On the highway's south side stood the

Battle Axe Inn in the late 1930s. Mount Hood was clearly visible then because forest fires had burned much of the timber from the village to the tree line. Ralph Eddy photo.

The lobby of Battle Axe Inn. The lovely lodge was destroyed by fire in 1950. Ralph Gifford photo.

Lige Coalman's Government Camp Hotel nearing completion on the left. Yocum's Mountain View Inn, later known as the Annex, on the right, circa 1912. Photographer unknown.

three-story Government Camp Hotel, built by legendary mountaineer Lige Coalman between 1910 and 1914, and the smaller Annex built by pioneer climbing guide Oliver Yocum in 1900. (The genesis of its name escapes me.)

Near them was Hill's Place presided over by jovial Charlie Hill. In 1930 it featured hamburgers and creamy milkshakes, but after the repeal of prohibition in 1933, Hill's Place became known as the best beer stop between Bend and Portland.

The view of Mount Hood from the Loop Highway then was better than in later years because forest fires early in the century had burned much of the timber between Government Camp and the tree line.

SWIM

A mile or so east of town was Swim, a mineral springs resort with a cluster of cabins, a large warm water swimming pool and its own post office. There was even an airplane landing field at Summit Meadows, although the only plane known to have landed there prior to 1930 crashed when the pilot attempted to take off again. Maryanne Hill, who now owns and operates the Government Camp Water Company and several other businesses and properties in Government Camp, told me that she and her family lived in Swim then and that she has a photograph of herself seated on the plane's wing after the ill-fated landing. The unknown pilot survived.

CASCADE SKI CLUB UPS & DOWNS

Cascade Ski Club had converted three surplus Portland portable school buildings into a clubhouse on swampy land behind the Government Camp Hotel and had reshaped the north face of Multorpor Mountain to create a ski jumping hill qualified to hold sanctioned Class A, B and C championships. It had an elevated judge's stand, which provided a fine platform for photographing the events.

For the next dozen years an annual jumping tournament combined with the Oregon

Cascade Ski Club's jumping hill on Multorpor Mountain, 1932. CCC crews later cleared the hillside of fire-killed snags. Photo-Art Studios photo.

Winter Sports Association's Winter Sports Carnivals attracted as many as 10,000 visitors to Government Camp on tournament days.

WYMOND TRIES THE SKI JUMP

On that sunny day in January when our family arrived at Government Camp cars were parked for half a mile on each side of the highway. Word that Cascade Ski Club had been awarded the first ever PNSA Class A ski jumping championships for the following year, combined with crisp clear weather, had attracting a sizable crowd anxious to watch

practice jumping on the newly completed hill.

Father had stopped the car in the street while Wymond and I grabbed our skis and headed for Multorpor and Mother found a comfortable spot for coffee in Battle Axe Inn. Father parked the car and soon caught up with us as we joined other spectators and skiers trudging across frozen Collins Lake toward the jumping hill.

(Note: Twenty years later the state rerouted Highway 26 south of Government Camp and built an overpass to provide safe access from the village to Multorpor.)

As we approached the hill we saw skiers

Skier coming off the Class A takeoff in 1937. Wymond tried the Class C takeoff in 1930.

leaping off the hillside, soaring through the frosty air and landing gracefully on hard-packed snow. It was our first sight of a ski jump. "Come on George, we can do that," Wymond called out, hurrying us on.

In Montana when I was 8 years old and Wymond was 9 we both had been taught the rudiments of the Arlberg ski technique by Father's nephew Dr. Lawrence Henderson, who had learned it in Austria from its creator, Hannes Schneider.

In 1922, after practicing medicine on the Flathead Indian Reservation for three years, Lawrence had decided he would rather be an ophthalmologist and sailed to Vienna to study eye surgery. That winter he spent holidays in St. Anton, Austria, and at the Hannes Schneider Ski School he learned the new Arlberg ski technique that was sweeping Europe.

When Lawrence returned to Missoula he bought skis for Wymond and me and taught us the rudiments of downhill skiing, but he had learned nothing about ski jumping. Wymond's skis were 8 feet long and made of pine, with double grooves in the bottoms, while my maple skis were shorter and had single grooves. We were carrying those same skis when we arrived at Multorpor and stopped to watch in wonder as Cascade's nationally ranked jumpers – Hjalmar Hvam, John Elvrum and Corey Gustafsson – made long seemingly effortless jumps from the Class A takeoff.

NOT THE ARLBERG WAY

Then Wymond realized that his long heavy skis with double grooves were really designed for jumping, and when we reached the hill he hefted them onto his shoulder and began climbing to the Class C takeoff. Reaching the top of the inrun he strapped them to his loose-fitting loggers boots and calmly pointed them straight down.

He managed to stay upright until he

reached the takeoff then sailed a dozen feet through the air with skis and poles flailing, landed on his back, bounced once and tumbled to the bottom. As he was getting back his wind, I gathered his skis and poles to clear the way for other jumpers. Then to Father's and my surprise he took back his skis and promptly headed back up the hill.

Before the day ended Wymond's persistence paid off. Father had left early to join Mother for lunch at Battle Axe Inn, but Wymond wouldn't give up. He soon learned that ski jumpers don't carry poles, and after getting some other tips from bystanders finally made a couple of short jumps without a fall.

I did not try jumping. Instead I practiced what Lawrence had taught us but no one seemed to have heard of: the Arlberg technique. It was six years before Timberline Lodge's first ski instructor, Otto Lang, introduced the technique to Mount Hood.

Comparing notes over hamburgers at the new Rhododendron Log Lodge on our way home, we realized that although Lawrence's Christmas skis no doubt had been the best available at the Missoula Mercantile Company in 1923, they were at least seven years behind the curve by 1930. Furthermore jumping skis had three grooves, not two.

That first trip to Hood was wonderfully climaxed when Father drove us to Swim for a fast plunge into the steaming pool.

SWIM – HOT WATER OR HOT AIR?

The source of the hot water at Swim remains a mystery to me today. When I began working for the Forest Service in 1936, I was told by one old-timer that the "hot mineral water" in the swimming pool at Swim actually was just plain creek water heated by a boiler hidden up in the woods. Certainly when I felt the water

Resort of Swim, covered in snow, Feb. 17, 1929, with cabins in back, and bath house and pool in front. Mike Hermann photo, courtesy of Mazamas.

"Before long Father bought Wymond a pair of proper downhill skis, and when one of mine broke he made a new pair for me by hand. They were so admired that he made three more pairs, selling them to friends for $5 a pair."

in the fork of Camp Creek that runs through the site of Swim in 1936 it wasn't a bit warm. However another old-timer who had worked on the highway crew when the Barlow Road was realigned from Meldrum Meadows higher up the mountainside assured me that the creek had been warm before dynamite was used to install a culvert to carry the spring water under the new road.

Maryanne Hill had been 5 years old when she lived at Swim, and when I asked her about the hot springs she couldn't confirm either story. I am sure only that when Wymond and I dove off a snow bank into the pool in 1930, it had been steaming hot.

A QUARTER CENTURY OF DISASTERS

By 1955 every one of the hotels, restaurants and other facilities with highway frontage had either burned down or been destroyed. Even the ski jump eventually was abandoned, its structures removed and the land allowed to revert to forest. Battle Axe Inn was one of the last landmarks to be lost, burning to the ground in a spectacular fire in the fall of 1950.

As the Depression deepened, the resort at

Swim closed, and the swimming pool became part of a Forest Service campground. By 2005 only a few broken concrete walls overgrown by forest remained to attest to its former existence.

NOT JUST A SPORT – A WAY OF LIFE

That intoxicating introduction to Mount Hood convinced us that skiing indeed was not just a sport but a way of life. Before long Father bought Wymond a pair of proper downhill skis, and when one of mine broke he made a new pair for me by hand. They were so admired that he made three more pairs, selling them to friends for $5 a pair.

CASCADE'S NEW CLUBHOUSE

In 1938 Cascade Ski Club bought new property on the north side of the loop highway, moved the clubhouse there and lovingly restored it, only to have it crushed by snow load early in WW II. Many older members who were not in the military joined together to clear debris from the site and make it ready for reconstruction when the club could become active again. Among them were community

Cascade Ski Club Clubhouse, as it appeared in 2005. It had been extensively remodeled since it was rebuilt on this site in Government Camp in 1955. Bonnie Henderson photo.

leaders Albert R. Bullier Sr., Fred H. McNeil, Harold Kelly, H.J. "Sandy" Sandberg, Vern Caldwell, Fred VanDyke and Boyd French Sr.

In 1955 club president George Riggs devised a plan that allowed members to buy $100 first mortgage bonds to raise $10,000 to pay for building the splendid clubhouse that now occupies the site. All the labor was provided by member volunteers under foreman Bill Hughes, the only paid workman. I took weekly progress photos of the construction and circulated them in the club's bulletin, *Multorporean*, to encourage the bond sales.

Then one day I received a phone call from the secretary of Aaron Frank, Chairman of Meier & Frank Company, saying that Mr. Frank wanted to see me. I was fearful of a confrontation, for I was vice president of the National Ski Association and Mr. Frank was an official of the Amateur Athletic Union, and the two organizations had been at odds over

skiing's place in the Olympic Games. Aaron Frank was an imposing figure, and I was uneasy as I crossed the wide office to his desk and responded to sharp questions about Cascade Ski Club. Then he smiled and signaled his secretary, who handed me a check large enough to pay for the last few bonds to build the new clubhouse. Few in the club were aware that Aaron Frank had been a member years before and continued to receive the *Multorporean*.

14 MILES BY CANDLELIGHT

As the winter waned Wymond and I soon were spending most weekends either skiing on Mount Hood or climbing trails in the Columbia River Gorge, often with a growing cadre of equally obsessed classmates – both boys and girls – who would remain our friends for years to come.

There were several bus schedules a day

up and down the Columbia River Highway, and by making an early start we could ride to Multnomah Falls and climb 4,000-foot-high Larch Mountain before lunch, then return to the Falls in time to take an evening bus home.

When we first started hiking in the Bitterroots in Montana, Father had taught us how to fashion an excellent trail light from an empty number ten round metal fruit can with one end removed. We would cut a hole the size of a candle in the side of the can, leaving the edges of the cut poking inside, and thrust a candle through so that it would be held in place by the sharp edges of the hole. Then we would make a bail with a piece of stiff wire fastened from top to bottom of the outside of the can. When the candle was lit the bright lining of the can cast a broad cone of light on the trail ahead. A sturdy candle resisted wind and would last for miles – and it never ran out of batteries.

One evening in late spring Wymond and I took the bus to Eagle Creek, hiked 14 miles up the Eagle Creek Trail by candlelight, and reached Wahtum Lake in time to watch a spectacular sunrise over Mount Hood. As we started back down, a log at the lake's outlet spun under me tossing me into the water. After emptying my boots and wringing out socks, we walked the squishy 14 miles back to the highway and caught an afternoon bus home.

Fourteen-year-old boys are very resilient!

16 HIGH SCHOOL DAYS

JOYFUL YEARS

1930 and 1931 were joyful years for our family. Wymond got his driver's permit and although I wouldn't have one for more than a year Father let us both drive the Hupmobile. Our first trip after school ended was the Columbia River Highway to Astoria, then down the Oregon Coast on the Roosevelt Highway (named for Theodore, not Franklin), which became the Oregon portion of newly designated U.S. Highway 101. There were few bridges across the rivers, and the many ferry rides were exciting. I remember long stretches where we drove on the beach, with Mother cautioning, "Keep it under 70 boys."

We drove through much of Oregon and Eastern Washington those summers but never visited our old homes in Missoula, Lewiston or Klamath Falls.

On another trip we drove to Lake Quinault and around the Olympic Peninsula where the Olympic National Forest soon would become Olympic National Park. On a side trip up the dramatic Elwha River we stopped at Sol Duc Hot Springs to soak in the hot mineral baths which Mother felt eased her rheumatic pains. From there we took the two-hour car-ferry ride from Port Angeles across the Straits of Juan de Fuca to Victoria, where we stayed at the elegant Empress Hotel and spent a day at Butchart Gardens.

Wymond and I were into acrobatics then, and when we visited the British Columbia House of Parliament we waited for a quiet moment, then turned handsprings right down the carpet of its austere main aisle before making a quick exit through a side door.

ONCE AGAIN A HOME OF OUR OWN

Just when Wymond and I had figured out how to build scooters from roller skates, apple boxes and short 2-by-4 boards to race down steep, winding Wyberg Lane from our house on The Alameda, Father and Mother announced that they had bought a new home at 541 East 31st St. North near Knott – just a few blocks from Grant High.

(Note: Almost every street name and address in Portland was changed in 1931 and 1932. Numbered streets were redesignated as avenues and house numbers were resequenced. Thus our new home address became 2611 N.E. 31st Ave.)

TO EACH HIS OWN

The lovely home in the new upscale Dolph Park district presented only one problem; who would get the neat bedroom with a dormer? One of the two upstairs bedrooms had a cozy dormer with a window looking out on the tree-lined front street, while the other had a larger storage closet and a built-in bookcase but only a single window with little view. Father assumed that Wymond would have priority for the dormer room, but Mother proposed a different solution.

Wymond had a substantial collection of poetry books and literature by writers such as Edgar Allen Poe, Guy de Maupassant, Henry Thoreau and Ernest Hemingway along with The Dialogues of Plato – many of which I have but still haven't read. My interests ran toward action and adventure books and stories of reporters and photographers in the days of

Wymond Henderson, Milton Henderson, Paul Henderson and George Henderson in Portland,
fall 1930. Milton and Paul were sons of Father's brother Clint Henderson.

cutthroat big city newspaper competition.

Mother's wise suggestion was that Wymond take the smaller room with bookshelves and Father buy him a full-sized desk with lots of drawers and a spring-loaded shelf for his Underwood typewriter. Then I would get the room with a dormer and a small unfinished desk that would fit into it. Once again Mother had averted a crisis while each of us felt that he had come out ahead in the deal.

Father encouraged her to get high quality furnishings, so she bought solid mahogany dining room and bedroom furniture and two of the newly created Karastan domestic oriental rugs. She also had the hand-fed coal furnace converted to a modern sawdust burner.

Father reveled in those luxuries. They, along with the family's two years of expensive living and travel and the cost of the house and car, must have taken most of the money he had left from sale of the farm. He passed the examination for a real estate license and set up an office at home, with Wymond applying his artistic talent to designing attractive business stationery and outdoor signs. His confidence was undiminished when finally he turned his full attention to the unfamiliar business of selling houses and making a living from the commissions. Soon the reality of the Great Depression would dawn upon him.

COLLEGE GOALS

Grant High School offered three different four-year courses, each leading to a high school diploma: college preparatory, classical and general. Wymond and I assumed that after high school we would go right into college, so we both chose college prep, which required three years each of math, English, science and history and two years of a foreign language. By taking five subjects a semester instead of four and not taking a daily study period, I graduated in four years with five years of high school credits.

I surely didn't get straight four-points, but I must have been proud of the report cards for I still have all of them from high school and most of them from grade schools in Montana, Idaho and Oregon. My only poor grade was in Latin, where I just barely passed the two-year course. In senior year I wrote for the *Grantonian*, the school newspaper, and was business manager of the school annual, *Memoirs*.

Wymond excelled in writing, history, political science, philosophy and debate but had little time for matters that didn't interest him, such as taking examinations, turning in homework, or learning to write legibly or spell adequately. A typing course mitigated his handwriting problem, and a generation later an electronic spell-checker could have solved another. His teachers praised his compositions, often reading his essays to other classes, but despite his fine intellect, his academic record when he graduated in June 1932 was well below the level that might have gotten him a college scholarship.

ROSE FESTIVAL GYMNASTS

We both earned letters in gymnastics even though there was little such training in school. An English translation of a German gymnasts' handbook was our guide as we spent most lunch hours and much after-school time working out on the horizontal and parallel bars and flying rings and practicing tumbling on the wood-chip-covered ground at Grant Park. Along with classmates George Young and Noble Dutton we developed a gymnastics routine that we performed in Multnomah Stadium during the 1932 Portland Rose Festival.

RICHES TO RAGS – AGAIN!

The Great Depression reached its low point that year and stayed there for the next seven years!

President Herbert Hoover was a brilliant

economist and humanitarian, but he failed to see the full significance of the nation's economic stagnation and ran for reelection in 1932 under banners proclaiming, "Prosperity is just around the corner" and "There'll be two chickens in every pot and two cars in every garage."

When the election was over it was the severely crippled Franklin D. Roosevelt who was inaugurated President in March 1933, and who in his inaugural speech soberly proclaimed, "All we have to fear is fear itself." But it would be almost a year before many actual jobs were created by the New Deal.

UNEMPLOYMENT AT TWENTY-THREE PERCENT

Father's timing in starting a new career in real estate could hardly have been worse. Thirteen million Americans had lost their jobs since 1929, and unemployment peaked at 23 percent. Housing prices were plummeting, and soon people found that the sale price of their homes brought less that the balance owing on their mortgages. Some experienced realtors survived but Father was not among them. He told us later that he had not sold even one house in his few years in the business.

There was a well equipped YMCA branch on Sandy Boulevard about a mile from home, and that became my athletic club. At first Father could well afford the annual dues, and I finally learned to swim and play basketball, eventually joining industrial league teams. Wymond and I had spent so many summers in logging camps and working after school the rest of the year that we hadn't learned many team sports. I never did own a baseball glove.

George Riggs and I became counselors at the YMCA's Camp Collins on the Sandy River and at Camp Meehan on Sprit Lake, Washington, and when Father's money ran out I became the beneficiary of Portlander Wilbur P. Reed's charity, which paid my YMCA dues.

SELLING CHRISTMAS CARDS IN JULY

In the hot summer of 1932 Wymond and I spent several weeks selling Christmas cards door-to-door. An enterprising printer with a family to feed had set up shop in his basement to handprint personalized Christmas cards. Our job was to solicit orders and get customers to sign contracts. The printer would add the buyer's name and message and in a few days one of us would return to the customer's door with the finished boxes of cards and ask for payment in cash.

It was a sorry business. Harried housewives were captivated by seeing their names and messages in colored print but seldom had cash at hand, nor did they want to let us take away their precious Christmas cards if they didn't pay. I must have rung the doorbells of half the houses north of NE Broadway between 33rd and 60th avenues that summer.

It was a relief to return to the backbreaking work of moving tons of sawdust by wheelbarrow up driveways from the street and into basements for 50 cents a double truckload. A strong boy could earn a dollar or more a day that way.

I also worked for the Northeast YMCA as counselor, basketball coach and swimming coach during my last year at Grant. Wymond had graduated in June and worked part time as box boy at a Skaggs grocery store, and then in the fall he got a full-time job as warehouseman and janitor at the downtown F.W. Woolworth variety store. It paid $15 a week, and he stayed with its mind-dulling drudgery for almost four years, finally escaping in 1936 by joining the Merchant Marine.

A TORTUROUS TIME

The Great Depression was a torturous time indeed for our parents. Father took out a high-interest-rate second mortgage loan on the house, but after spending the proceeds he had no other assets or source of income. We continued to live in our lovely home only because if a dwelling was well-maintained by the borrower, the lender often would accept interest-only payments on a loan rather than foreclose when there was little likelihood of finding a satisfactory buyer. Father kept his end of that unwritten bargain by reshingling the roof, painting the house and replacing the concrete sidewalk and driveway. He also provided the materials.

Wymond and I had precious little money left each week after making the interest payments and buying groceries. Father supplemented our diet by gathering dandelion, lamb's quarter, mountain sorrel and other wild greens from vacant lots and along the railroad tracks for Mother to cook and serve in salads.

Margarine was much cheaper than butter, but its pasty white color was unappetizing and the law prohibited manufacturers or stores from coloring it before sale, so Father laboriously hand-mixed it with vegetable coloring.

A ROCK-SOLID MARRIAGE

Mother and Father's marriage bond seemed never strained by these difficult times but rather to be tempered to renewed strength. I don't remember that anyone railed against our poverty, and each seemed to find ways to overcome obstacles the way a rock climber searches out finger-holds in a granite face.

Mother's rheumatic pain and disability was a sorrow to us all, but it seemed not to get worse from lack of money for doctors. Her inner strength must have made her a role model for the rest of us.

DENTISTS FOR BETTER OR WORSE

I don't know that we had a family doctor, but Mother insisted that we boys go to the dentist every year, and that brought my only really frightful memories of the time. Fillings

cost $2 and inlays $5 but it cost an extra dollar if the patient asked for Novocain. Since Father and Wymond didn't take the painkiller what could I do? One time I delayed too long and lost a tooth – but I still have most of the rest of them.

Father had bragged to us that he would "as soon attend a tooth pulling as a taffy pull" and suddenly he had a chance to prove it. After years of neglect he finally went to the Oregon Dental College where treatment was quite inexpensive and sometimes free, but when he learned that the minimum cost for his many needs was far beyond his ability to pay he declared, "To Hell with it, pull 'em all," and they did! He came home that night with a full set of "temporary" dentures which he wore for many years.

SCHOOL YEAR IS CUT SHORT

It seemed as if the few people we knew who thrived during the Depression were those working for the federal government or receiving government or railroad pensions. They and others with steady incomes benefited from low prices, particularly in service industries.

Portland newspapers were 2 cents daily and a nickel on Sunday. A typical lunch of entree, salad, dessert and coffee cost a quarter. A cup of coffee cost a nickel with free refills. There was a cafe at S.W. Third and Morrison called "Buttermilk Corner" that kept pitchers of buttermilk on the counter with a sign, "All you can drink for a nickel." I often brought stale bread from home and made that my lunch.

In the fall of 1934 Wymond and I saved up for weeks in order to have $5 to take the family to the Multnomah Hotel for Christmas dinner. The full dinner with salad, roast turkey, mashed potatoes, pumpkin pie and coffee cost a dollar each – and we proudly left a dollar tip.

The Multnomah County School District ran out of money in the 1932-33 school year, so schools were closed a month early, and my

"...savoring hot coffee in our only really dry camp under the shake roof of an abandoned miner's cabin..." George Riggs photo.

A rare dry moment in camp in the Spirit Lake country.

Class of 1933 was the only one ever to graduate in May instead of June.

A SCHOLARSHIP AT WILLAMETTE UNIVERSITY

When I graduated from Grant High School, Willamette University offered me a full scholarship and arranged for jobs at the *Salem Statesman* and the state library to pay for room and board, but with Wymond's $15 a week at Woolworths and my after-school jobs providing the family's only income, I had no choice but to decline the scholarship. Wymond had shouldered the greatest burden while I was finishing high school, and now it was time for me to pick up my share.

Although the workday in retailing generally was 8 a.m. to 6 p.m. six days a week, we both managed to stay active in our favorite sports – skiing and climbing – which made for mighty low-cost recreation. We wore the same boots for both of those sports, and skis, poles and boots lasted several years. There were no tows or lifts to pay for, and we took our lunches from home. One-day ski trips to Government Camp depended upon rides from someone's parents until we were old enough to drive, and everyone shared in the cost of gas and oil.

THE SPIRIT LAKE COUNTRY

Grant High School classmates George Riggs, George Young and I hoped to make a week-long backpack trip during the late summer of 1932. A remote wilderness of old growth forests, gem-like lakes and restless streams stretched north from Mount St. Helens to beyond Spirit Lake and halfway to Mount Rainier. It hadn't yet been officially designated a wilderness but was simply known as "the Spirit Lake country," and we yearned to hike its trails, cross its rivers and scale its peaks. During other summers at Camp Meehan we had made day hikes to peaks and passes where

the entire panoply had spread before us.

When we met at the Northeast YMCA to plan our trip, the obstacles appeared insurmountable. George Riggs' Model T Ford was not capable of making the trip, so we would need a different car. Young had a pack board but Riggs and I did not, so we would have to buy or borrow two or make them ourselves. Finally, we did not have any money to buy gasoline and food.

Then from an unexpected source came a glimmer of hope. Willard F. Rouse, secretary of the Northeast Y, had overheard our talk. He was in his early thirties, had a 10-year-old son, loved the outdoors and best of all owned a 1920 Buick touring car. But he couldn't drive the car because it had a flat tire, and wasn't registered. He couldn't afford to buy a tire or pay the car's $5 annual registration fee.

If we three 16-year-olds would include him on our 60-mile backpacking expedition, perhaps we could strike a bargain. Rouse lived in a big house with a full basement and a sawdust-burning furnace, and he was about to order his winter supply of sawdust, but access to the basement was so difficult that it was hard for him to get anyone to move the sawdust into the basement after it was dumped in the street. Furthermore he had promised his son Bobby a week at Camp Meehan on Spirit lake, which would free Rouse for our hike, but he had no way to get Bobby to camp and back.

If we boys would put away the sawdust, he would use half of the $10 he had budgeted for that job to pay the Buick's registration fee and would use the other half to buy a retreaded tire – and Bobby could ride with us to Camp Meehan and back.

We had second thoughts when we saw that the sawdust had to be carried in garbage cans up a steep driveway and around to the back of the house then down a back stairway and across the basement before being dumped in a far corner. It took the three of us three days – but a deal was a deal!

Willard F. Rouse, George Young and George Henderson on the summit of Mount Margaret. Mount Rainier in the distance. George Riggs photo.

GOD'S GREAT MEMORIAL

As from Mount Margaret's jagged spire-like teeth
I view the vast expanse reclining 'round;
Impressed by the stillness so profound,
Inhale a high-flung fragrance with each breath
And see the lovely green and bluish wreath
Of forests holding riches yet unfound,
Or gaze upon St. Helens' snowy mound
And at the glittering lake that lies beneath,

I ask, "Did chance alone produce it all?"
But shrinking from that thought when seen in full,
I, pondering, seem to hear an answering call,
And realize that deep within my soul
I know a King who, far from earthly hall,
Rules over nature -- His own memorial.

by George M. Henderson
From Grant High *Memoirs* 1933

TRAPPER NELSON MEETS A SKUNK

Trapper Nelson pack boards had been invented in 1929 and were far better than the loose canvas packsacks and hard wooden pack boards used for Forest Service fire packs. They were expensive, but Father had made us fine skis by hand, so we decided to try to make our own packs patterned after Trapper Nelsons.

From the Hirsch-Weis tent factory at the west end of the new Burnside Bridge we bought enough scraps of waterproof canvas for two packs, then found several short pieces of oak flooring at a construction site and set up our factory in George Riggs' basement. I was a little nervous about that at first, because George's younger brother, Frank, had recently brought from the woods a black-and-white baby skunk which made itself at home in the Riggs' basement sawdust pile. Mrs. Riggs didn't seem to object, and the skunk had us outgunned, so there never was a confrontation.

Each pack board required two pieces of flooring bent into shallow bows and two short uprights of straight-grained fir. We had watched Father bend the tips of skis by steaming them until they were limber and then forcing them into molds made by driving spikes into a plank. George Riggs devised a steam chamber from a 2-foot length of sewer pipe, plugging one end with wood and running a short hose from the other end to the spout of his mother's tea kettle, which he sat on an electric hot plate. Then we steamed and shaped the pack frames just as Father had done with the skis.

We finally gave up on sewing the heavy canvas either by hand or on a home sewing machine and paid a seamstress at the tent factory to do the job.

Our homemade Trapper Nelsons were a real success, and I used mine later for a 90-mile ski trip down the Oregon Skyline Trail. In the 1950s, when aluminum-framed Kelty backpacks revolutionized the market, I donated my homemade Trapper Nelson to the Forest Service's Historic Ranger Station at Clackamas Lake, where it is on display.

UNCLE WILLIE AND THE THREE GEORGES

Although Willard F. Rouse was our boss at the YMCA and twice our age, it turned out to be a happy liaison. We dubbed him "Uncle Willie," and he enjoyed not having to tell us apart since we all three were named George.

Snapshots of that disparate quartet taken on our inaugural trip hang in our Mount Hood cabin. One shows Uncle Willie, George Young and me atop the dramatic spire of Mount Margaret as it looked before the explosion of Mount St. Helens devastated it 50 years later. Below the photo is a poem I wrote for the Grant High School yearbook. The photo and poem appear on the preceding two pages.

SIX WET BUT HAPPY DAYS

My memories of that hike are a series of vignettes, one or two for each of the six days. Hurrying down Norway Pass on the first day under too-heavy packs as we tried to beat the rain to our first campsite at Shovel Lake. Scrambling to the top of Mount Margaret on the trip's only sunny day. Stumbling into a patch of devil's club when we lost the trail down Miners Creek on day three. Laughing as we watched Uncle Willie slip from a log he was using to walk across Green River – until we realized that our only supply of eggs was in his pack. Savoring hot coffee in our only really dry camp under the shake roof of an abandoned miner's cabin. Finally clambering soggy but happy into the Camp Meehan speed boat that met us at the head of Spirit Lake.

Recalling those scenes would help us face some of the dispiriting times that lay a decade ahead in WW II.

17 MOUNT HOOD CLIMBS – 1933

Old Timberline Cabin under 20 feet of snow. The skier is Wymond Henderson.

FIRST ASCENT

"Tea 10 Cents" read a sign neatly lettered on a hand-split cedar shake in the snow on the very top of Mount Hood. An arrow pointed toward the fire lookout perched on the eastern end of the narrow summit ridge.

I took another step upward and suddenly was peering over the top of the mountain and down its north face where it falls sheer for a thousand feet to the broken ice above Ladd, Coe and Eliot Glaciers. My hands scrabbled to find a grip in the loose snow.

Every muscle had been limp with fatigue a moment before, but now adrenaline was pumping, and I felt that if need be I could run to the lookout cabin to reach its security.

You can climb Mount Hood for the first time only once, and although I've climbed it more than 50 times since, I remember best that first ascent on July 23, 1933, when I was 17.

WYMOND, MALCOLM AND THE THREE GEORGES

There were five of us on the climb, all from

Grant High School. We had skied together much of the winter and hiked trails in the gorge in summer. A few weeks earlier when George Riggs, George Young, Wymond and I had climbed 5,000-foot-high Mount Defiance and were standing on its top gazing at Hood's snowy majesty, we had decided that we were ready to try for its summit.

"I'll bet we could see the Pacific Ocean from the top," I said, to which Wymond promptly challenged, "You'll never know because you cannot climb that high." George Young laconically suggested, "Let's climb it and find out."

George Riggs ignored us. He was inured to our internecine rivalry and began seriously pondering the possibilities. He was a thoughtful planner who had climbed Hood once already and who had acquired enough parts to rebuild a 1920 Model T Ford that sometimes provided transportation for our hikes.

Finally Riggs said, "Well, Mount Defiance here is 5,000 feet high, and Larch Mountain is over 4,000, and we've had no trouble climbing either of them, but Mount Hood is 11,225 feet, so from the trailhead at Government Camp to the top is a 7,225-foot climb, and the air is pretty thin up there!"

That caught our attention.

"Wouldn't we need ropes and crampons and a guide?" I asked. The question hung in the air. I had climbed Larch Mountain earlier with a Trails Club party, which included 20 men and women of all ages led by mountaineer Mike Hermann, but that laborious 13-mile round trip over an easy trail with frequent stops to "split the party" had turned me off on the concept of a guided climb.

Mike had carried an ice axe on the Larch Mountain hike, so the next day I asked him about equipment. He said that Curtis Ijames had climbing equipment for rent from his home on Southeast Madison Street. "He's one of our finest climbers," Hermann said. "Tell him I sent you."

Accordingly we set out to find Ijames. Madison was a tree-lined, two-lane street with attractive older homes, and Ijames' basement was stuffed to the ceiling with outdoor gear.

He had steel crampons to rent for a dollar a weekend and steel-tipped alpenstocks for 25 cents, but he was a careful man and he wanted to assure himself that if he rented us equipment, both it and we were likely to return in good order.

First he urged us not to climb without a knowledgeable leader, but when it seemed likely that we wouldn't heed that warning, he reviewed our experience. He said our speedy climb of Mount Defiance was "only a good warm-up" for Mount Hood, but he finally agreed to rent us the needed gear.

We learned that Ijames was a member of the elite Wy'east Climbers, whose members had made first ascents of many routes on Northwest peaks and were the area's primary volunteers for search and rescue work. (Note: In 1937 Barney Macnab, a member of the Nile River Yacht Club, and Wy'east climber Everett Darr worked with the Forest Service to create the Mount Hood Ski Patrol, and Wy'easter Hank Lewis was hired to serve on the weekends as the first paid patrolman; all others on the patrol were volunteers.)

CLIMBING TIPS FROM IJAMES

We completed our outfitting with a trip to the Hirsch-Weis canvas products factory on West Burnside Street to buy "tin pants." They were made of waterproofed canvas and were so stiff that they would stand up by themselves, but they were favored for glissading back down the mountain.

When we returned later to pick up the equipment, Ijames gave us some sound advice on mountain climbing safety along with a photo he had taken of the mountain on which he drew in the safest climbing route. I relied upon his advice for many years to come.

Ranger leading the way on the Blossom Trail.

RANGER JOINS THE TEAM

It was evening when the five of us parked at Raffertys in Government Camp, shouldered our packs and crossed the highway to the start of Blossom Trail. We knew the trail well, for that winter we had climbed it on skis many times, but even if we were to lose the way, Ranger would have put us right.

Ranger was the Raffertys' legendary mixed breed collie who loved to climb the mountain and would attach himself to a party every few days, sometimes summiting twice in a single day. We took it as a good omen when he deigned to join us instead of several other groups starting up that night.

We followed the old wagon road for the three-mile climb to Camp Blossom, where a climber's shelter called Timberline Cabin had been built in 1916. It would be another three years before construction of Timberline Lodge would begin a mile to the east.

Ranger seemed to feel that his proper place was at the head of our party, and he settled into an even pace, only dropping back from time to time to check on each of us. He didn't waste energy chasing chipmunks as many dogs do.

The trail wound up through the lush forest of Douglas fir, lodgepole pine, hemlock and cedar, highlighted by red rhododendron buds and green shoots of huckleberry bushes. Soon the candle-like white blooms of beargrass and delicate trilliums would follow them. At around 5,000 feet the trail vanished under the snow pack, and when we neared the tree line at 6,000 feet only dark rock ridges blending with the greens and browns of subalpine trees provided contrast with the snowy landscape.

Timberline Cabin was everything it needed to be and not one thing more. It was large enough to sleep 20 or more climbers but small enough to be heated by a single primitive wood stove. It was high enough for its upper gable entrance to be used even when the snow was 20 feet deep, but it also had a ground level entrance for summer climbers. Inside there were ladders to reach the several levels of double bunks, and on the outside a ladder was spiked to the wall to gain the gable entrance.

It wasn't an architectural gem, but from

under our drooping eyelids it seemed a thing of beauty when Ranger led us there in the dark. We found empty bunks, rolled our blankets out on the bare boards and were asleep in a trice.

A SCARY "BREAKFAST IN BED"

I awoke with a start from a dream that someone was frying eggs on my stomach! The dream was almost true for Ole Lien, one of the climbing guides, had lit his tiny Svea alcohol stove in the adjacent bunk and was calmly cooking breakfast. The memory of our 1923 Pablo sawmill fire flashed before me. It was almost two a.m. and time to start anyway, so I woke the others and we crawled outside and ate our own breakfast on the snow.

Oddly enough my dream became reality as Ole Lien eventually did burn down old Timberline Cabin! I learned that some 24 years later the Forest Service decided that the cabin was a fire hazard and assigned Ole to burn it and dispose of the remains. Only the

Ole Lien at timberline, 1931. Jim Harlow photo courtesy of Anne Harlow Trussell.

ancient garbage dump and some rocks from the chimney identify its location today.

Ranger was waiting for us when we emptied our packs of everything but crampons, lunches and warm clothes and fell in with other climbers who already had started up, their swinging flashlights looking like a chorus line of earthbound fireflies.

The few hours of fitful sleep had partially restored our muscles, but our spirits lagged until the first light of sunrise crept across the wheat fields of Eastern Oregon and set alight the Cascade peaks to the south, then bathed the snow beneath our feet with a golden glow as it spilled down into the Willamette Valley.

A picture I took almost two years later of George Riggs and Ranger facing the sunrise on the south side of Mount Hood won first prize and $2.50 in the *Journal* photo contest.

We held a steady pace, alternating the lead, until we reached Triangle Moraine at the top of Palmer Glacier near the foot of Crater Rock, where we stopped to strap on crampons and shed extra sweaters. Triangle Moraine is the first point of potential danger on Hood's popular south side climbing route. A misstep there when the snow is frozen hard could send a climber on an ever-steepening slide into the head of White River Glacier on the east.

TIME FOR CRAMPONS

When the snow is soft it is easy to kick in safe steps – in fact, Forest Service packers regularly took strings of pack horses loaded with lumber and supplies right into the crater, whence it was backpacked to the summit – but when the snow is frozen, crampons are needed, as are ice axes for chopping steps.

It was 6 a.m. and we were at 9,500 feet, so the snow still was frozen, but with crampons and steel-tipped alpenstocks we were adequately equipped, although we hadn't yet learned the technique of self arrest to use in case of a fall. Fortunately none of us fell.

We had made good time because we didn't take rest stops but instead slowed to a wedding-step pace whenever one of us called a rest. Father had taught us that on our first short climb in the Mission Range of Montana 10 years before.

As we climbed around the base of Crater Rock, we soon were aware that Mount Hood is indeed an active volcano! In an area called the Hot Rocks, snow melts as soon as it falls and hydrogen sulphide-laden steam curls up through fumaroles from the volcanic caldera below wafting, its sickening rotten egg odor into the already oxygen-starved atmosphere.

Crater Rock is at about 10,500 feet. By the time we got there, I wasn't sure I had the stamina to make it to the top. It was the first time that I had been above 10,000 feet, and we learned that oxygen shortage affects people differently. Riggs, Young, Malcolm and I were short of breath and lethargic. Still we relished the lunch of hard-boiled eggs and ham sandwiches that Mother had packed for us. However Wymond had a sensitive stomach and soon lost his appetite and then his breakfast. He decided to stay at Crater Rock while we went on.

CROSSING THE CREVASSE

Avalanches and changes in ice and snow patterns vary the climbing route from year to year and in 1933 the way was several hundred feet farther west than when I last climbed a half-century later. A large crevasse that opens in the ice at the foot of the Chute every spring usually can be circumvented or else crossed on snow bridges, but that year a long wooden ladder had been laid across it.

George Young was a gymnast in high school and confidently walked upright over the shaky ladder, but the others crept across on hands and knees. As I peered down between the rungs at the seemingly bottomless gash of blue-green ice, I shuddered to think of crossing it again on the way down!

Above the crevasse some climbers roped themselves together in groups of two or more and made their own trail – the standard mountain climbing technique – but we did not have a rope. After crossing the crevasse we grasped a 1,000-foot-long line installed and maintained by the Forest Service and used arms and legs to struggle upward. Climbing the Chute that way was pure drudgery. From time to time we passed exhausted climbers who had stopped for breath, but the pace was dictated by the slowest person on the rope.

AN ABYSS OF ICE AND ROCK

Our fright was palpable as we crested the summit ridge and suddenly peered down the other side of the mountain onto the near-vertical walls of ice and rock above Eliot Glacier. The incongruity of the sign at the top of the Chute, "Tea 10 Cents," was lost on us, but its message of warmth and stimulation sustained us as we made our way to the lookout cabin along the narrow ridge, feeling as though we were balancing on a tightrope.

Ray Lewis was the lookout that year, and he was doing a thriving tea business. Between periods of searching the forest for smoke, he poured steaming hot water into tea bag-laden tin cups stretched out to him by dozens of exhausted climbers who had chosen that sunny weekend for their first climb of the year.

To make the tea, Lewis had backpacked kerosene up the mountain to fuel the small stove, then melted snow for water. Fire lookouts were paid only $60 a month, so every 10 cents he got for a cup of tea was appreciated.

The building had two levels. The 8-foot-square cupola housed the original model of the famous Osborne Firefinder along with a telephone, maps and binoculars, while the stove, a cot, a table and two chairs occupied the 12-foot-square main floor.

The place was bedlam, with people sitting and sprawling in every open space. More than

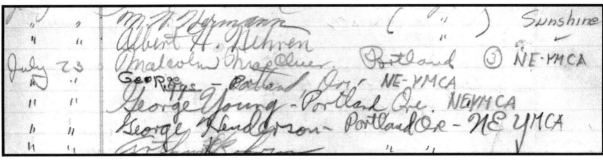

Above – George Riggs (left), George Young, Malcolm MacCluer and I in front of the Mount Hood summit lookout, July 23, 1933. Below, our signatures from Mazamas' summit register.

two hundred climbed the mountain that day, and several who signed the summit register became lifelong friends, including Boyd French Jr., Marjorie French (Simmons), Donal French, Russ McJury and Bill Hackett.

Ole Lien, who had cooked his breakfast on my bunk in old Timberline Cabin that morning, was leading a Mazamas climb that included Oregon orator laureate Frank Branch Riley, Cloud Cap Inn owner Homer Rogers and Homer's daughter Kate.

Wy'easter Hank Lewis (not related to the lookout) climbed the mountain for the second day in a row and wrote in the summit register, "A climb a day keeps the doc away." He later was hired by the Forest Service as the first patrol chief of the Mount Hood Ski Patrol.

HOT TEA AT LAST

After handing the lookout my dime, I savored the first cup of tea I had ever drunk, curled up on a lumpy coil of climbing rope in one corner, and fell asleep.

A RUDE AWAKENING

It seemed only a few moments until George Riggs shook me awake, exclaiming, "We were afraid that you'd fallen off the mountain!" He reminded me that Curtis Ijames had advised us to get down to Crater Rock before the sun hit the Chute and rocks began rolling. I was yearning for another cup of hot tea, but George Young and Malcolm were waiting at the door, so I grabbed my pack and joined them.

Stepping from the lookout and facing north across the Columbia River to the tumbling mass of Washington's Cascade Range we saw 14,410-foot-high Mount Rainier in the distance, with the round 9,671-foot cone of Mount St. Helens on the left and massive 12,307-foot-high Mount Adams on the right. (Note: The elevations I use here are from the U.S. Geological Survey contour maps I purchased in the 1930s. All the elevations have been revised since.)

For a few minutes we ignored our hurry and pointed our cameras for photos I still treasure, then we carefully balanced our way back along the narrow ridge to the Chute.

DODGING BOULDERS

As we took hold of the lifeline to start down, we saw that there still were climbers coming up, so we had to step around them carefully, while keeping an eye on the cliffs where rocks already were breaking loose and bounding across the slope. Only a few came our way, but dodging them was frightening – and no one had a safety helmet in those days.

At the big crevasse we were in no mood to dally and hardly hesitated as we scrambled across the ladder. Circling around Crater Rock with its steaming fumaroles, we rejoined Wymond and dropped to Triangle Moraine.

The sun had turned the ice of early morning into soft corn snow, so we wrapped sweaters around our crampons, stuffed them into packs and plopped our backsides onto the snow for an exciting glissade down Palmer Glacier, using alpenstocks for steering and speed control. Our waterproofed tin pants were super slick, and glissaders ahead of us already had worn a track nearly a foot deep.

Below 8,000 feet the slope no longer was steep enough for sliding, so we took long, leaping steps most of the way to Timberline Cabin. By then our breathing was back to normal, so we stopped only long enough to pick up bedrolls and eat the last of our oranges. Somehow Ranger had kept pace with our exuberant descent, so we fell in behind him, and in less than an hour we were back at Rafferty's devouring hamburgers and huckleberry pie and ready to pile into George Riggs' crowded coupe for the ride home.

Early Monday morning, on limping legs and with sun-scorched faces, we shared the fun of returning the climbing gear to Curtis Ijames and trying all at once to tell about our successful ascent.

FATHER AND AUNT JENNIE CLIMB

Later that summer our Aunt Jennie Miller, Uncle Carl's wife from Des Moines, Iowa, visited us in Portland and was so fascinated with our climbing stories that she asked Wymond and me to take her to the top.

We agreed quickly, but Mother wasn't so sure. She remembered that Aunt Jennie had been an adventurous and athletic youth but wondered whether we boys were qualified to guide an inexperienced Midwestern housewife up Oregon's highest snowcap. She asked Father's opinion, and he offered a neat solution; he thought that we might need help, so he would go along!

Although there were yet no plans to build a hotel at timberline, the new gravel road to Phlox Point was free of snow so a few days later we left Portland about midnight and drove the Hupmobile right to the 6,000 foot level. It was

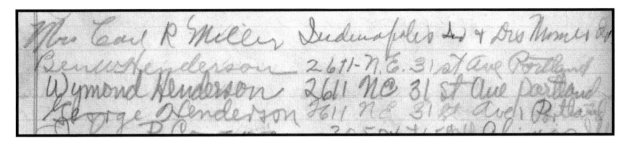

Wymond and I led our Father, then age 68, and Aunt Jennie Miller up Mount Hood on Aug. 17, 1933. Above are our signatures from Mazamas' summit register.

a pleasant moonlight night, and the change in altitude didn't seem to dampen Aunt Jennie's enthusiasm a bit as she stared up at the 5,000 feet of mountain yet to be climbed.

Things went smoothly until we reached Triangle Moraine and sat down to strap on crampons. Then we were made aware that Father was the most capable mountaineer among us. While Wymond and I watched, not fully alert to the danger, Aunt Jennie began to slide toward the edge of White River Glacier. Father quickly dropped below her, using his alpenstock for self-arrest, and blocked her fall.

As we continued to climb and reached the Hogsback, the altitude began to take its toll on us all. We had come from sea level to 11,000 feet in only nine hours, but Father was determined that Aunt Jennie reach the summit. He quietly encouraged her as she crept across the ladder over the big crevasse. He then placed himself behind her on the fixed lifeline and boosted her foot by foot ahead of him all the way up the Chute and guided her along the knife-ridge summit to the lookout with its restorative 10-cent cups of tea.

FOUR HOOSIERS SIGN THE SUMMIT REGISTER

I have no photos of the climb, but the Mazamas still have the Mount Hood summit register books in their archives. With the help of their historian, I verified dates and names on many of our early climbs. On the page dated Aug. 17, 1933, are our signatures as clearly shown on the previous page. A photocopy of the full page hangs on my wall today!

After that climb Wymond and I shared our chagrin as we realized how much tougher physically and mentally Father was at almost 70 than we were in our early teens, even though we then were active in climbing, backpacking and skiing. Most of his exercise in the previous four years had consisted of gardening and walking to the store.

THREE CLIMBS IN TWO MONTHS

George Riggs and I climbed Mount Hood again on Aug. 27, 1933, with John Mountain and two of George's relatives. I don't remember their names, but we all reached the summit and signed the register. It was my third climb that summer. Photos of two of those climbs are on the wall of our cabin in Government Camp.

CHRISTMAS WITH LIGE COALMAN

The previous December George Riggs and I had spent a delightful week with Elijah Coalman, who had built the lookout on Mount Hood in 1915. Each Christmas the YMCA conducted a skiing expedition to Camp Meehan at Spirit Lake on the northern slope of Mount St. Helens, where Coalman was the caretaker and cook. We were anxious to go but had no money, so we hired on to wash dishes to pay our way. It was a great week. Twenty

Lige Coalman at Spirit Lake, late 1920s. Harriet Park Cramer photo courtesy of Owen Cramer.

boys with skis and packs were trucked up the Toutle River as far as possible. From there we skied to camp, where we stayed in cabins.

Spirit Lake was at 3,200 feet elevation, and timberline on Mount St. Helens is at about 3,900 feet. Each morning after breakfast the paying campers would climb almost 1,000 feet to timberline to spend the day skiing. It didn't take George and me long to organize our breakfast dishwashing job so that we could finish in time, to race up to timberline and join the others by the time some of the less experienced skiers got there.

Elijah Coalman was a delightful person and a fine raconteur who spent many evenings after supper spinning yarns with the campers in front of the blazing fireplace in Camp Meehan Lodge. He told us about climbs, mountain rescues and personal injuries experienced in his legendary 586 Mount Hood climbs.

He had retired as a fire lookout on Mount Hood in 1920 after several serious injuries and stopped climbing Mount Hood about 1928, but he continued to lead YMCA campers on summer climbs of Mount St. Helens into the mid-1930s. It was difficult for us to realize that he was only 51 years old when we knew him.

Less than a decade later I was to be part of a crew that dismantled the Mount Hood lookout cabin that Coalman had built a quarter-century before.

HISTORY OF THE "LIFELINES"

Guides Doug and Will Langille were the first to fix thick ropes to aid their clients up and down Mount Hood when they guided from Clould Cap Inn on the north side in the 1890s. Later Elijah Coalman and his crew installed fixed ropes on the south side when they built the first lookout on the summit in 1915. As more people climbed the mountain on their own and the commercial guides faded away, maintaining the fixed ropes became the job of the Forest Service. The Forest Service called the ropes "lifelines" because they made the mountain safer for thousands of less-than-expert climbers.

From 1938 to 1940 while Boyd French Jr. was the lookout at Lone Fir near Silcox Hut, he and I climbed the mountain many times each summer to ensure that both ropes remained securely anchored. Then in the fall came the hazardous task of pulling both lines up to the summit and storing them in the lookout. Rolling rocks were at their peak then, and safety helmets were not yet in vogue.

After World War II, while still on military furlough from the Forest Service, I volunteered to help pack a new lifeline to the Hogsback and string it on up the Chute to the summit, anchoring it to boulders and stabilizing it with steel posts just as we had done in the 1930s.

I don't know when the lifelines were discontinued, but in 1986 when I last climbed the mountain, there was no lifeline.

On top once more. I made my most recent Mount Hood climb on May 31, 1986; 53 years after my first ascent on July 23, 1933. The fire lookout and the fixed-rope lifelines were gone, but the big crevasse and the crowds on the summit were there as before.

18   MOUNT ST. HELENS AND MOUNT ADAMS - 1934

MARCHING WITH THE BLUE EAGLE

It was like marching in a socialist workers' parade in Moscow, but I was beaming, because the New Deal had just dealt me a job in the middle of the Great Depression. President Roosevelt's National Recovery Act of June 1933 was designed to drastically reduce unemployment, and it had accomplished that goal in some cases by mandating a 40-hour workweek. That meant that S.H. Kress & Co., whose usual workweek was 54 hours, had to hire more workers for its Portland variety store. On Sept. 16, 1933, I got one of those jobs.

The NRA's Blue Eagle was emblazoned on a flag that flew beside the Stars and Stripes at the head of a parade of new jobholders marching up Portland's Fifth Ave. and down Sixth in tribute to the New Deal.

When the Supreme Court eventually declared the whole scheme unconstitutional, I was the only "NRA boy" to survive the resulting staff cut at Kress & Co., and my high school record helped qualify me for the company's intensive management training program. The salary would stay the same, but the workweek jumped to nine hours a day, six days a week, with a week's annual vacation after the first year. Seeing no farther ahead than the $13.50 a week salary, I grasped the opportunity.

A SQUARE PEG IN A ROUND HOLE

There hardly could have been a worse fit. I was determined to be a journalist, but the company expected me to think only of rising rapidly in its management ranks. Later I realized that manager Orin Bradshaw had been praised for recruiting so likely a candidate for the company's training program, which gave him a personal stake in my success.

It didn't take long for our interests to clash. I enrolled in a freshman journalism course at the University of Oregon Extension, where the instructor was a reporter for the *Oregon Journal*. Mr. Bradshaw quickly scotched that by scheduling me for window trimming on the nights of my classes. The company training program required correspondence study and monthly letters from me to Mr. S.H. Kress himself in New York, avowing loyalty to the company and to those extracurricular activities appropriate to the company's interests.

MORE MOUNTAINS TO CLIMB

When I arrived at work one Monday morning, weary and sunburned from two nights and a day spent climbing Mount Adams, Mr. Bradshaw counseled me not to refer to the hazardous sports of climbing and skiing in my letters to Mr. Kress.

Despite working six days a week at our variety store jobs, Wymond and I spent most weekends climbing glacial mountains or lesser peaks in summer or skiing in winter.

MOUNT ST. HELENS

Mount St. Helens was fun to climb before it blew its top! Its symmetry and its cape of smooth glaciers made it more welcoming than

Above: Ken Johnsrud (right) and I on our first Mount St. Helens climb on June 16, 1934. Below: Mount St. Helens from the north in 1939 showing Spirit Lake in the foreground. Ken and I started near timberline and climbed the Dog's Head route in the left center. Brubaker photo courtesy of the Mazamas.

its neighboring "Guardians of the Columbia," 11,225-foot-high Mount Hood or 12,307-foot-high Mount Adams. On June 16, 1934, when I first reached its ice cream cone shaped-summit with high school classmate Kenny Johnsrud, its elevation was 9,677 feet, but when I climbed it 53 years later with Bill June on Aug. 5, 1987, its summit had become the ragged rim of a steaming crater and measured only 8,364 feet high.

The volcanic eruption on May 18, 1980, had blasted away 1,313 feet of the mountaintop, triggered the largest landslide in recorded history, filled Spirit Lake with rock and mud, killed 57 people and devastated 229 square miles of rich timberland.

That first climb had been a high-spirited mountaineering event concluding with signing the summit register, eating lunch on the steps of the abandoned lookout cabin, and admiring the encircling tableau of lakes, forests and snowcapped peaks.

A MOUNTAIN CLIMBER AT 72

After the eruption the mountain was closed to climbing for several years, but by August 1987 the Forest Service allowed limited climbing on a permit basis, and I was ready. I was 72 and had climbed Mount Hood the year before. Because the climbers' bivouac on the south side of Mount St. Helens was well below timberline, the length of the two climbs would be comparable. My partner was William June, a vice president of Portland General Electric Company and a graduate of the Sierra Palisades School of Mountaineering in California. I did not realize that he, too, had climbed Mount St. Helens before the eruption and had climbed Mount Rainier. Since neither of us knew the new route or climbing conditions, we decided to drive to the end of the road on Tuesday afternoon, cook steaks by a campfire and be ready for an early start on Wednesday.

We were up at 3 a.m., and after a hasty breakfast and climbing the two miles of trail to timberline, we broke out of the trees. In the gray dawn light had our first close-up view of the mountain's steep south face. Suddenly the warm image of the peak I'd always held dissolved into an eerie feeling that the tranquil snow-covered slope was a hollow shell that might collapse under the weight of our steps.

The anxiety waned as we settled into a steady pace, alternating between kicking steps into the steep snowfields and picking our way among the boulder-strewn ridges. As we neared the summit the foreboding returned, and well it may have, for the snow field seemed simply to drop from sight. I drove my ice axe in to its hilt but could not tell whether there was solid ground beneath us or if we were treading on a snow cornice created by the winter's persistent southwest wind.

We hadn't roped in for the climb, but now we uncoiled a 100-foot line. Bill used his ice axe to belay one end, and I tied to the other and crept toward the crater's edge, testing with my axe. We were on a cornice, but as I gingerly peered over the edge, I could see that the snow was many feet deep. Steam was rising from the cauldron below, and after throwing a rock into its midst, I scrambled back the hundred feet to the comfort of Bill's belay and switched places so that he, too, could take home the memory of spitting into a live volcano.

The weather was mild, and as we looked beyond the crater to the north we could see Mount Rainier serenely surveying the scene as though contemplating the desecration that would be wrought by a comparable explosion of its 14,410-foot-high mass. It was a memorable day – probably my last climb of a glacial peak. (I'm writing this in 2005.) The climb had taken less than five hours and the descent about two, so we were back at the car shortly after noon.

A MESSAGE FROM THE PAST

I recall clearly having made a second climb

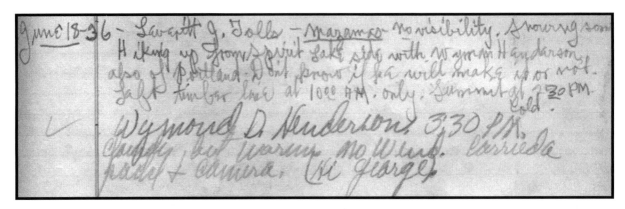

Wymond's signature from Mazamas' Mount St. Helens summit register. "It was a message from the dead, because in 2005 when I first saw it, Wymond had been dead for 50 years and I didn't remember that he ever had climbed Mount St. Helens."

of St. Helens in 1934 because it almost ended in disaster. On our first climb that year Kenny Johnsrud and I had delighted in glissading down the mountain's steep north face, sliding with our feet together and leaning back on our alpenstocks, but when I tried that glissade on the second climb a few weeks later I suddenly broke through a snow bridge and dropped into a shallow crevasse beneath. We foolishly had taken off our crampons for the slide but fortunately were still roped together, so I wasn't hurt. It was a lesson I never forgot.

I don't know why that second 1934 climb isn't in the register, but the Mazama's historian found a 1936 entry that was both startling and heart-warming to me. It is dated June 18, 1936, with brother Wymond's bold signature followed by, "(Hi George)." His entry was just below that of another old friend, Leveritt Tolls. It was a message from the dead because in 2005 when I first saw it Wymond had been dead for 50 years and I didn't remember that he ever had climbed Mount St. Helens.

MOUNT ADAMS 1934 – ANATOMY OF A LIGHTNING STRIKE

The bolt of lightning knew exactly where it wanted to go.

With an earsplitting clap of thunder it struck the lightning rod atop the Mount Adams lookout. While some of its electrons peppered the sheet metal flashing on the roof, the main bolt followed the cabin's grounding system down the outside wall, drove a hole right through the wire-reinforced window and pounced upon its quarry inside: a half-ton bundle of diamond-tipped steel drill bits that were stored behind the wooden bench where we four weary climbers were dozing.

It was July 15, 1934, and Keith and Elwood McCoy and Dick Mansfield, all from White Salmon, Wash., and I had just reached the summit of the 12,307-foot peak when a thunderstorm swept across the Columbia River and engulfed the mountain.

After venting its fury on the drill bits and setting alight a straw broom, the lightning bolt followed grounding cables to earth, leaving the four of us lying on the rough plank floor. As we regained our senses and threw the blazing broom into the snow, we congratulated one another on the miracle of our survival and began to assess the damage.

The only traces of the bolt's instantaneous presence were damaged flashing, the burned broom and the hole through the reinforced window – the rest of the window glass wasn't even cracked!

When we had first reached the summit

Approaching the fire lookout on the summit of Mount Adams. As the photo shows, the isolated building was a natural lightning rod. Mike Hermann photo, courtesy of the Mazamas.

Dick Mansfield (left), Keith McCoy and Elwood McCoy resting by the diamond drill outfit about halfway up the south side of Mount Adams, July 15, 1934.

that morning, I was surprised to see a string of packhorses standing beside the summit cabin. The Forest Service had abandoned its fire lookouts on both Mount St. Helens and Mount Adams a few years earlier. However, we learned that Adams' dormant crater was thought to have major deposits of sulfur, gypsum and alum, which White Salmon entrepreneur Wade Dean hoped to bring to market by a series of underground shafts and surface conveyors. His Glacier Mining Company was using the old Forest Service cabin as its base for exploration.

The horses belonged to veteran packer Jack Perry, who was making regular supply trips to the summit. When he spotted the approaching storm he had hustled the pack string off the peak ahead of the lightning strike.

Thunder was still rumbling in the darkened sky as we fled the lookout, bounded down the first thousand feet or so to the false summit and - ignoring tired legs - hurried down the remaining 5,000 feet to the trailhead. I made it home at 11:30 p.m., in time for a few hours' sleep before going to work Monday happy to be alive. Keith McCoy returned to the summit during the summer of 1935 to operate the diamond drill for the mining company. Meanwhile I submitted a short article and a photo on the sulfur mining to the *The Oregonian*, which ran in the July 27 issue.

A ROUND TRIP ON COOPER SPUR

Two weeks later, on July 29, 1934, Bob Dail and I climbed Cooper Spur on the north side of Mount Hood for the first time. We learned the hard way that although it usually is important to make an early start, especially on the south side where the sun starts rocks rolling soon after dawn, the problem is not always the same on a north side climb. Since neither of us knew that route, we started the climb from Cloud Cap Inn at 1:10 a.m.

A cold moon was shining, and the snow had a solid crust that persisted until we reached Tie-in Rock, where it changed to ice too solid for safe climbing, even with crampons! I've never forgotten taking turns chopping 450 steps with our ice axes between the 9,000-foot level and the summit, which we finally reached almost eight hours later after reestablishing the anchors of the lifeline. Returning the same way, we had the worst of both worlds, for in the narrow gulch just below the summit the ice had thawed, sending rocks of all sizes thundering past our unprotected heads.

ON ASSIGNMENT FROM *THE OREGONIAN*

In another two weeks, on Aug. 12, 1934, I was on the summit of Mount Adams again – this time on assignment to do an expanded story for the *Oregonian*.

That was Wymond's idea. When I described our lightening-disrupted climb and showed him snapshots of horses on the summit, he thought that the story would support more complete coverage and urged me to make a proposal to the *Oregonian*. I was reluctant. I didn't have a proper news camera. We knew no one at the Glacier Mining Company. We both were working six days a week so would have only one day and two nights for the project. The last obstacle was the biggest, we had no money to buy gas for the family's aging Hupmobile, and it had not been driven in months.

But Wymond overrode each of my objections, and we went together to see Bob Notson, then night city editor of *The Oregonian* who eventually became publisher. Wymond was bold and persuasive, and to my surprise, Notson agreed to take the story and even advanced us $5 for gasoline!

We phoned Wade Dean and told him that two *Oregonian* reporters were coming to White Salmon the next weekend to write a story and take pictures of the sulfur mine. He was more than cordial, assuring us that Jack Perry and

Above: Jack Perry's six horses nearing summit of Mount Adams carrying supplies to the sulfur miners. Below: Some of the horses at the summit lookout. Both photos were taken Aug. 12, 1934, and accompanied my second article for The Oregonian.

his packhorses would be on the summit that day and volunteering to have a spokesman from the company accompany us. We hadn't realized until then that publicity was an important ingredient in getting financing for such a mining speculation.

The ailing Hupmobile was almost our undoing. Hardly were we started thn the radiator began to steam. We found that it would go only about 20 miles between water refills, so it was almost midnight when we steamed up in front of Dean's attractive White Salmon home. We were greeted by Dean and several associates who had been waiting since nine o'clock to join us at a buffet supper.

It was Dean's turn to be surprised when two teenage boys stepped out of the limousine carrying crampons, alpenstocks and Mother's Kodak folding postcard camera. I was just out of high school, and Wymond was 19.

In spite of our obvious inexperience we were warmly welcomed. The people of Klickitat County were anxious to encourage the mining project, knowing that it could bring jobs and prosperity to a community struggling in the depth of the Great Depression.

We gladly accepted their offer to drive us to the trailhead at Cold Springs near Mount Adams' 5,700-foot timberline. We'd had no sleep, and it was almost dawn when we started the climb, but somehow we reached the summit ahead of the packhorses.

A NOD FROM EDITOR NOTSON

The second newspaper article was a triumph for Wymond and me and was my first real journalistic coup. It pleased Wade Dean too and even brought a favorable nod from quiet-spoken editor Notson. It appeared in the Sept. 2, 1934 *Sunday Oregonian* as a full column story accompanied by two three-column photos of Jack Perry and his horses.

The Oregonian paid us $16.40 for the weekend's work, which was more than either my weekly salary of $13.50 a week at S.H. Kress & Co. or Wymond's $15 a week salary at F.W. Woolworth. I still have the pay slip.

A FOUR-BITS-A-WEEK CAMERA

I had several more small but tantalizing journalistic successes that resulted from climbing and skiing, both on Mount Hood. One was a short article that appeared in the *Oregon Journal* about Mazamas Maxine Faircourt and Leveritt Tolls getting stuck in the Crater Rock Shelter on the south side in a storm in April 1935. One week later, on April 27, George Riggs and I climbed Mount Hood with Ranger. The photo I took of the two of them facing east into the sunrise won first place in the *Oregon Journal's* photo contest on May 10 and included a cash prize of $2.50.

The award winning photo of Ranger and the resulting monetary prize was an inspiration. I realized that my little folding Brownie camera was limiting my ability to take professional photographs and that I needed better equipment. After 11 days of intense shopping I bought an excellent used newspaperman's camera from Sandy's camera store for $42, paying $2 down and the balance over two years at 50 cents a week. I used it for freelance travel and sports stories that I sold to *The Oregonian* and *Oregon Journal*, finding a lame excuse to explain my photography "hobby" when Mr. Bradshaw noticed the bylines.

I do recall that Mr. Kress once sent Mr. Bradshaw a note of approval for a dry goods window display I built featuring several of Mother's antique handmade quilts. He didn't know that I had taken the photo of the display with the same news camera that I used in my sub-rosa freelance work.

When the store remodeled its lighting, Mr. Bradshaw let me purchase an obsolete reflector fixture for 50 cents, but I didn't tell him that I would use it in a photographic enlarger I was building in our basement.

George Riggs and Ranger at sunrise on the south side of Mount Hood, April 27, 1935. I took this photo with a Kodak folding Brownie camera and it won first prize in the hobbies, sports and recreation category of the Oregon Journal's *photography contest.*

I WAS THE FIRST TO REVOLT

Wymond and I were careful that no one in either the Kress or Woolworth stores knew that we were brothers, because association with employees of a rival store was forbidden. In those days ocean freighters tied up to discharge and load cargo along the waterfront between the Broadway and Hawthorne bridges, and we often met at the docks to eat lunch and dream of escaping our dime-store shackles and shipping out to other worlds.

Reading Richard Halliburton's *The Royal Road To Romance* and Alice Hobart's *Oil For The Lamps of China* solidified those dreams, and eventually we both would break free.

By December 1935 it seemed that the deprivations of the Great Depression were going to stretch on forever, and I was ready to gamble that I could earn more as a freelance writer and photographer than the $13.50 a week that S.H. Kress still was paying me. Wymond was willing to stick it out a bit longer on his $15 a week salary at Woolworth until I got on my feet and could again contribute to the families' living expenses.

With a sense of grim satisfaction, I gave notice to Mr. Bradshaw right at the start of the store's busiest week, just before Christmas, but the tough-minded manager didn't even give me the satisfaction of suggesting that a raise might have been in sight.

19 SKIING THE SKYLINE TRAIL – 1936

"Truly it was a dream of a place to ski." Ralph Day and I on Park Ridge Feb. 28, 1936. A few moments later Everett Lynch, who took the picture, joined us to make the first recorded winter descent into Jefferson Park.

JEFFERSON PARK

Teetering on a snow cornice at the rim of Park Ridge, I could see framed between my ski tips icc-bound Russell Lake a thousand feet below and the mile-wide col of Jefferson Park stretching to the buttress of 10,495-foot-high Mount Jefferson a scant two miles away.

Moments before a capricious wind had swept the Park clear of fog, and now we could reach our goal of skiing into the park – if we dared schuss the tantalizing slope at our feet.

The last five days had been a stormy hell as five of us battled deep snow, raging winds and numbing cold to push a route for adventure skiing from Mount Hood to Mount Jefferson.

EIGHTY MILES ON SKIS

I had just turned 20 and had climbed Mount Hood, Mount Adams and Mount St. Helens, so I thought I was quite an able mountaineer, but this attempt to complete the 80 mile trek by skiing down into Jefferson Park itself was to deal a harsh blow to that self-confidence.

The 80-mile trek had begun at the Wapinitia Highway near Mount Hood on a chilly Sunday morning in February, and we planned to reach Detroit Ranger Station on the Santiam Highway by Sunday night.

OUT OF A JOB IN THE GREAT DEPRESSION

After more than two years of mind-numbing drudgery as a $13.50-a-week trainee at the S.H. Kress & Co. variety store, I had quit that job cold, gambling that I could make a career as a photojournalist. It was an insane move to make in the depth of the Great Depression, and I was soon wallowing in regrets.

Then Foster Steele, a man with a vision, entered my life. He was the assistant supervisor of the Mount Hood National Forest. There was an upsurge of interest in downhill skiing right then, and Mount Hood was in the spotlight.

Following years of fruitless agitation by winter sports enthusiasts for a hotel to be built at the tree line on Mount Hood, suddenly the Works Progress Administration had decided to create jobs for unemployed craftsmen and women by putting them to work building a luxury ski lodge to be owned and administered by the Mount Hood National Forest.

To Forest Service brass it was as though a baby had been left on the doorstep of a confirmed bachelor along with a note saying that the foundling's upbringing would be the responsibility of the reluctant foster parent.

A MAN OF STEEL

The concept was so counter to the culture of national forests that most administrators were aghast, but to Foster Steele it was a welcome challenge. As a boy in the 1890s, the veteran outdoorsman had carried the mail on skis through snowbound mountains in Idaho, and soon after national forests were established in 1905, he became a forest ranger.

Steele knew that responsibility for the new resort would devolve to the agency's regional office and finally to the Mount Hood National

Foster Steele measuring water content of the snow at Clackamas Lake Feb. 24, 1936.

Forest, but he had a broader vision: "Why not encourage adventure skiing in Oregon's Cascades similar to the hut-to-hut skiing popular in Europe's Alps?" he wondered.

THE BRASS WERE NOT IMPRESSED

Tolerant smiles greeted the balding, white-haired forester in the winter of 1935 when he proposed establishing a series of ski huts along the Oregon Skyline Trail and volunteered to lead an expedition to assess feasibility.

Despite the skeptics, the indomitable Steele recruited Clackamas Lake District Ranger O.J. Johnson to join him on a preliminary trek, and in mid-February the two set out to survey a route, planning to stay overnight in existing summer ranger stations.

The first day's 10 miles from the Mount Hood Highway to Clackamas Lake went well, but their plan to ski 22 miles the second day to a cabin at Olallie Meadows was thwarted by a fast-moving blizzard, and they ended up surviving the night bivouacked in an

Otis J. Johnson, Clackamas Lake District Ranger, surveying his territory on the high ridge between Olallie and Brientenbush lakes, March 9, 1935. Foster Steele photo.

abandoned sheepherder's wanigan at Warm Springs Meadow. Although they planned to ski into Jefferson Park, they only got as far as Breitenbush Lake. From there they followed the snowbound road down the west side of the Cascades to Breitenbush Hot Springs.

Steele was undaunted and immediately began planning another attempt for the next year. To provide an additional ski hut on the route he had a new guard station built at the site of the old sheep camp, and when Ranger Johnson retired that summer, Forest Supervisor A.O. Waha appointed as his successor Everett Lynch, a young ranger with skiing experience in northeastern Washington. Rounding out the expedition would be L.A. "Bud" Waggener, a rugged 21-year-old Mount Hood Forest engineer who was anxious to go even though he wasn't a skier, and 18-year-old office assistant Ralph Day, who was a good skier.

FORTUNE SMILES

That was when fortune smiled on me. Foster Steele wanted the skiing world to hear about Oregon's challenge to Europe's Alps, but because he couldn't count on help from the regional office public affairs staff, he turned to his friend Marshall Dana, Editor of the *Oregon Journal* for advice.

I had been contributing feature stories and outdoor photographs to Portland newspapers and magazines since July 1934, so with the advice of the *Journal's* City Editor Arthur Crookham, Northwest Editor Fred H. McNeil and Sunday Editor Sam Raddon, Dana suggested that the Forest Service invite me to join its team. Steele had no way to hire me for the job, but the newspaper would pay me for whatever stories and photographs they ran.

When I walked into Steele's office the next

My homemade pack, specially modified to carry and protect my camera gear. Everett Lynch photo.

day I was awed by his invitation. Would I join an official Forest Service party on a weeklong ski trip from Mount Hood to Mount Jefferson with food, housing and transportation provided, knowing that the *Oregon Journal* was ready to run stories and pictures I submitted? No 20-year-old skier and aspiring journalist had ever received a more alluring offer.

It didn't take me long to get ready. I was proud of my camera – a well-used 1910 model German Ica Reflex with an f 1:4.5 Carl Zeiss Tessar Jena lens. I had bought it from Sandy's Camera Store for $42, making payments of 50 cents a week for two years. Knowing the camera would be in for rough treatment, I built a sturdy plywood box padded with cotton that filled a fourth of the space in my homemade Trapper Nelson pack board. My seven-and-a-half-foot-long hickory skis had been handmade by my father.

On a cold, rainy Sunday in February Bud, Ralph and I met for the first time at the Mount Hood forest headquarters in Portland where "Shorty" Porter from the Zigzag CCC camp had been sent to pick us up. We climbed into the back of a canvas-topped, stake-body truck

for the chilly two-hour trip to Summit Ranger Station where Foster Steele and Ranger Lynch joined us for the the drive to Blue Box Pass.

I liked Everett Lynch from the start. He was a slow-speaking, pipe-smoking woodsman whose wry humor often caught people off guard. He hadn't seen much of his new district yet, nor had he known Foster Steele until recently, so the expedition must have appeared a bit fanciful to him. Only Steele and I knew the country well, for in past summers I had hiked the Oregon Skyline Trail and had made several trips into Jefferson Park.

A MOTLEY CREW

It was a motley crew especially when it came to what we wore. Steele and Lynch were dressed in uniform chokebore pants, high-laced boots and ski caps. Waggener and Day wore ski pants, caps and stiff-soled ski boots, and I had on logging camp-style woolen clothes, Bergman boots and a sealskin cap.

When we unloaded at Blue Box Pass, the snow was falling so fast that the plows barely could keep the highway open, and I wondered if we would really start our trip in such a storm.

Foster Steele left no doubt as he climbed out of the truck's cab, selected a sizable item from the pile of supplies, loaded it into his own pack, strapped on his skis and called out, "You men divide the rest and I'll start ahead." It was the last ever said about sharing the weight. From then on we competed to be sure that each of our packs was as heavy as any other.

We planned to follow the Skyline Road. In 1936 it dropped directly from Highway 26 at Blue Box Pass to Clear Lake, which it circled before joining the present road near Clear Lake Butte. We expected our first mile to be a swift downhill run, but instead when we caught up with our leader he was breaking trail knee-deep in new snow and stepped aside to make way for another trailbreaker. That became our routine for most of the next 50 miles – as each

The motley crew at the start of the expedition at Blue Box Pass, Feb. 23, 1936. I'm at left; to my left are Foster Steele, Bud Waggener, Ralph Day and Everett Lynch.

leader tired he would drop to the back of the line and allow another to take over.

We skied across frozen Clear Lake trying to adjust to skiing with heavy packs. As the trail led into heavy timber we finally achieved a steady pace. It was close to dark when we spotted the warm glow of a gasoline lantern shining through the window of the old log ranger station at Clackamas Lake.

VENISON STEW

When we pushed open the door, we were assailed by a blast of warm air filled with the scent of venison stew simmering on the pot-bellied stove. Forest guard Paul Dennis and his wife lived in the Packer's Cabin that winter to care for the district's string of horses and mules, and he kept the phone line to the Summit

Paul Dennis and wife greet Foster Steele and party at the Packers Cabin at Clackamas Lake Ranger Station, Sunday, Feb. 23, 1936. Awaiting inside was a hot venison stew.

and Bear Springs ranger stations working, so they knew our plans and had prepared the welcoming supper.

A new residence and headquarters building were built in 1935 by carpenters on relief rolls of the Emergency Civil Works Administration and young enrollees in the Civilian Conservation Corps (CCC). Lynch was anxious to see his new facilities, so we stayed two nights and spent time shoveling snow off roofs. We also skied to the upper end of the lake to see how a colony of beavers were faring in the cold. The shallow lake was completely frozen. Steele believed the beavers had moved downstream, possibly as far as the main Clackamas River, but might return in the spring. The power company dam that created Timothy Lake hadn't yet been built.

WARM SPRINGS MEADOW AT LAST

Foster rousted us out of our blankets at five o'clock on Tuesday morning, reporting that the weather looked worse than on the first day, so

there was no point in waiting any longer.

Worse it was! As we started up Dry Creek hill the wind had risen to a small gale that filled our tracks behind us. Foster started in front as usual, but soon his skis were sinking 15 inches into the new snow. Finally he decreed that to assure steady progress without rest stops, each man would break trail for only one hundred steps then drop to the back of the line. Foster never missed his own turn, either.

It was only three miles to the crest of the divide that separates the Willamette and Deschutes river drainages. From there the trail dropped quickly into Warm Springs Meadow, which was partly sheltered from the wind by Peavine Mountain on the west. As the climb steepened and our packs seemed to grow heavier, we bent our heads into the wind, picturing a swift downhill slide after we crossed the summit.

That was not to be. Even on the downhill our skis sank several inches, and to keep moving we had to push with our poles just as we had going up. It was nearly dark when we reached

Foster Steele, Everett Lynch and Bud Waggener in front of the Warm Springs Guard Station, Feb. 25, 1936.

the sheep camp where Foster and O.J. Johnson had spent a miserable night in the herder's wanigan the year before. Our spirits soared as we sighted the new Warm Springs Guard Station tucked in a lodgepole pine thicket.

A FROZEN SKY

At dawn on Wednesday we walked out of the cabin at Warm Springs Meadow into a world so still and cold that it seemed as though a block of ice could be cut right out of the ominous atmosphere. The slate gray canopy of sky looked like all the heat of the earth was trying to push up through it, while a blanket of cold air held the ground in a tight grip, and there was no current of air to mix the two.

"It's a temperature inversion, and a darned cold one," said Foster. "Don't touch your metal bindings without gloves or you'll likely lose some skin." His thermometer read 10 degrees below zero. The wind had stopped during the night and the only snow falling was from moisture being crystallized out of the clear air.

"We'll need to watch for frostbite," he continued, "and there isn't much relief in sight. If we get some wind to stir up the air, the temperature on the ground will rise, but then the wind chill might prove even more dangerous."

Our schedule called for us to ski 20 miles that day and to spend the night at Breitenbush Lake Guard Station, which had been winterized and had food cached for a three-day stay. But we didn't make it.

A CHERRY-RED STOVE

My right thumb gave the first warning. The snow was firmer than before, and soon the five of us were strung out along a half-mile of trail. Bud Waggener had adapted quickly to skis and took more than his share of trail breaking, and I accepted the challenge, so the two of us were in the lead. Then I realized that despite the exertion my right thumb had been numb for an hour or more. Shucking off the canvas outer mitten and heavy wool glove I saw that the skin was dead white.

When the others caught up Foster looked for signs of frostbite on all our faces and inquired about any other numb fingers or toes. "Don't try rubbing your thumb in snow, George," he warned. "That would just make it worse." Everett Lynch quietly pulled from his pack a spare pair of wool mitts to replace my gloves, and then other exchanges were made among the group.

We hadn't seen an animal since leaving Clackamas Lake, but as we climbed between Pinhead Butte and Sisi Butte we suddenly realized that we were being watched!

The party had spread apart again, with Bud in the lead, when I spotted the tracks of a big cat – no doubt a cougar – in the smooth path of Bud's skis. Bud was out of sight in the trail ahead, and no one was in sight behind me. I

On Wednesday, Feb, 26, the temperature dropped to 10 degrees below zero, our party was stalked by a cougar and I got frostbite. We never made it to Olallie Lake.

called for Bud to wait, and when Foster Steele, who was next in line, caught up he commented, "Yep, that fellow's tracks are in the trail between you and me too." He said that cougars are inquisitive animals and that this one might have been watching us for quite a while, but only now had we gotten far enough apart for him to come between us without being seen.

Foster was worried, but not about the cougar. We were less than halfway to Breitenbush Lake, which was a thousand feet higher and likely much colder. "We're just not equipped to ski another 10 miles in this temperature," he finally said. "There's an old log ranger station at Olallie Meadow a couple of miles ahead. We'll stop there for the night, and George can thaw out his hand."

The best thing about the abandoned log cabin was a large stack of firewood that had been left by a CCC crew that summer. I was the only one with frostbite, so after helping reassemble the stovepipe on the sheet metal stove and melting snow for water, I soaked the

thumb in warm water until feeling was restored – then suffered agony during the last stages of thawing. Foster checked it and commented, "I've had worse," which I took as both kudos for my stoicism and speculation that there wouldn't be permanent damage.

"You could throw a cat between those logs," he said as he helped drive wedges of firewood into spaces where the chinking was missing. The little stove glowed cherry red, but its heat could barely be felt three feet from the source. We had brought bags of smokechasers' emergency rations from Warm Springs Meadow, so after dark we ate a cold dinner of tinned corned beef, canned Boston brown bread, canned peaches and powdered coffee.

The fire would have to be kept burning all night, so two-hour shifts were set for each person to stay awake and stoke the stove. Lynch, Waggener and Day had cut a bushy hemlock tree and stripped the limbs, providing a soft layer of boughs to insulate our blankets from the cold plank floor.

"When we arrived at Breitenbush Lake only a corner of the guard station roof showed above the snow." Bud Waggener (left), Foster Steele, Everett Lynch & Ralph Day, Feb. 27, 1936.

OLALLIE BUTTE – A SKYSCRAPER

When we started up the trail at dawn on Thursday, the deep freeze was loosening its grip. The lookout cabin on top of 7,200-foot-high Olallie Butte almost touched the bottom of the overcast, and a stiff east wind streamed snow from the treeless summit. As we passed Lower and Spoon lakes, the trail again crossed briefly to the west side of the Cascades, then swung east to Olallie Lake Guard Station.

SKIS ON ICE

The cabin was nearly buried in drifts 10 feet deep, so we passed it by and coasted out onto frozen Olallie Lake where I called for a stop to take pictures. After five days of storms I had begun to lose hope of making the spectacular midwinter photographs that I had promised to the *Oregon Journal*. Clouds still engulfed Mount Jefferson, but the sky was clearing to the north, and I was rewarded with a dramatic scene of our skiers in the center of the icebound lake, and beyond them, Olallie Butte and the northern Oregon Cascades stretching to 11,225-foot-high Mount Hood.

The Ruddy Hill Fire a decade earlier had swept through the forest above Horseshoe Lake from Double Peaks, Upper Lake and Gibson Lake right down to the north edge of Breitenbush Lake, creating open slopes dotted with tall hemlock and cedar snags. It was our first opportunity for a fast downhill ski run – and neophyte skier Bud Waggener learned a new word, *sitzmark!*

(Note: Sixty years later when I camped near Gibson Lake, natural reproduction had restored those burned-over slopes, and the subalpine lakes and meadows were interspersed with wildflower-carpeted ridges.)

BREITENBUSH LAKE

Nineteen thirty-six was a record year for deep snow and below-zero temperatures up and down the Cascades. Snow tunnels connected many buildings in Government Camp, and we ice skated all winter on Collins Lake near Multorpor Hill. It was no surprise that we could ski right across every lake along the summit that year. When we arrived at mile-high Breitenbush Lake only a corner of the Guard Station roof showed above the snow.

Early morning view of Mount Hood and Olallie Butte from lower Park Ridge, Feb. 28, 1936.

The building had been winterized and a new door built high in the gable end. We crawled through it and brought out shovels that Bud, Ralph and I used to dig out the front door and windows. Foster and Everett lit the Coleman lantern, fired up the cook stove, melted snow for water and fixed the first real meal we'd had in two days.

It was a night of pure luxury. Insulated by its mantle of snow, the cabin warmed in a hurry. Our bellies were full, and after rolling our blankets out on comfortable cots with real mattresses, we fell asleep trying to forget the frigid night before at Olallie Meadow.

JEFFERSON PARK AT LAST

The blizzard blew itself out during the night, so at dawn Lynch, Day and I left for the 12-mile round trip into Jefferson Park. Steele and Waggener weren't downhill skiers, so they decided to wait at Breitenbush. We knew that we must travel fast, but the spectacular landscape of snow-laden trees, sparkling peaks and azure sky dictated many photo stops.

After we passed Pyramid Butte the route ahead was clearly defined, so I left the others and climbed to the top of a ridge. There I took one of the best photographs of the trip (see above), then hurried to catch up with Everett and Ralph. It was past noon when we finally reached the 7,018-foot summit of Park Ridge, and it would be dark in a few short hours.

A THOUSAND-FOOT SCHUSS

"Should we try it, George?" Everett asked as we peered excitedly into the park a thousand

Ralph Day sliding onto Russell Lake after a 1,000-foot schuss down Park Ridge. Everett Lynch photo.

feet below. Suddenly I realized the burden that was mine as the only one of the three who knew the country. Ranger Lynch was trusting my judgment, and Foster Steele was counting on my pictures to help him demonstrate the skiing potential of Jefferson Park and thus justify the expedition itself.

Was there time to ski into the park and then return to Breitenbush Lake before dark? Strangely the possibility of an injury or a broken ski didn't occur to me. We were 30 miles from the nearest road and had no radio. If help was needed, one of us would have to ski out to Detroit and bring back a rescue party on skis or snowshoes. Neither snow machines or helicopters had yet been invented.

I was 20 years old, and I really wanted to schuss that challenging slope, and the others did too. Everett returned my nod, and the three of us tipped our skis over the edge. Two tremendous tumbles later I coasted excitedly

onto the ice of Russell Lake with equipment intact, and shortly Everett and Ralph arrived, also wearing broad smiles. The afternoon sun was shining directly into the park, so we took more photographs before commencing the long climb back up Park Ridge.

CONSEQUENCES

Our ardor cooled quickly when we reached the top. Daylight was fading, and the sun had softened the snow so much that instead of a fast four-mile glide back to the guard station, we might have to pole to keep moving. Pyramid Butte and Ruddy Hill, our best landmarks, seemed far away and would recede behind other ridges as we descended. My self-confidence began to ebb as we scraped the climbing wax from our skis, rubbed on paraffin and graphite, and took compass readings on Pyramid Butte. It would be a race against nightfall.

After the first mile we realized that in order to maintain some speed. we were allowing the slope of the terrain to pull us too far west, and in the fading light landmarks were disappearing in a confusion of ridges. Then came the final blow to self-confidence. As we rounded a small ridge, Pyramid Butte loomed ahead but on our right, when it should have been on our left! We stopped to consider the options. Should we push on by flashlight when we weren't even sure where we were, or should we seek a sheltered place to contrive a snow cave? Without a tent, food or stove, the outlook was bleak.

MOONLIGHT

Suddenly Ralph cried, "What's that light?" and pointed to the high ridge on the east.

"It's the moon!" replied Lynch with unaccustomed vigor, and as we watched, the moon slowly appeared above the horizon, bathing the mountains in sparkling white light. Not once during our stormy trek had moonlight

Ralph Day and I on Park Ridge in a race to reach Breitenbush Guard Station before dark, Feb. 28, 1936. Everett Lynch photo.

penetrated the overcast sky. Foster may have been aware that the moon was entering a new phase, but none of the others were.

Then we realized that I had mistaken Bear Point for Pyramid Butte, each of which was more than 6,000 feet high with a lookout cabin on its top. It meant that we were rounding Pyramid on the west instead of the east and were about to drop into the narrow gorge of the frozen Breitenbush River.

Taking off our skis, we kicked steps down the side of the snow-filled gorge, then took turns stamping a trail through breakable crust up the moonlit river bottom. Two hours of climbing put us on the north side of the ravine, where we could hear Bud Waggener shouting for us from the outlet of Breitenbush Lake. Seventy years later he told me that he had followed our tracks almost to the top of Park Ridge that morning then returned alone – pretty daring for a first-timer on skis!

(Note: As I was writing this memoir in 2005, 70 years after that first Skyline Trail trek, I wanted to check my memory of that lifesaving moonrise and found, on the Naval Observatory Web site, that indeed the moon was about half full on that night in 1936.)

BREITENBUSH HOT SPRINGS – OUR LEADER CRASHES

If Foster Steele hadn't broken his leg on the way out, we could have made the 26-mile downhill run to Detroit Ranger Station the next day as scheduled. Foster and Bud had started out early, allowing Everett, Ralph and me an extra hour's sleep. After breakfast we closed up the guard station and started off in high spirits to catch up, clattering down the first few miles of icy road grade in a half-hour before coming upon Foster seated on a snow bank massaging his right leg! Bud had gently removed one of the Supervisor's high-topped boots, exposing a rapidly swelling ankle.

Foster Steele wasn't about to give up! He insisted that we put the boot back on and lace it very tight so that it would act as sort of a walking cast and then help him to his feet. Gritting his teeth he took a step, but if Bud hadn't caught him, he would have collapsed onto the snow – he certainly wouldn't be able to walk the remaining 23 miles to Detroit anytime soon.

Everett emptied blankets, food and extra clothes from his own pack and struck out to get help. It was only nine o'clock and he hoped to ski the 10 miles downhill to Breitenbush Hot Springs by noon. If the phone line to Detroit was working, he could report the accident to Ranger McClannaghan. If the line had been broken during the storm, he would have to ski another 13 miles, because the road to Detroit had been closed by snow since fall.

A COLD NIGHT AHEAD

It appeared that the four of us were facing a cold night ahead, so Ralph and I decided to make a toboggan from our two pairs of skis and use it to pull Foster down to the hot springs. He didn't argue but speculated that even if he couldn't walk, he might be able to "shuffle along" on his skis, so he asked Bud to put them back on for him.

Ralph and I headed back up the trail to find suitable saplings to use for thwarts for a toboggan, then we laced the parts together with clothesline. All skis were made of wood, and many had holes drilled through their tips to aid in such an effort. Several of us carried clothesline that we could loop around our skis as emergency climbers.

By the time our toboggan was ready, Foster and Bud had disappeared down the trail, so we set out after them on foot, dragging the sled. It was a sunny day, and soon we were sinking boot-deep in softening snow and were bathed in sweat. After an hour we hadn't yet caught up with the two, so we disgustedly dismantled the toboggan and put our skis back on.

GRIT AND GUTS

When we finally reached our quarry, Foster was also sweating as he doggedly shuffled down the well-broken track, supporting himself on his poles, with a steadying hand from Bud.

"The pain isn't any worse when I shuffle along like this than when I stand still," he said through clenched teeth, "but if I stop and let it cool down I don't believe I could get started again." We took turns skiing beside him, and he never stopped his painful plodding until we reached the hot springs and he could plunge the aching limb into a tub of steaming mineral water. Then Bud dove into the pool but quickly scrambled out, sputtering that beneath the hot surface was a layer of very cold water. Ralph and I soon helped him stir it up.

A THWARTED RESCUE

Everett had reached the springs less than an hour after leaving the accident and had phoned the bad news to Ranger McClannaghan in Detroit. When McClannaghan learned that the assistant supervisor of the Mount Hood National Forest had broken his leg and was awaiting rescue 23 miles up the Skyline Trail, he lost no time putting a snow plow and road graders to work attacking the snowbound road. As we climbed out of the pool, we could hear the roar of heavy engines, for in just eight hours the crew had opened a single narrow roadway all the way from Detroit.

Assistant Ranger Kermit Linstedt driving a Forest Service sedan was behind the snowplow, followed by a stake-bodied truck, so within the hour we all were enjoying a hot dinner with the McClannaghans in Detroit and made it back to Portland shortly after midnight.

CENSORED

I don't remember how the rescue itself had been planned, but certainly if Foster Steele hadn't made it to the hot springs on his own there would soon have been a team of mountaineers with toboggans and survival gear on their way. How surprised they would have been had they found the victim lolling beside a swimming pool. X-rays the next morning in Portland showed that iron-man Steele had indeed skied those last 10 miles with a clean break in the small bone of his right leg.

Foster insisted that his accident not be reported to the press. There were three daily newspapers in Portland then – the *Oregon Journal*, *The Morning Oregonian* and the *Daily News Telegram* – and none ever learned the full story. The *Journal* made the most of its access to my reports. The following paragraph from the Sunday edition reflects our enthusiasm.

Now, on the morning after the storm, we stood atop the 6,800-foot rim of Jefferson Park gazing at what no man had seen before – Mount Jefferson and the 'hanging garden' lying smooth and white under the low mid-winter sun. Truly it was a dream of a place to ski.

20 A DOLLAR HERE, A DOLLAR THERE

Future site of Timberline Lodge. Forest Service Engineer Ward Gano, right, Forest Guards Jerry Lymph, center, and George Calverley pause in survey of water supply for the new resort in May 1936. Mount Jefferson is in the distant background.

The 1936 Skyline Trail ski trip had helped launch my career as a freelance photo journalist, but the Depression's grip still was firm, and I spent the next two months earning a few dollars at a time from sales of stories and pictures to newspapers, selling advertising in struggling magazines, doing publicity for local Red Cross fundraising, taking pictures of window displays for Meier and Frank Co., photographing dentures and other products for a dental supply company and the like. After paying for supplies, there were few dollars left to help Wymond pay for the family's food.

BONNEVILLE DAM CHRONICLE

Bonneville Dam was under construction, and the publisher of the *Hood River News* started a weekly newspaper called the *Bonneville Dam Chronicle* to serve the sprawling community that had grown up east and west of Cascade Locks. I hired on as its reporter, advertising salesman and circulation manager. There was no salary – only commissions – and I was not a savvy enough salesman to make a living that way, so finally I gave up and hitchhiked back home to Portland.

I worked several weeks in April 1936 for the Bonneville Dam Chronicle, *but I was not a savvy advertising salesman, and Mount Hood was calling.*

MOUNT HOOD CALLING

There were two good reasons for me to visit the Mount Hood National Forest office when I got home: one, to ask Foster Steele how well he was recovering from his skiing accident on the Skyline Trail, and two, to see if there was a chance for me to get a summer job on a lookout or fire crew.

After saying proudly that he hadn't missed a day at the office despite his broken leg, Foster announced that already he was planning another Skyline Trail ski expedition for 1937 and invited me to go again. Of course I accepted, but that was almost a year away, and he said that although there were no summer fire protection jobs open, there was a temporary need right then at the site of the new Timberline Lodge for a few workers who could ski. He sent me to see project engineer Ward Gano in the regional office.

THE ELUSIVE WATER SUPPLY

A little-known fact about Timberline Lodge was the uncertainty about its water supply. In the rush to gain final funding before winter closed in, the subject was yet unresolved. There were plans to build two rock-faced storage tanks on a ridge just above the lodge to receive melt from the snowfields and glaciers, but was there enough water flowing in the bottoms of Salmon River and nearby canyons to provide a reliable source of water for domestic use and fire protection?

It was then May, and engineer Ward Gano was lining up a five-man crew to help him find the answer by digging shafts through the snow to canyon bottoms to determine the water flow at that time of year. On Foster Steele's recommendation, Gano put me on his crew along with George Calverley (who in summer was a horse packer), forest guard Jerry Lymph and one other. Gano and I were skiers and the others were not, but they needed jobs, so they borrowed skis and showed up at Government Camp anyway.

COWBOYS ON SKIS

We loaded supplies for two weeks on our backs and skied up Alpine Trail to the snowbound Phlox Point Guard Station, near where the Pucci chairlift now is located. The road from Government Camp was still under 10 feet of snow. At the end of that three-mile, 2,000-foot climb Calverley proclaimed, "When the good Lord gave me bow legs to straddle a horse, he never meant for me to fasten a pair of skis to them."

We lived in the little cabin half-hidden in trees near the 6,000-foot level, and each morning, sometimes in sunshine and sometimes in snowstorms, climbed a thousand feet higher on skis to excavation sites that Gano had selected. The drifting snows of winter had made it hard to tell from the surface where the actual canyon bottoms would be, but after using shovels to dig shafts as long as 40 feet and as deep as 30 feet, and hauling blocks of snow to the surface with ropes and buckets, we finally reached several streambeds and found that the flows clearly were not adequate.

Gano then shut down the job and called on CCC crews under Forest Service direction to install a pipeline and pumping system from a spring a mile below the lodge. I was out of a job again, but the timing was perfect, for right then I got my first big break as a journalist.

A PHOTO JOURNALIST AT LAST

The Oregon Winter Sports Association, which had been a leading advocate for a hotel at the tree line on Mount Hood, decided to launch a campaign to tell the nation about the new hotel and asked *Oregon Journal* City Editor Arthur Crookham to suggest someone to handle the publicity. He recommended me.

The idea of staging a ski tournament in June

Looking up a 40-foot snow tunnel while digging for the elusive water supply for Timberline Lodge in Salmon River Canyon. Ward Gano in foreground and Jerry Lymph in distance.

Jack Meier (left), Berger Underdahl, in Royal Rosarian white uniform, and Jim Mount look over the ground for the Rose Festival Ski Tournament on June 14, 1936. The idea of a ski race in June to bring attention to the start of Timberline Lodge construction came from the fertile brain of Berger Underdahl.

to bring attention to the start of construction of Timberline Lodge came from the fertile brain of Berger Underdahl, a native of Bergen, Norway, and the first president of the Oregon Winter Sports Association. For years he and other enthusiasts had enjoyed summer skiing on Mount Hood's upper snowfields, even though it required climbing two or three thousand feet on skis from the loop highway just to get started. Now that the road from Government Camp would be kept open all winter, wasn't it time to tell the world that skiing was a year-around sport in Oregon?

A NO-BUDGET NATIONAL SALES CAMPAIGN

Sun Valley had just opened, and renowned promoter Steve Hannigan had so focused the nation's attention on that spectacular resort that it seemed as if handfuls of movie stars and socialites had been sprinkled across Idaho's Sawtooth Range. That was the competition I faced when association director Dale Cowen offered me the job. I was short on experience as a press agent, but they didn't have much money, so we quickly reached an agreement.

Well, Sun Valley had Steve Hannigan, but I had lovely 18-year-old Delores Enebo, Crown Princess of the 1936 Oregon Winter Sports Carnival. My 20-year-old hormones must have been in overdrive, for I was able to convince Princess Delores to pose on a snowfield at the site of the new lodge wearing nothing but skis, boots and a one-piece swimsuit.

The photo of Delores' warm body silhouetted against the icy background of Mount Hood's snowfields and glaciers was picked up by wire services and appeared in more than 100 newspapers in the United States, from the *Boston Globe* to the New Orleans *Times-Picayune*.

Delores Enebo at the future site of Timberline Lodge on the south side of Mount Hood, May 1936. Her photo appeared in more than 100 North American newspapers.

THE GOLDEN ROSE RACE

Billed as America's first international midsummer ski championship and featuring the Mazamas Cup Race, it was held on June 14, 1936, as the final event of the Portland Rose Festival. It drew competitors from two nations and was carried on a national radio hookup, helping to give credence to the Association's slogan, "Roses to Snow in Ninety Minutes."

We devised some dramatic publicity events to draw spectators. The most bizarre was a ski jump built right in the Civic Auditorium (now the Keller Auditorium) with the inrun starting at the ceiling and the outrun dropping into the orchestra pit. Wooden planking was covered with canvas and sprinkled with soap flakes in lieu of snow. Several Cascade Ski Club jumpers made successful leaps, and to climax the event, Hjalmar Hvam strapped a pair of wooden barrel staves to his boots in place of skis and made the jump without a fall. The event got good newspaper coverage and drew large crowds for two nights. Hvam also made

"We devised some dramatic publicity events." Hvam jumping over the rose garden.

dry land ski jumps over blooming roses in the Washington Park rose garden in June, and all three Portland newspapers printed pictures of that stunt too.

TIMBERLINE'S WANDERING CORNERSTONE

A ceremony marking the laying of the cornerstone of Timberline Lodge was a highlight of tournament day, and only a few of those present realized that the stone was laid in the wrong place. Jack L. Meier, chairman of the event, knew, and so did I, for I had arranged the deception. It happened this way.

When Oregon WPA Administrator E.J. Griffith and I visited the site the previous day, we realized that the cornerstone's location would be hidden from the mountaintop by a tree-covered ridge, so when newsreel and press photographers recorded the event, Mount Hood would not show in the background. The WPA crews had located a boulder of the right size coughed up eons ago from the mountain's flaming crater. It was swinging from the boom of a power crane ready to be deposited at the site selected by the engineers when I appealed to Griffith to revise the location.

The engineers were adamant and the construction crew anxious to get on with the job, but the WPA chief had a sense of history, and the clanking crane was redirected to a point a hundred yards away so that Mount Hood's majestic summit was aligned perfectly beyond the stone. Following the ceremony, the oft-moved monolith was returned to its rightful resting place to become a permanent part of the lodge's foundation.

Response to the publicity was a press agent's delight but turned out to be an embarrassment

E.J. Griffith (left), WPA administrator for Oregon, and James Frankland, USFS regional engineer, laying the cornerstone for Timberline Lodge, June 14, 1936. USFS photo.

Mazama President Ed Hughes with the Mazamas Cup awarded to Hjalmar Hvam, winner of the first Golden Rose Race, June 14, 1936. Mazamas withdrew their sponsorship in 1937.

to the Forest Service and WPA. Race day dawned sunny and warm, with participants and early-arriving spectators scattered from timberline to Crater Rock, but the just-opened gravel road from the highway was not passable for private cars, so visitors were shuttled up the road in WPA construction trucks. The resulting traffic jam at the highway junction might have been tolerable had not a drenching thunderstorm trapped hundreds at timberline waiting for rides back down the mountain.

Those who coped with the chaos were rewarded with a spectacular ski tournament and colorful cornerstone ceremony. Boyd French Jr. won the downhill race, a 3,000-foot schuss from Crater Rock to a rose-garlanded finish arch at the site of Timberline Lodge, but Hjalmar Hvam won the slalom and combined titles so was awarded the Mazamas Cup, donated by Mazamas' President Edward J. Hughes. The following year the Mazamas decided that ski racing did not fit with the club's emphasis on mountain climbing, so they withdrew the cup, and the race was renamed the Golden Rose.

That acquaintance with the Portland Rose Festival resulted in my becoming president of the festival after World Ward II and melding those dissimilar interests by staging international ski jumping tournaments right in downtown Portland in 1951 and 1953, using shard ice for snow.

My job publicizing the midsummer ski races ended June 14, and on June 15 I started work for the Mount Hood National Forest. For the next eight years I worked summers for the Forest Service and winters for the Winter Sports Association and Timberline Lodge.

George Riggs, chairman of the Rose Festival committee for Cascade Ski Club, myself, Rose Festival program director, and George Halling, Rose Festival Association president, looking over the final plans for the 155-foot ski jump in Multnomah Stadium rearing its immense frame in the background, May 23, 1951. Oregon Historical Society photo, CN #013413.

21   A Shiny new Badge And A Model T Ford

When Foster Steele offered me a summer job as a forest guard on the Mount Hood National Forest, my first reaction – boundless joy – was quickly tempered by the question, "Can I afford to accept?"

The $60-a-month salary would be 10 percent more than the $13.50 a week I had been paid at S.H. Kress before I quit six months earlier, but the Forest Service job would require a car and a uniform, and I had neither. In 1936 such jobs were at a premium, though, and I thought that if I could just finance the car and uniform up front, I might make it through the summer and hope for a job with the Oregon Winter Sports Association again in the fall.

Nudelman Brothers, which specialized in mens clothing, was the official supplier of Forest Service uniforms, and I still have a warm feeling toward them for selling me a uniform for 10 percent down. Next I bought a 1924 Model T Ford through the want ads for $25 – $5 down and $5 a month – and with George Riggs' help soon had it in good running order.

I was a mighty happy 20-year-old that June as I loaded the Model T with food, blankets and rainy-weather clothes. I putt-putted at 10 miles an hour or so up Laurel Hill, turned down the Skyline Road at Blue Box Pass and reported to Ranger Everett Lynch at Clackamas Lake ready to begin work repairing telephone lines and trails until snow drifts melted on the road to my first guard station at Olallie Lake.

BLUE BOX PASS

Did you ever wonder how Blue Box Pass got its name? The story is worth telling. One hundred years ago before the Forest Service built fire lookout cabins on mountaintops, forest rangers patrolled on horseback or afoot watching for forest fires. Since radios were unreliable in the mountains the rangers kept in touch with dispatchers by telephone. Phone lines were hung on trees along main roads and trails, with sturdy waterproof telephone boxes built well above the normal snow levels every few miles. An early ranger, Joe Graham, devised a clever system of wooden levers that automatically switched the telephone to the

Blue Box in 1915. USFS photo.

line when the box door was opened, then switched it back to a lightning arrestor when the door was closed.

One of the first of those boxes was built in 1912, painted blue and located where the Oregon Skyline Trail crosses Highway 26 several miles east of Government Camp. That box is no longer there, but a highway marker still identifies the site as Blue Box Pass.

HOW NOT TO HANG A TELEPHONE LINE

As "Gil" Gilbert braked the stake-body truck to a sudden stop, I jumped down from the tailgate for a look. A snag about two feet through lay across the gravel road along with a small hemlock tree from which hung a white telephone line insulator. Under it all was a section of the trail to High Rock Lookout. A trail crew's job was to maintain roads, trails and telephone lines, and here we had come across damage to all three in one place.

Gil Gilbert was in charge of the crew, which included newly married Irwin Hull, son of veteran packer "Win" Hull, who had worked on the Lakes District before, and Joe Daniel and me, both new to the Forest Service. I was pleased when Gil handed me the telephone lineman's gear and tree climbing spurs and told two of us to locate the ends of the broken line and hang the insulator up on a different tree.

THE UBIQUITOUS FOREST SERVICE PHONE LINE

The ubiquitous Forest Service telephone lines were marvels of simplicity and reliability. They required only a single number nine iron wire strung on trees and needed no outside electric current. Every lookout and guard station had a phone connected to a simple hand-operated switching station, usually the district dispatcher, and weather-proofed telephone boxes were located strategically along trails and roads. But if the phone line broke, there was no way to report fires or carry on business until the line was repaired.

While the others began swamping limbs from the downed trees and cutting them into logs to roll off the road, I selected a 10-inch jack pine on which to rehang the phone line. At the base of the tree I strapped on the climbing spurs and took along an insulator, pliers and a hand axe. I sensed the others were watching as I drove in one spur and then the other, only to have both slice free as I put weight on them.

"Lean your knees away from the tree," shouted Irwin, who had built phone line the year before. I must not have heard him, for with a rush I clambered several feet back up the tree before both spurs slipped out again, and in a panic I grabbed the tree in a bear hug

Pack mules loaded with #9 iron wire to run phone line to a fire lookout. USFS photo.

and lost considerable skin sliding back to the bottom. It probably was a good time for me to lose some face before my peers anyway.

Before I tried again, Irwin showed us how to use a lightweight block-and-tackle called a "come-along" to bring the broken phone lines together and splice them using less than two feet of wire. Although the tree had broken the wire that time, if a phone line isn't fastened solidly to a tree, it should hang in the insulators with enough slack that it can be pulled to the ground by a falling tree without breaking. Unless it falls into a pool of water it usually continues to work while lying on the ground.

Irwin then showed us both how to use the climbers by leaning back against the safety rope and driving the spikes into the tree at an angle. Then we assembled the split insulator around the phone line with a short piece of number nine hanger wire, and I succeeded in climbing the tree while holding the line in front of me on the safety rope and stapled the hanger wire to the tree. I learned later that it was fortunate that the dispatcher didn't decide to ring the High Rock Lookout right then, for with my spikes in the tree I was perfectly grounded, and the high voltage of the phone ringer could have given me quite a jolt.

MY KINGDOM FOR A CHAIN SAW

If we had had a chain saw we could have cleared the two fallen trees from the road in short order, but it took much longer using a six-foot, two-man bucking saw to cut them into logs and roll them off the road with cant hooks. Although loggers were beginning to use chain saws in the woods, the first one I ever saw in the Mount Hood forest was one that the regional division of engineering turned over to George Lasher and me at Zigzag a few years later with instructions to test it out and write an operating handbook on its use for snag falling in forest fires. My vague memories of that project are mostly of the difficulty we

had getting the heavy machine to start. Once started, it required two men to operate and a third man to watch out for "widow-makers." That was because snags often have broken tops or limbs that would shatter and fall from the vibration of the saw and couldn't be heard or seen by the sawyers.

Twenty years later when I was in banking, I was involved in helping logger Joe Cox from Klamath Falls finance his revolutionary chipper saw chain, which under entrepreneur John Gray became Omark Industries and dominated the market worldwide.

RIDING THE RAILS TO GUARD TRAINING CAMP

Before World War II the Clackamas River watershed from Estacada to the crest of the Cascades was a vast roadless wilderness, with the only access a narrow gauge railroad built years before to serve Portland General Electric Company's Three Links hydroelectric power plant. The Forest Service could use the railroad and had freight and passenger cars equipped with railcar wheels for use by the district headquarters near Three Links, but there was no auto or truck access. With its major tributaries Fish Creek and the Collawash River, the Clackamas was a significant source of water power and a storehouse of prime old growth timber that remained inaccessible for logging for several more years.

That was the setting for the 1936 Guard Training Camp where 120 summer lookouts and forest guards gathered in late June to hone their skills in fire control and forest management.

The camp was located at the North Fork Guard Station at the point where the auto road from Estacada met the railroad.

Most attendees were students at Oregon Agricultural College or another forestry school, and many had worked for the Forest Service before. I had not had any training since

Above: Passenger train at Big Eddy, Clackamas River, July 1923. Before World War II the only access to the Clackamas River watershed was via this narrow gauge railroad. USFS photo. Below: Guard training camp at North Fork Guard Station, Clackamas River, 1936.

high school, so I looked forward to the course. I could handle saws, axes and other tools better than most, but I knew little about the Osborne Firefinder and plotting courses by map, compass and survey markers. There also were sessions on livestock grazing and the laws and practices of fish and wildlife management.

Those not assigned to lookouts or guard stations were on trail crews or fire crews, but they all would be available for fire protection and for contacts with recreationists and other forest users.

When our contingent arrived by truck from Clackamas Lake on Sunday, I had my first opportunity to meet the legendary Harold Engles, new district ranger at Zigzag, who had decided to walk the 40-some miles by trail across the mountains from his ranger station and reached the training camp ahead of those who had ridden around by truck. The next winter he and four other rangers and I made the second 80-mile ski trip down the Oregon Skyline Trail from Mount Hood to Mount Jefferson and Detroit Ranger Station.

Guard Training Camp was nothing like Army boot camp, but the training was intense from dawn to dusk and included techniques for fighting ground fires, crown fires and fires set by lightning in dead snags. We learned that most forest fires are suppressed by digging fire lines around them and knocking down flames with dirt rather than dousing them with water. The training included practice on live fires set near the camp, with a tanker truck and fire pumps standing by just in case.

A CAMPFIRE PERMIT CRISIS

From Guard Training Camp I headed directly to Breitenbush Lake Guard Station and quickly learned that handling people could be a more complex problem than handling forest fires.

The campground was not supposed to be open for a few more days. Several families

anxious to be first to fish the lake had dug away the snow on the road between Horseshoe Lake and Breitenbush Lake and virtually lifted their cars over the last snowdrifts; they were happily camped in prime locations around the lake, fires glowing, when I arrived. Campers were required to have permits before lighting fires, and I had learned at guard camp how to politely ask them to show me their campfire permits, but of course they had none, because no fire guard had been there to issue them one.

I've made better decisions, but as I stood there surrounded by bright eyed-kids and their unsure parents, all of whom I felt sure were admiring my brand new uniform with its shiny new badge and Stetson hat, I simply sat down and wrote out a fire permit for each family. In a few days Hal Harrison, a Washington State University forestry student, arrived in his 1920 Hupmobile touring car to take up his assignment at Breitenbush Lake where he had spent the previous summer, and I moved to my assignment at Olallie Lake. I might have asked him how I should have handled the campfire permit problem – but I didn't.

THE INDIANS CALLED IT "KLALELLI" LAKE

Olallie, or *Klalelli* in the Chinook jargon, means huckleberry, and until 1930 Olallie Lake was the southern terminus of the Oregon Skyline Road. It nestles against 7,020-foot-high Olallie Butte, and its blue waters mirror 10,497-foot-high Mount Jefferson. On its western shore stands the sturdy log and stone Forest Service guard station that truly saddles the crest of the Cascade Range, for Olallie's waters drain eastward into the Deschutes River, while adjoining Head Lake is a tributary of the Willamette River on the west. That idyllic setting was my home for two adventurous summers and was the mantra that I sometimes called to mind during moments of stress in World War II.

*At Olallie
Lake on my
21st birthday,
Aug. 19,
1936. Mount
Jefferson
is in the
background.*

Clear Lake Butte Lookout, 2005. When I was a forest guard in 1936 the lookout was 60 feet higher. Jeff Thomas photo.

THE "FIREPROOF" SOUTH END

The south end of the Lakes District was at higher elevations than the surrounding country – much of it was above 5,000 feet. Snow could lay there until late summer, so sometimes when fire danger was high, one of us was sent north to increase protection there. Frequently when a lookout spotted a fire near his location, the dispatcher would send him to fight the fire immediately and send one of us from the south end to temporarily man the lookout.

That happened to me one August day in 1936 when the lookout on the 100-foot-high tower atop Clear Lake Butte was sent to quell a lightning fire, and I was told to take over his station until he returned. For whatever reason I had the hood off my Model T when the call came, and I hopped into the car without replacing the hood. As I reached the top of Clear Lake Butte it started to rain, so before starting up the tower's 150 steps, I pulled off my heavy canvas rain jacket and threw it over the Ford's engine to keep it dry.

When I was about halfway up, I turned to look back and saw the jacket blazing merrily atop the car, which I had parked beside one of the tower's wooden legs. In my hurry I must have let it touch the car's hot manifold. Taking the steps back down three-at-a-time, I pulled away the burning coat and doused it in a rain puddle, then made sure that the tower was undamaged before renewing the 100-foot climb to the top.

The busy night spent recording lightning strikes allowed little time to think of the small fire-scorched auto awaiting me below, but next morning I hurried down to check the damage. The four coils that fire the spark plugs on a Model T were soaking wet as were the plugs themselves, but worst of all, the insulation around the wires connecting the coils to the plugs was burned clean, leaving the four copper wires bare. Attempts to start the car were futile, so I bundled the coils, plugs and wires into the wet rain jacket, carried them up to the lookout cabin, started a fire in the stove and put the engine parts into the tiny oven to dry.

When the lookout returned I made knife cuts in strips of cardboard to separate the bare wires and reassembled the parts. The car's starter wouldn't work, but after only a few spins with the hand-crank, the brave little engine burst into life.

I made it back to Olallie Lake and replaced the hood, but then as I stepped into the guard station, I was assailed by a strong odor like baking bread. My sourdough starter had escaped its pot, flowed over the top of the cook stove and looked like it was headed for the back door – so I had a cleanup job to do. Father had told me about the sourdough biscuits and hot cakes he made when he was a gold prospector in Montana, so I had gotten a starter from a camp cook and kept it working on my stove.

Sourdough contains live yeast and should be used regularly or else stored in a cool place with lots of room for the dough to rise. Before getting the fire call I had added flour, water and potato peelings to my start so that it would be ready for the next meal. Then in my hurry I had left it on the warm stove where it had gone right to work.

LONELY ON THE FIRE LINE

I smelled the smoke before there was any sign of a fire. It was a still, clear morning, and there would be a downdraft in the canyon, so I turned uphill, grabbing small trees to help me hunch the fire pack. Then I saw it – flames licking at the base of a blackened stump and along the length of a lightning-struck snag which lay where it had fallen. A widening circle of fire was creeping up the duff-covered hillside.

It had been a raucous night of dry lightning flashes punctuated by earsplitting thunder, then in the storm's calm aftermath a narrow column of white smoke rose above the deep Clackamas

River gorge. The lookout on 5,700-foot-high West Pinhead Butte 50 miles south of Mount Hood was the first to report the smoke to dispatcher Paul Dennis at Clackamas Lake Ranger Station, followed soon by the Peavine Mountain Lookout a few miles north, but neither could see to the base of the fire. Then as Dennis plotted those azimuth readings on his fireman's map, the lookout on RHO Mountain several miles to the west spotted the smoke and phoned in his sighting.

Triangulating the three azimuth readings indicated that the fire was on the steep canyon wall at about 3,000 feet elevation with no road closer than Warm Springs Meadow, 15 miles north of Olallie Lake.

SECONDS COUNT, LET'S GO!

Two long and two short rings: The jangling of the phone on the guard station wall had jarred me awake at dawn, and as I mumbled "Olallie Lake" into the mouthpiece, I sensed from Paul Dennis' response that he hadn't been to bed at all. He had dispatched members of the trail crew to other fires that lookouts had seen flare up after lightning strikes during the night. Now that the storm had passed, he probably was hoping for a respite, but fear of a major forest fire in the heavily timbered Clackamas River drainage was a constant source of worry.

Forest guards were nicknamed smoke chasers, and I was about to earn the title. As Dennis read out the coordinates on the fire's probable location, I cudgeled my brain to recall what I had learned in Guard Training Camp. Spreading a fireman's map on the floor, I drew a line from the fire to the closest point on the Skyline Road and used a protractor to determine a course between the two.

To follow a compass course over such terrain was a real challenge. No landmarks were evident, no creeks, no meadows, no cliffs – just a very steep tree-covered canyon with the fire perhaps a mile below the road and a quarter-mile above the river.

After telling Dennis where I expected to leave the road, I pulled on my clothes, ate some cold breakfast and loaded the fireman's pack into the Model T Ford. I recalled that the pack contained a one-day food ration in a cloth sack emblazoned with the words: "SECONDS COUNT, LET'S GO."

I had been just plain lucky to have come within a hundred yards of the fire when I first smelled smoke, because most of the smoke was going straight up. I used the pulaski to scrape a quick fire line ahead of the creeping ground fire, throwing the dirt into the burned-over ashes, and then used the shovel to dig down to mineral earth and throw damp dirt onto the flaming log and stump. (A pulaski is a double-bitted fire tool with one bit a sharp axe and the other a sharp grub hoe.)

It must have taken more than an hour to drive from Olallie Lake to where I left the car and then to crash down through the underbrush to the fire. I knew there would have been an increase in the volume of smoke since the fire was first reported, but as I continued to knock down the flames with dirt and to tear apart the log and stump with the pulaski, I hoped the lookouts could tell that the fire was being worked on. The nearest telephone was Red Box in Warm Springs Meadow, so there was no way to make a report until I had the fire out and returned to there or to Olallie Lake.

A smoke chaser was expected to stay at a fire until it was dead out. If it appeared to the lookouts that it was getting out of control, I would be sent reinforcements. The possibility of an accident never was mentioned. After all there was a first aid kit in the fire pack!

I learned two important lessons that day. First, fighting fire alone is mighty exhausting work, so take along plenty of water, extra food and a few candy bars; second, watch your back trail. By noon I had emptied my canteen, drunk the juice from the can of tomatoes in the fire pack, and eaten the entire tin of baked beans.

Then when thirst forced me to leave the still-live fire and rush down to the river to drink and refill the canteen, I almost panicked when I turned back up the hill and realized that seen from below, the forest looked unfamiliar with no landmark to guide me.

I did find my way back to the fire that day, and by dark I was sure that the fire wouldn't flare during the night. I rolled up in the canvas fire pack cover for a fitful sleep. Although the food was gone, I stayed on the next day, feeling around the fire for sparks with my bare hands. By mid-afternoon I headed back to the road, confident that I could report that the fire was out, even though I knew that fire in deep duff can sometimes punk along for many days.

When I reached Olallie Lake and reported my first lonely day and night on the fire line to Ranger Lynch, his only comment was that since it was Saturday, I might as well take the rest of the day off. I had gotten to know Lynch pretty well a few months earlier when he, Foster Steele, Ralph Day, Bud Waggener and I spent a week together skiing the Oregon Skyline Trail, so I recognized his laconic response as his own brand of Irish humor.

THE METAMORPHSIS OF RED BOX

Red Box at Warm Springs Meadow south of Clackamas Lake was the last original phone box in use when I began working for the Forest Service. They built a new guard station there the previous fall to provide a winter stopover for Skyline Trail skiers, so Red Box was no longer needed as a trailside reporting station.

Ranger Lynch felt that we had been mighty fortunate that the fire I had managed to put out deep in the Clackamas canyon hadn't gotten out of control. None of the lookouts who reported it could see below the canyon rim, so they hadn't been able to spot the smoke until it was well above the treetops. As a result, it was decided to give Red Box a new life as a lookout by moving it to the top of nearby 5,617-foot-

high Sisi Butte. The Skyline Road ran within a half-mile of the summit, but we would have to go the remaining distance on foot.

The fire danger remained high, and before the move was completed, dispatcher Dennis decided that a temporary lookout was needed right away and told Hal Harrison and me to take the telephone box to the top of Sisi and begin reporting lightning strikes from there.

We drove to Warm Springs in Harrison's open-top touring car and realized that the only way to get the telephone equipment installed on the mountain would be to move the entire structure. It weighed close to 400 pounds even without the needed half-mile of number nine iron wire.

Harrison was a sturdy Washington State College football tackle, and neither he nor I was about to tell Dennis that we weren't up to the task. We piled the whole shebang onto the rear seats of the open car, and while I sat in the back, holding the load, Hal steered us along the narrow road to where a pack trail turned up the mountain. There we cut two saplings, and spiked them to the sides of Red Box and headed up the trail like two bearers carrying the sedan chair of an Oriental potentate.

Later that year other workers added a tent and firefinder. The arrangement served until a standard lookout cabin was built in 1937, and Red Box was reborn as Sisi Butte Lookout, which stood for another 20 years.

UNTOLD TALE OF THE PACIFIC CREST TRAIL

Here is the previously untold story of how Hal Harrison and I secretly rebuilt a critical section of the Pacific Crest Trail by hand. We were finishing our 1936 summer jobs as forest guards at Breitenbush and Olallie lakes and were fed up with settling squabbles between horsemen, hikers and motorists over use of the scenic road between the two lakes.

The Pacific Crest Trail had been built early

South end of the Clackamas Lake District from Olallie Butte. Olallie Lake in the foreground.

in the century as a pristine route to ride or hike from the Columbia River to the California border. Over the years automobiles had begun using the trail faster than it could be rerouted, and conflict between the two uses sometimes reached the boiling point. (Note: The Oregon portion of the Pacific Crest Trail was known as the Oregon Skyline Trail before the present three-state trail was conceived.)

After sorting out many conflicts between the two groups, we scouted out the high mountains to the west and decided that there was a feasible route through open subalpine country that would require only a few miles of new trail. We proposed to District Ranger Everett Lynch that if weather and fire conditions permitted, Harrison and I would undertake to do the job ourselves that fall. Lynch responded that the plan was highly irregular. He pointed out that no survey had been made, the Pacific Crest Trail should be built to the highest standards of grade, tread and drainage, and most importantly, there was no money left in the budget for trail construction, so there was no way that he could authorize the plan.

In those years after the First World War, Forest Service discipline had a sharp military tilt. Fortunately Assistant Supervisor Foster Steele, who would have to allow if not actually approve our plan, was a free spirited woodsman who had been known to find ways to do the impossible. Lynch passed on our proposal to Steele, and he decided that such a trail would be valuable in case of a lightning strike in the remote area. Since there was still money in the budget for fire suppression, Harrison and I could work on the trail project until weather shut it down.

It was a delightful fall, and we undertook with vigor to meet our self-imposed challenge. Each morning we shouldered saws, axes and grub hoes and with Lucky, my exuberant half-grown German shepard pup, drove Harrison's Hupmobile or my Model T, whichever one was running best that day, to the trailhead on Olallie Lake. Then we hiked several miles to our work site, built trail until late afternoon, and often returned cross-country down the mountainside to where we had left the car. One day at quitting time we found ourselves at the top of the high cliffs bordering Horseshoe Lake, so we passed Lucky from hand to hand as we scaled down to the lake.

Foster Steele must have been quietly keeping track of our progress, for near the end of the job he met us one day with two hand-carved Pacific Crest Trail signs, which we proudly posted. Thereafter, instead of having to travel five miles on the dusty gravel road from Olallie to Breitenbush Lakes, hikers and horsemen could follow the scenic new trail.

The route passed Top Lake, Eloise Lake, Cigar Lake and Timber Lake, then wound for several miles among sub-alpine meadows below Twin Peaks and Double Peaks. Along the way a stop could be made for a dip in sun-warmed Indian Lakes or Red Lake, sharing the tranquil scene with a thriving herd of elk that summered there. Beyond the Indian Lakes basin the trail climbed the shoulder of Ruddy Hill, then dropped down to intersect the road from Breitenbush Hot Springs at the outlet of Breitenbush Lake. In ensuing years the Pacific Crest Trail has been rebuilt in many places but at this writing it still follows that lake-strewn route, which we built in 1936.

BREITENBUSH LAKE

Breitenbush Lake is nestled at the foot of Campbell Butte, its waters lapping a wildflower meadow fed by creeks gurgling down from the Papoose Lakes. Sadly the Breitenbush Lake campground has fallen into ruin. The Forest Service Guard Station is gone and dozens of rustic tables, benches and safe campfire sites built by CCC and WPA crews have been broken or used for firewood.

This eyesore exists amidst such natural beauty because in 1972, a century-old battle over the location of the Mount Hood National Forest and the Warm Springs Indian Reservation boundary was settled in favor of the Confederated Tribes of Warm Springs. Sixty-two thousand acres of land, including Breitenbush Lake, were transferred from the national forest to the reservation.

What a warm gesture of friendship it would be for the Warm Springs tribes to restore the facilities at this cultural crossroads and invite outdoor lovers again to use and enjoy them as guests of the tribes.

A SHEEPHEREDER, HIS DOGS AND A BURRO

Recreationists often overlook the many valuable uses of national forests other than the most controversial ones: protecting the environment and harvesting timber. Grazing sheep and cattle is significant among those uses and has been a major source of income to the Mount Hood National Forest through the years. It is a colorful bit of Americana.

In past years there had been many more sheep ranches in the high desert country east of the Cascades, most of them operated by first-or-second-generation Irish and Basque immigrants who grew forage to feed in winter and in the spring grazed their bands on leased allotments of public land.

In the early part of the century many such bands were driven up the eastern slopes of the Cascades in the spring, moving steadily higher as the growing season advanced, and by midsummer they would cross the summit and continue grazing down the west side to the edge of the Willamette Valley. Then as fall approached they recrossed the summit, feeding on the new growth, and were back on home ranches before winter.

Wide swaths called stock driveways were cut across the mountains and seeded to provide forage for the moving bands. The driveways connected the best grazing land en route, and among those favorite forages was Warm Springs Meadow. A sheepherder and his dogs handled each band, and one job of a district ranger was to see that no part of the allotment was overgrazed and that proper fire and sanitation practices were observed.

The herder usually carried his supplies in a two-wheeled canvas-covered cart drawn by a burro. It was one of those wanigans that Ranger O.J. Johnson knew had been abandoned at Warm Springs Meadow and that served as a bivouac for him and Foster Steele on their blizzard-blighted ski trip in 1935.

The herder, his dogs and his burro often were the only visitors a lookout had during a summer of fire watching. During my first year as guard at Olallie Lake, I spent a week relieving the lookout on High Rock, which overlooks several miles of a sheep driveway. One time a herder gave me a mutton roast from an animal that hadn't been able to keep up with the band, and I spent hours on the telephone with other lookouts seeking a recipe that would render it edible. I found that with enough A1 Sauce, I could eat almost anything when I hadn't had fresh meat for a month.

As might be expected, the various uses of these forest resources often are not mutually compatible. Hiking in summer on trails covered with fresh sheep manure is unpleasant enough, but it is quite unacceptable to have to pitch your tent in a meadow blanketed with the stuff, so grazing in scenic areas has been sharply curtailed. Nevertheless many delightful recreational sites owe part of their beauty to the bands of sheep that grazed in them over the past half-century.

LITTLE CRATER LAKE

One time when I was checking on a band near the lookout, I located the herder and his wanigan in the middle of what now is the prime recreational destination of Little Crater Meadow. The dogs were running across the backs of the sheep, making sure that none would fall into unfenced Little Crater Lake, and the herder assured me that the band would be moved toward Timothy Meadow before the pasture was overgrazed. The dam that created Timothy Lake hadn't yet been built, but that meadow now is entirely submerged.

Today Little Crater Meadow is hip-deep in a lush stand of grasses and wildflowers thriving on the fertile earth enriched by 50 years of sheep grazing. A wheelchair-accessible trail has been built from Abbott Road to the now safely fenced Little Crater Lake. A few months ago while recovering from a broken hip I shuffled across that trail with my walker and enjoyed gazing at my reflection in the 70-foot-deep volcanic pool just as I first had done 70 years before.

22 SKIING THE SKYLINE TRAIL AGAIN – 1937

Tom Terry (left), Reinhardt Haack, Everett Lynch, Harold Engles and Roy Weeman at Abbot Road on the first day of the trip, March 4, 1937.

Foster Steele organized a third Skyline Trail ski trip in 1937 with Everett Lynch as leader and asked me to go again as writer and photographer. I was then publicity director for the Oregon Winter Sports Association and was glad to accept, as the two assignments fitted well together.

Long distance voice communication by radio was an emerging science, and the Forest Service decided to take along a new radio called an SPF (Semi-Portable Fone) to test its practicability in the mountains in winter. Ranger Roy Weeman, a communications specialist, was a member of the team along with Zigzag District Ranger Harold Engles and two stalwart younger skiers, Reinhardt Haack from the Mount Hood Forest staff and 16-year-old Cascade Ski Club downhill racer Tom Terry.

The radio with batteries and hundred-foot-long antenna weighed more than 40 pounds, and while some of us were discussing how to

Roy Weeman operating the new radio under field conditions.

During the winters of 1936 and 1937 all the lakes in the high Cascades froze solidly. Roy Weeman (left), Reinhardt Haack, Tom Terry and Everett Lynch crossing Olallie Lake. Olallie Butte in the background.

distribute its weight, Harold Engles tied the whole unit on top of his already heavy pack and carried it all the way.

The 80-mile trek began on March 4 at Blue Box Pass and finished at Detroit Ranger Station on March 11. After testing our mettle the year before, the storm gods relented with moderate temperatures, clear skies, many miles of pleasant skiing and not one real crisis. The expedition was so relaxed that at one point I found a cornice and practiced gelandsprungs.

The radio field tests produced mixed results. Although the SPF equipment was designed for use only within a 10-mile radius, Ranger Weeman was able to make contact at various times with Summit Ranger Station in Government Camp, KBDT at Herman Creek in the Columbia Gorge and KBAA at the Forest Service radio laboratory in Portland. Its reliability was deemed adequate for emergencies, but its weight and bulk would limit its practical use by skiers and hikers. I was glad to be able to use the radio to send brief daily dispatches to the *Oregon Journal*.

BIVOUACING PLAN THWARTED

Plans to spend a night in Jefferson Park without a shelter were thwarted by a fast-moving storm. Here is how I described that frustrating day in a story carried in a Sunday edition of the *Journal*:

A storm that moved in early in the afternoon blighted the earlier plan to bivouac in Jefferson Park that night so we holed in at the Breitenbush Lake Guard Station. At 6 a.m. the following day we started for the Park but as the storm had not abated we left cameras behind. Then after three miles of climbing the sun broke through the sweeping clouds for a moment, and the photographer returned for his equipment. Following a six mile round trip back to the cabin he rejoined the party with his camera just as the storm again obscured all visibility.

Park Ridge was gained at the height of the

storm *with a 35-mile wind driving stinging sleet across the 7,018-foot summit. Although Mount Jefferson was less than two miles distant across the valley the storm obscured any sight of it. When there was no sign of a break a half-hour later the party turned skis northward again for the fine runs that mark the winter route between Breitenbush Lake and the Park.*

Then the elements took pity on this group of skiers who had come so far for a mid-winter glimpse of Mount Jefferson and just as a good vantage point on the return trek was reached the wind began sweeping away clouds and the 10,495-foot summit reared into view. It was a fine opportunity for photographs.

Reinhardt Haack and Tom Terry on top of Park Ridge at the height of the storm. Winds of 35 mph and whiteout conditions prevented us from skiing down into Jefferson Park. After we turned around the storm abated, and we were able to see the mountain.

The north side of Mount Jefferson from a ridge above Shitike Creek, March 9, 1937.

RACING TO THE HOT SPRINGS

Wednesday dawned clear and cold, and we raced one another down the 13 miles of powdersnow-covered trail to see who could be first to dive into the Breitenbush Hot Springs pool. What a contrast that run was with the rough, icy roadway that had been Foster Steele's nemesis the year before. We stayed the night at the hot springs, and on Thursday skied the last 10 miles to Detroit Ranger Station, where we were met by a truck with Foster Steele in the passenger seat, anxious to hear our report on the expedition.

FOSTER STEELE'S DREAM FULFILLED

The newspaper story on the expedition concluded with this announcement:

If you like to ski and would enjoy a little real adventure thrown in plan to take the Skyline Trail on skis next winter. Food and blankets may be cached at the shelters during the summer by arranging with the Mount Hood forest office in Portland.

Tough mountaineer Foster Steele's goal of establishing alpine-like hut-to-hut skiing in the Oregon Cascades had been implemented!

23 INDIANS AND BEADED BAGS

At first I didn't see the buckboard with two Indians when it pulled up opposite my Toll Gate Guard Station one August midday in 1938, so I didn't know how long they had waited. They were a colorful pair – his hair hung below his shoulders in two long braids, and he wore a soft buckskin shirt and held the horses' reins in brightly beaded gloved hands.

In contrast she was wrapped in a bright Chief Joseph blanket from Pendleton Woolen Mills.

It was an incongruous tableau, with the horse-drawn wagon stopped in the shade of two bigleaf maple trees beside a replica of the toll gate that had been built on the historic Barlow Road in 1846. The tranquility was fractured from time to time by automobiles

Warm Springs Indian encampment on Zigzag Mountain. Mount Hood in the background.

that shared the narrow road. Samuel Barlow had located the toll gate where the Zigzag River ran close to Zigzag Mountain, making it difficult for wagons or cattle to avoid paying the toll, and the Mount Hood Loop Highway followed the same route in the 1930s.

I learned that these were the vanguard of a contingent of Indians from the Confederated Tribes of the Warm Springs who came from Eastern Oregon each year to pick huckleberries on Zigzag Mountain. They had come to the guard station to get campfire permits for the encampment. It had been a long drive from their reservation at Warm Springs, and they had yet to climb the four-mile road up the mountain to reach the berry fields.

My eyes were drawn to the intricate beadwork on his gloves and on a buckskin bag

Warm Springs Indian building a traditional hot rock sweat lodge on Zigzag Mountain.

Black bears were fair game for Indians in the huckleberry fields.

that she was carrying. I set out to bargain, but neither of them seemed to understand, and without comment they turned the wagon up the West Zigzag Road.

The next day when I drove up to check out their camp, the scene could as well have been from a century earlier. Pitched on a low rise near a stand of timber was a large tepee with smoke rising from its top, and seated before it was a brightly robed Indian holding a papoose. More tepees clustered below, and beyond them huckleberry bushes stretched toward the horizon, dominated by Mount Hood's snowy bulk six miles to the east. Forest fires earlier in the century had cleared Zigzag and East Zigzag Mountains of timber, leaving acres of dead snags and providing ideal habitat for huckleberries and bears.

There were few Indians in sight, and I supposed that most of the women and older

Beaded gloves and bag made from buckskin by a Warm Springs Indian.

children were picking berries. I learned later that some of the men had other pursuits in mind including bear hunting.

On my next trip to the camp one of them proudly showed me the skin of a fair-sized black bear that he had shot, and another man was building a sweat lodge beside the stream. Diffident at first, the Warm Springs' reserve soon faded and they invited me into their tepees and even posed for pictures.

Although many of the berries were dried in the sun, some families had come by car and would drive home to Warm Springs to do the canning. The Forest Service had built a fire lookout cabin on East Zigzag a few years before, but it wasn't in use that year, so there were few cars on the road.

I kept watching for beaded gloves or other handicrafts for sale or trade, but I was disappointed that none were offered.

A SURPRISE VISIT FROM THE WARM SPRINGS

A year passed, and the next summer I was back at Toll Gate when I glanced out the door and saw the same horse-drawn buckboard stopped by the road with the same pair of colorfully dressed Indians waiting patiently on the seat. To my delight when I went out to their wagon, I was handed not one but three pairs of fringed buckskin gloves, each ornamented with bright patterns of delicately sewn beads, and a beaded bag much like the one the woman had carried the year before.

I had asked for just one pair of gloves, but perhaps the enlarged order was intended to make up for the year's delay in delivery.

24 MOUNT HOOD'S SECRET BACKSIDE

Until foresters and CCC crews carved Timberline Trail out of the steep slopes of Mount Hood's north side in 1938, few people were aware of the vast wilderness that stretches from the waterfall-laced north shore of the Columbia Gorge to the mountain's summit.

Lying like a huge lasso draped around the two-mile-high peak, Timberline Trail skirts icy glaciers, penetrates stands of old growth timber and falls into cool canyons in what the Forest Service considers some of the most remote and spectacular mountain country to be found in the West, and yet its points of access by auto are barely an hour's drive from Portland.

HOOD FIRST ENCIRCLED IN 1890s

Cloud Cap Inn climbing guides were the first to circle Hood on foot. Government Camp guides Oliver Yocum and Lige Coalman duplicated the feat in the early 1900s; however these were high-elevation traverses far above tree line and required some skill and special mountaineering equipment.

Wy'east climbers James Mount and Ralph Calkin made the first recorded circuit of the mountain on skis in 1934, starting and finishing at Cloud Cap Inn. Sometime later Wy'easter Russ McJury and the legendary Gary Leech duplicated the feat but started and finished on the south side. Today the south side start and finish has become the normal route. Either way the ski encirclement, like the mountaineering encirclement, is a major expedition requiring skill and technical equipment, and relatively few people attempt it.

AROUND-THE-MOUNTAIN TRAIL

The Forest Service planned to build a trail to circle the mountain at timberline in 1938, and a route was surveyed the previous summer. The plan was for the trail to cross high on Yocum and Cathedral Ridges, nudge the snouts of some of the mountain's nine active glaciers, and ford the streams below others. It was a spectacular route, but the survey crew had lacked experience with the multifarious weather patterns that prevail in the high Cascades, and in 1938 the construction crew found that even by midsummer some of the marker stakes that had been set in 1937 had not yet emerged from the mountain's icy grasp.

District Ranger Engles faced a tough decision. An inaugural horseback trip over the trail by Forest Supervisor A.O. Waha had been laid on for that fall, so should Engles count on another month of good weather that might allow the crew to finish the trail as planned, or should he reroute the last segment over a less weather-sensitive course? I am not sure how he squared it with the regional office, but he decided to abandon the authorized survey. It turned out to be a wise decision, for it was several years before the high mountain route could have been used.

RAMONA FALLS - A WALL OF WATER

Instead of crossing the Sandy River basin near Reid Glacier at 7,000 feet, the revised route dropped to about 3,000 feet and crossed the river near Upper Sandy Guard Station,

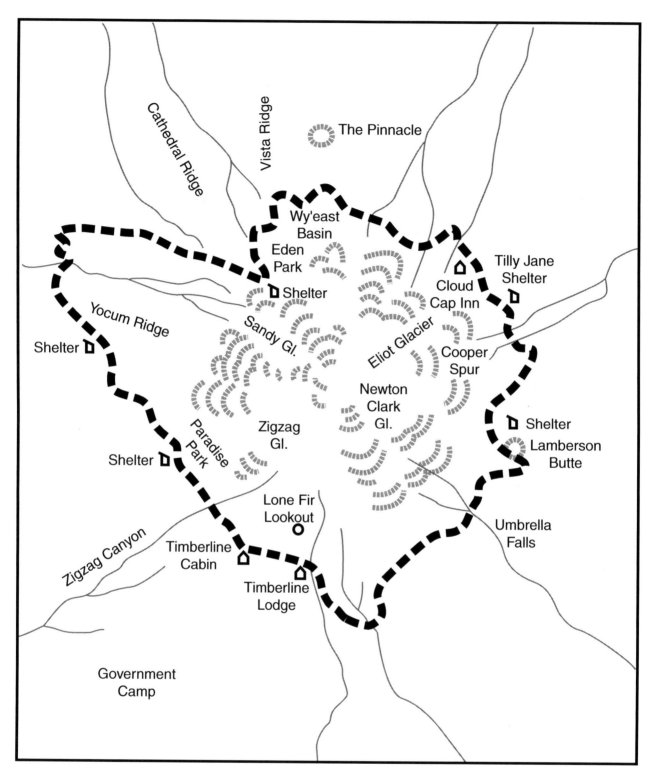

Map of Mount Hood showing Timberline Trail after its construction in 1938.

Forest Supervisor A.O. Waha, Parkdale District Ranger Stanley Walters and Packer Irwin "Win" Hull on Timberline Trail just above Zigzag Canyon in September 1938. Mississippi Head, Zigzag Glacier and Mount Hood in the background.

then climbed to the spectacular wall of water that is Ramona Falls.

In September when the trail was just barely completed, Engles, Ranger Maxwell Becker and I became the first to hike it on foot, and Supervisor Waha, Parkdale District Ranger Stanley Walters and Packer Irwin "Win" Hull were the first to ride it on horseback. It was a near thing though, and those of us in the lead sometimes spotted trail crew members skittering out of sight around a bend ahead of us as they added final touches to their work.

As the riders were saddling up at the stables at the beginning of the trip, Engles had signaled Becker and me to join him ahead of the others to avoid walking in the horses' dust. We soon realized that his real purpose was to show that the almost 40-mile trek could be made faster on foot than on horseback.

WHERE EAST MEETS WEST

At the junction of the new trail and the summit climbing route there were carved signs indicating Paradise Park to the west and Cloud Cap Inn to the east and pointing both east and west to Eden Park, for that pristine meadow is just halfway around the peak.

We had decided to circle clockwise so followed the tree line past Timberline Cabin, the primitive forerunner to Timberline Lodge, then plunged into and out of Sand Canyon, Little Zigzag Canyon and Zigzag Canyon before leveling off again at 6,000 feet in the glacier-fed gardens of Paradise Park. Nestled in the park among wildflowers and brilliant mountain ash berries was the first of six open-faced stone shelters newly built along the trail by artisans of the WPA and CCC.

At the Upper Sandy Guard Station, September 1938. Max Becker photo.

Switchbacking down Sandy River Canyon for 3,000 vertical feet to the Upper Sandy Guard Station, the trail forded the river and climbed to the spectacular wall of water that is Ramona Falls. Arriving well ahead of the horsemen, we suddenly realized that we had gained no time, because we had to wait for the packhorse that carried all of our lunches.

An open faced log-and-shake shelter with a reflecting fireplace at Ramona Falls made it an enjoyable overnight camping spot for those planning a four-day circuit of the peak.

From Ramona Shelter the trail climbed almost constantly up Bald Mountain, gaining more than 2,400 feet of elevation in seven-and-a-half miles, ever shifting its setting of trees and streams but always keeping the same backdrop of high rearing ice and snow. Next came Yocum Ridge, then Cathedral Ridge, the most difficult upper part of which I had climbed that July when the Sunshine Route was blocked by crevasses.

Had we been carrying heavy packs we probably wouldn't have beaten the pack string into camp that warm afternoon, for I recall hearing the horses gaining ground behind us from time to time, but then packer Win Hull would stop to give them a needed rest while we steadfastly plodded along in Engles' wake.

Dropping off Cathedral Ridge, the trail entered alpine meadows, snow flecked until late August. That made the difference, and we were stretched out on the velvety grass of Cairn Basin a few hundred feet from the snout of Ladd Glacier when the others arrived.

Stone shelters also had been built that summer in Cairn Basin, Eden Park and Elk Cove, providing delightful camping spots along the 10 miles of subalpine meadows that stretch from Cathedral Ridge to Cooper Spur.

EDEN PARK – THE HALFWAY MARK

Because we planned to make the trip in two days, we spent the night at Eden Park – the halfway point – then made an early start the next day so that we could reach Gnarl Ridge Shelter, 6,500 feet high on the rim of Newton Clark Glacier, by lunchtime.

At midmorning we came to historic

The disparate delegation that skied to Cloud Cap Inn to survey the area as a possible site for a destination resort. Jim Lill (left), John Litchfield, Andy Anderson, Arne Udelius, George Sheppard and Bob Webb. George Henderson photo courtesy of Arne Udelius.

Cloud Cap Inn, which is the only place except Timberline Lodge where Timberline Trail touches a road. At that time the inn was operated by Mr. and Mrs. Boyd French Sr. and their daughter Margie. The French family also owned the skiing facilities at the Ski Bowl.

Cloud Cap Inn was built in 1889 and is now listed in the National Register of Historic Places. Its fascinating history from the days when guests were brought up the mountain by horse and carriage from the railroad depot in Hood River is recounted in Fred H. McNeil's *Wy'east the Mountain.*

SUMMIT TRAMWAY PROPOSED

During the economic boom days of the 1920s, there were plans to build a tramway from Cooper Spur to the summit of Mount Hood, but the Depression of the '30s was blamed for loss of needed financing.

COOPER SPUR SKI RESORT URGED

In the year following our first round-the-mountain trip, hopes were high in the Hood River Valley that Cloud Cap might soon be developed into a year-round destination resort, and winter sports enthusiasts petitioned the Union Pacific Railroad to consider building a Sun Valley-like resort on the mountain's east side. In response the railroad sent Sun Valley Ski School director John Litchfield to survey the skiing terrain, and Union Pacific's Western public relations chief Jim Hays invited a group of us headed by Jim Lill of Hood River to meet with Litchfield at Cloud Cap Inn. The story and photos appeared in *The Oregonian* on Dec. 13 and the *Oregon Journal* on Dec, 14, 1940.

It was a disparate delegation. Hays didn't ski nor did he realize that the six-mile road to the inn was snowbound. Of course Litchfield was a fine skier. Bob Webb was the ski columnist for

The Oregonian. Boyd French Sr. was president of Cascade Ski Club and the operator of Cloud Cap under Forest Service permit. Andy Anderson, Arne Udelius and George Sheppard were members of the Hood River Crag Rats climbing club, and I represented Timberline Lodge.

Jim Hays turned out to be the toughest of us all. He struggled almost to the timberline wearing a raincoat and slick-soled galoshes buckled over dress oxfords, then to our amazement skillful skier Litchfield had Hays step on the back of his own skis and ride with him back to the highway.

A FRUITLESS EFFORT

That effort bore no fruit, but after World War II the Hood River enthusiasts renewed their efforts, and largely through the pioneering work of Crag Rat Jack Baldwin they convinced the Forest Service to allow development of an entirely new ski area below Newton Clark Glacier known as Mount Hood Meadows.

GNARL RIDGE IS HIGH POINT

From Cloud Cap Inn our 1938 Timberline Trail inspection continued past Tilly Jane Campground, following the summit climbing trail to another new stone shelter with a fine view overlooking Eliot Glacier, Mount Hood's largest body of ice. Soon the trail reached the highest point on Timberline Trail, Gnarl Ridge, on the rim of Newton Clark Glacier near the head of deeply eroded Polallie Creek. From that vantage point most of the Oregon and Washington Cascades stretch in easy view – Mount Rainier, Mount Adams, Mount St. Helens, Mount Jefferson, Three Fingered Jack and Broken Top.

Next came nine delightfully scenic miles past glacier-fed Newton Creek and Clark Creek, delicate Pencil Falls, Heather Canyon, sprawling Umbrella Falls and the headwaters of Hood River and finally to a crossing of often turbulent White River.

SKI LIFTS MEET HIKING TRAILS

Beyond Umbrella Falls Timberline Trail now shares a mile or so of Hood River Meadows with the chairlifts and ski trails of Mount Hood Meadows resort.

I'm not sure what Engles, Becker and I proved, but we did beat the pack string back to Timberline Lodge. I must say that the riders looked mighty content in their saddles as their mounts carried them up those last two steep miles out of White River and across Salmon River Canyon to trail's end. (Note: The goal of some hikers today is to don running shoes and circle the mountain in a single day.)

Earlier in the year *The Oregonian* had agreed to buy a feature story and pictures of the new trail to use in a Sunday travel section, but editor Edward Miller decided to hold it over until the next summer. The half-page layout with photos finally ran on Aug. 13, 1939, so although I had completed my trip and my story in September 1938, I was not paid until a year later because newspapers paid for freelance stories only upon publication.

25 YOCUM RIDGE AND CATHEDRAL RIDGE

Lin Bowman (left), Jack Bennett, Horace Mecklem Jr. and I in front of Timberline Lodge after a successful climb of Cathedral Ridge, July 24, 1938.

CATHEDRAL RIDGE – JULY 1938

I climbed Cooper Spur in 1934, but since then I had skied and climbed almost exclusively on the south side of Mount Hood. So three skier friends and I decided to investigate the glaciers and climbing routes on the north side. I was working for the Forest Service in 1938, and the job included maintaining the lifelines on the south side and Cooper Spur, so the climb was a real busman's holiday for me. My compatriots were Horace "Hod" Mecklem, a Dartmouth College ski jumper, and Linden Bowman and Jack Bennett, both Cascade Ski Club racers.

Hod's sister Janet drove us to Cloud Cap Inn early in the morning July 24, and we began by climbing up Cooper Spur and dropping down to Eliot Glacier, intending to traverse it and reach the summit via the Sunshine Route. However, the season was late, the bergschrund near Horseshoe Rock was melted out, and we weren't able to cross the resulting moat and ice wall. We then traversed horizontally west across Upper Coe Glacier to Cathedral Ridge and followed its loose shale crest to the summit, passing the top of Yocum Ridge, which Jim Mount and I tried to climb the next year.

Three climbers followed us up the last part of the route and also signed the Mazamas register at the lookout. Their names were Wilfred Buhler, Ed Rankin and Morton A. Werner, all of the Yakima, Wash., Cascadians. I took a good picture of them, and if any reader knows how to reach them I would be glad to send them a print.

We descended the south side to Timberline Lodge where we met Janet Mecklem, who had driven from Cloud Cap Inn. It had been my sixth Mount Hood climb that year, and I would make several more with Boyd French Jr. before we finished our weekly trips maintaining the lifelines down the Chute and Cooper Spur.

UNCLIMBED YOCUM RIDGE – 1939

By 1939 all the logical routes on Mount Hood had been climbed except one – Yocum Ridge. (Note: Even today many climbers would question my use of the work logical.) Several skilled and motivated individuals had probed its ramparts, and one of them, Jim Mount, thought he had found the key to overcoming its defenses.

Looking down at the three Yakima Cascadians who climbed upper Cathedral Ridge on the same day we did during July 1938.

Yocum Ridge is the stark, serrated crest that buttresses the western end of the mountain's summit and is sheathed in loose, rotten rock. Its near-vertical face offers neither footholds nor handholds, nor is its rock solid enough to hold pitons or other climbing hardware. Mild mannered James A. Mount was a member of the elite Wy'east Climbers and had made several first ascents on Pacific Northwest peaks, including Leuthold Couloir on Mount Hood with Ralph Calkin in 1932. He also was president of the Oregon Winter Sports Association, my employer.

When he phoned in late winter 1939 and asked me to join him on an attempt to climb Yocum Ridge that weekend, it put me in a quandary. He knew that I climbed Hood several times a year, but he did not know that I was neither a rock climber nor an ice climber.

Shunting aside my protests, he explained that he believed Yocum Ridge could be climbed in winter under just the right conditions. He was certain that the long season of repeated storms that winter had coated the rotten rock with a hard layer of ice, which would not only hold the rock in place but would provide a bold climber with a more trustworthy surface to climb. The key was to find a cold day and finish the climb before the afternoon sun started melting the ice. The last couple of days had had exactly the type of weather Jim was looking for, and the forecast was for several more days of the same.

I should not have agreed to go on the climb, but with the perspective of 66 years I am glad I did. As far as I know, self-effacing Jim Mount never talked about the attempt, and even his son Barry, an excellent climber in his own right, was surprised when climbing historian Jeff Thomas asked him about it recently.

We left Timberline Lodge before dawn, reached 9,000-foot Illumination Saddle at daybreak, roped up and put on crampons. It was a heavy snow year and no crevasses were showing as we traversed down Reid Glacier and started toward Yocum Ridge. The climb was steep from the start, but I decided that it wasn't going to be too tough after all, as Jim confidently climbed up to what later would be named the First Gendarme, setting belays for me to follow.

After a short traverse to the west he began working his way straight up the kind of sheer slope I had feared. He set another belay, pulled the slack out of the rope and again called for me to follow. Careful not to look down and supporting myself on the rope, I climbed up to him. As he stepped aside, I was startled to realize that his belay consisted of a foot or two of rope coiled around a slight mound in the ice. The only anchor holding the coils in place was the weight of his body.

At that moment I understood the fine line that separates a true rock or ice climber from many other mountaineers. We had crossed that line and I had reached my limit. It was time to go down, but Jim was not quite ready to give up. To my amazement and admiration he untied and soloed on ahead over some incredibly steep ground. I remained at the belay and took photos. When he returned he reported that the climb did not look feasible, and we retreated.

It was not until 20 years later, on April 10, 1959, that Fred Beckey and Leo Scheiblehner made the first successful ascent of Yocum Ridge by skirting the First Gendarme on the right. Thirteen years later, on March 1, 1972, guides Del Young and Terry Hiatt completed the second ascent, this time climbing directly over the First Gendarme. It is a tribute to Jim Mount's vision that both these parties climbed in winter. I have always felt to a near certainty that had Russ McJury or Ralph Calkin been in my place that day, Jim would not have turned around, and they would have climbed Yocum Ridge. Jim, gentleman that he was, always insisted otherwise.

Jim Mount at the base of the First Gendarme, Yocum Ridge, 1939.

26 DOWNS WITHOUT UPS

Timberline on Mount Hood in March 1933 before there were ski lifts. Curtis Ijames photo.

The year may have more than one season,
Yet I can remember but one,
The time when the rivers are freezin',
And mountains with whiteness are spun.

Two boards upon cold powder snow, yo-ho!
What else does a man need to know?
Two boards upon cold powder snow, yo-ho!
What else does a man need to know?

"Two Boards," by David Bradley, Dartmouth '38

There was no way to ski downhill on Mount Hood before 1936 without first climbing up on your own two legs – unless you were a ski jumper. In about 1930 jumper Ole Haugen chained an air-cooled Franklin automobile engine to a stump near the top of the Cascade Ski Club jumping hill on Multorpor and geared it to a cable and sled, which could pull several jumpers at a time to the top of the inrun. It was Mount Hood's first ski lift, but Ole was far ahead of his time, and downhill skiers would have to wait another six years to see a similar development for downhill and slalom skiing.

Until 1936, when the Forest Service opened the road from Government Camp to timberline for construction of Timberline Lodge, skiers depended on either "climbers" made of sealskin or strips of pleated canvas fastened to the bottoms of the skis or climbing wax, to allow them to walk uphill without slipping backward. Beginners usually shouldered their skis and trudged up the open slopes above Government Camp or walked across Collins Meadow, to Multorpor Hill where they could climb steeper slopes and practice turning or jumping on the way down.

Ole Johanson, Hermod Bakke, Hjalmar Hvam and John Elvrum ride Ole Haugen's cable sled to the top of Cascade Ski Club's jumping hill on Multorpor Mountain during a Feb. 24, 1935, ski tournament. The sled was the first known ski lift of any kind in Oregon. Oregon Historical Society photo, CN #012050.

Government Camp and the south side of Mount Hood from the top of Tom Dick and Harry Mountain in 1922. Numerous fires around the turn of the century had destoyed much of the timber below tree line, creating open slopes ideal for skiing. E.C. Blackwood photo.

When snow conditions were right, the Ski Bowl was our favorite place to ski, but we spent many days skiing down the Blossom Trail between old Timberline Cabin and Government Camp, or down the Alpine Trail between Phlox Point near the Wy'east Cabin and Summit Ranger Station. For those treks we'd cram food, sweaters and extra wax into our rucksacks in the morning, climb three miles to the timberline where we'd have lunch, then wrap the climbers around our waists and race one another back to the highway.

If there was powder snow we'd sometimes return down Sand Canyon, whose smooth, steep walls allowed rhythmic turns even by those just learning to ski. Then we could rejoin Blossom or Alpine Trail and wind through open glades dotted with young trees in the old burn that bordered Government Camp on the north. Trail skiing could be done in almost any snow condition – even in rain – if the only alternate would be to give up skiing for the day and return home. Sometimes we made the six-mile round trip twice in the same day.

GREAT FIRES SCORCH THE LAND

The treeless slopes above 6,000 feet provided fine skiing in spring and summer, but reaching them in winter from Government Camp was more like a ski mountaineering expedition. Thus most open slope skiing before there were roads or lifts was on hillsides cleared in former years by forest fires.

Until the U.S. Forest Service was created in 1905, there was little done to control forest fires on federal lands in the Cascades other than to protect homes and private property. Only timber owners and others with logging contracts on government land had the incentive, manpower and skill to battle a really large fire.

The 1918 Cispus burn in the Columbia National Forest in Washington (now the Gifford Pinchot) had sent flaming embers across the Columbia River and was said to

have ignited the fire that burned a portion of the Bull Run watershed in Oregon.

Two other disastrous fires, the Sherar burn and the Abbott burn, occurred at about the same time. They devastated large areas south of Mount Hood from Laurel Hill over Tom Dick and Harry Mountain, singeing the edges of Government Camp, then racing down Camp Creek, up over Veda Butte and Devils Peak to Salmon River, and south to High Rock and beyond. Early photos of ski jumps on Multorpor show the hill lined with dead snags that later were felled to reduce fire hazard.

When I last drove up the tree-lined road from Trillium Lake to Devils Peak in 2005 it was difficult to remember that 70 years earlier there were only a few green trees in sight along that ridge top.

THE SKI BOWL WAS BORN OF FIRE

Early in the century a stately stand of old growth cedar trees had thrived on the moist, wind-protected north face of Tom Dick and Harry Mountain, until a wildfire torched the great grove, leaving a ghostly forest of barren trunks. Multorpor Hill was the nearest steep skiing area to Government Camp, and it wasn't long before skiers began crossing from there to Tom Dick and Harry to test their skills among the whitening snags. Maryanne Hill told me recently that even before the Ski Bowl was given its name, she and other Government Camp youngsters often made that trek to Tom Dick for a day of racing practice.

It paid off for Maryanne, for she became a princess in the 1939 Winter Sports Carnival royal court and was among Cascade Ski Club's best women racers and was a candidate for the 1940 U.S. Olympic ski team.

A CALL FOR HELP

Then in 1936 there came a call for help from 2,000 feet above Government Camp.

Thousands of split-cedar shakes were needed to side and roof an unfamiliar feature on the mountain – the new Timberline Lodge. When foresters found that the soaring snags contained wood as solid as it had been when the fire struck, an environmentally sound solution to the problem was at hand. A Civilian Conservation Corp spike camp was established to fell the ancient monarchs, cut them into shake bolts and truck them to a shake mill at Zigzag Ranger Station, leaving behind a sturdy warming hut and many acres of steep clear-cut slopes.

A VERTICAL 2,000 FEET OF POWDER

From the top of Tom Dick and Harry down the west ridge past Mirror Lake to the highway, more than 1,800 feet of unbroken snow beckoned aficionados of extreme skiing. Soon the great basin was named the Ski Bowl and became known as the finest terrain in the Pacific Northwest for slalom racing.

THE WORLD'S FIRST SLALOM RACE

For almost a century Europe's Alps had been laced with railways and cable cars that carried sightseers to their summits, but even though ski touring was popular with some visitors, most of the grand hotels and resorts were closed in winter.

Then in the 1920s an unlikely pair of sportsmen, Sir Arnold Lunn and Hannes Schneider, triggered a change in all that.

Sir Arnold was an aristocratic Englishman and ardent mountaineer who, despite a crippling climbing injury as a young man, became an active skier, a prolific writer and editor of the *British Ski Year Book*. He managed his father's hotels in Switzerland during World War I, and Switzerland became his second home.

Hannes Schneider was the son of an Austrian cheese maker who had taught skiing to Austrian and German soldiers during the First World War. He developed a system for turning raw recruits into competent skiers in a few weeks and, after the Armistice, used the same teaching methods in his Arlberg Ski School at St. Anton. The Arlberg Technique, which stressed both skill and safety, was widely accepted and earned Schneider the sobriquet, "father of modern skiing."

Informal downhill races were bound to follow improvements in skiing skill, but it remained for Lunn and Schneider to formalize the sport. High on a mountain in the Swiss Alps is a bronze statue of Lunn bearing the following inscription.

It was here in Murren that Arnold Lunn set the first Slalom course in 1922 and organized the first World Championship in Downhill and Slalom racing in 1931.

The Austrians won that competition, the first downhill event ever sanctioned by the International Ski Federation. Five years later, in 1936, Lunn spearheaded a successful campaign to have downhill and slalom racing made a part of the Winter Olympic Games.

SIR ARNOLD LUNN VISITS TIMBERLINE LODGE

The first slalom races on Mount Hood were held in 1934 just above Timberline Cabin, a mile west of the future site of Timberline Lodge, with Boyd French Sr. as course setter. In 1936 Mount Hood was host to the Northwest's first downhill and slalom championship. In the fall of 1937 Sir Arnold Lunn visited Timberline while it still was under construction.

I had become acquainted with the legendary skier through correspondence, and he had published some of my articles and photographs in the *British Ski Year Book,* which led to his interest in Timberline Lodge. I met him at the airport, and we drove to the lodge where we met with Boyd French Sr., Hjalmar Hvam and Fred VanDyke. During the visit Sir Arnold sanctioned two new Mount Hood

Sir Arnold Lunn (left), inventor of modern downhill and slalom racing, congratulates Cascade Ski Club downhill and slalom champion Hjalmar Hvam at Timberline Lodge after a race on Nov. 21, 1937.

The first engineered ski tow in the Mount Hood area, March 1938. It was designed and built by Boyd French Sr. and his son, Boyd French Jr., with the help of many volunteers in the Ski Bowl during the winter of 1937-1938. Photographer unknown. Photo courtesy of Maryellen Englesby.

races, the Arnold Lunn Downhill and the Far West Kandahar, the latter to be held alternately at Mount Hood and Yosemite, Calif.

SUN VALLEY INVENTS THE CHAIRLIFT

New England led the way among U.S. ski areas in installing uphill devices, and by 1930 the Northeast had more than 200 of them ranging from rope tows and T-bars to the mile-long Mount Mansfield tramway at Stowe, Vt. Then in 1936 Union Pacific Railroad engineer James Curran invented the chairlift to serve guests at the new Sun Valley resort. That set off a revolution in the skiing industry – but there still wasn't even one permanent lift or tow on Mount Hood.

It remained for skier and engineer Boyd French Sr. to build the first one. In 1937 the Forest Service issued a permit for French, with the financial backing of Berger Underdahl, to build a rope tow up the back wall of the Ski Bowl. With the help of his savvy son Boyd Jr. and many volunteers he built the first really engineered tow on the mountain. The first test of the equipment occurred in 1938. I described the experiment in my *Journal* "Ski Scout" column on Jan. 30, 1938, as follows:

Boyd French's Ski Bowl tow was tried out for the benefit of a few ambitious runners who trekked into the Bowl in spite of insufficient snow last week. Those who wished to risk their necks winding among the yet-uncovered rocks and stumps reported having gotten more slalom practice in the one afternoon than they would have had in two months otherwise, for more than 20 rides down the 1,000 foot course were possible in 3 1/2 hours.

The 1,025-foot-long tow, which rose 350 vertical feet, was powered by a Ford V-8 engine that pulled an endless one-inch rope above the snow on automobile car wheels suspended on telephone poles. It officially opened to the

The Frenchs' second rope tow in upper Ski Bowl as it appeared in the winter of 1940-1941. It was west of the original tow and went to the rim of the bowl. Notice the belts worn by two skiers on the left. They were used to attach the skier to the moving rope with a special metal clip.

public on Feb. 13, 1938, and was similar to those in New England.

A year later the Frenches drew on the first year's experience to build two more tows, one with a vertical rise of 650 feet to carry skiers a half-mile from the highway into the bowl, and the other 1,600 feet long to extend the original tow to the rim of the bowl with a vertical lift of 750 feet.

In 1939 the Forest Service used CCC crews to clear snags and rocks from Multorpor Hill west of the ski jumps. That summer and fall Bill Hughes, Joe Bradbury and George Buhtler built a modern rope tow similar to French's tow. Many years later, after the ski jumping hill had been abandoned, the Ski Bowl and Multorpor were interconnected with trails and lifts to create a winter and summer playground for snow sports, bicycling and hiking.

HOW TO RIDE A ROPE TOW

Riding rope tows required considerable skill. On some tows skiers were issued a belt and a two-pronged metal rope-hook with a short piece of line attached. The rider would grab the fast-running rope with both hands and fasten the hook to the rope while being pulled rapidly up the hill, then let go with one hand and loop the clothesline into a metal ring on the belt but not tie it. If all went well he then could lean back and be pulled swiftly to the top. However if an unwary rider knotted the clothesline to the belt or allowed it to become fouled with the tow rope, or if the skier fell and the operator wasn't alert, the rider might be dragged into the safety gate at the top.

The new tows in Ski Bowl and the chairlift at Timberline were to have been ready to serve the national championships and Olympic tryouts in April 1939, but an early winter in the fall of 1938 delayed their construction. Consequently most racers and spectators had to climb from the bottom to the top of courses just as they had done in 1930 and earlier.

SNOWCAT TO THE RESCUE

There were two exceptions. Some of the women racers were taken to the top of the women's downhill course at 8,500 feet in the world's first Snowcat invented by Ira Davidson, foreman of the WPA crew of stone masons building Timberline Lodge. In addition Cascade Ski Club racers Grace Graham and Bob Rowan installed their portable Sweden rope tow at the bottom of the slalom course in the Ski Bowl, providing a small assist to both men and women competitors.

THE MAGIC MILE – MOUNT HOOD'S FIRST CHAIRILIFT

When Prince Olav of Norway dedicated the Magic Mile, Mount Hood's first chairlift, at Timberline Lodge on May 21, 1939, it heralded the end of the era of rope tows. Soon after returning from service in the Army's 10th Mountain Division in World War II, Boyd French Jr. replaced the Ski Bowl's ski tows with a high-speed chairlift, as did permitees at Timberline Lodge, Multorpor and Summit ski areas.

DOWNHILL AND SLALOM SKIING EXPLODE

In 1936 two Seattle skiers, Don Fraser and Don Amick, uncorked the bottle that released the genie of explosive downhill and slalom ski competition in the Pacific Northwest. Fraser and Amick were on the American ski team that competed in the 1936 Winter Olympic Games in Garmisch Partenkirchen, Germany, the first year in which the games included alpine skiing events.

When the team returned from Germany, the excitement of downhill and slalom racing came with them, followed by many of Europe's finest skiers and ski school instructors anxious to teach the Arlberg technique to Americans.

The world's first Snowcat was invented by Ira Davidson, foreman of the WPA crew of stone masons building Timberline Lodge. Shown above is the second version of the machine, which was engineered by the Forest Service using Davidson's original design. This Snowcat was used extensively during the national downhill championships on April 2, 1939.

The Magic Mile, Mount Hood's first chairlift, Feb. 20, 1940. Ralph Eddy photo.

Otto Lang, first head of Timberline Lodge's ski school. Midge Sperry photo.

OTTO LANG BRINGS THE ARLBERG TO OREGON

Otto Lang, one of Hannes Schneider's leading protégés, came to the United States with the ski meister in 1936 to appear in ski shows in Boston and New York. Instead of returning to St. Anton, he taught skiing in New England for a season, then opened America's first Hannes Schneider Ski Schools at Mount Rainier and Mount Baker. When Timberline Lodge opened in 1938, Otto became head of its ski school too, with Ariel Edmiston as assistant. A portable rope tow was installed on a slope just above the lodge and became known as "Otto Lang Hill."

NORDIC – ALPINE STANDOFF

Until then the Nordic sports of ski jumping and cross-country racing had dominated ski competition on Mount Hood, and rapport between the mostly Scandinavian jumpers and the burgeoning devotees of downhill and slalom developed slowly. Fortunately Hjalmar Hvam, who was Cascade Ski Club's top Class A jumper, also became a champion downhill racer, thus serving as a bridge between the two factions. However some ski jumpers continued to disparage Otto Lang and the Arlberg technique. Then one day Otto offered to "lay the track" for the annual Winter Sports Carnival jumping championships on Cascade's Multorpor Hill.

Skier coming off the B Jump at the 1937 Winter Sports Carnival. One of my favorite photos.

The one who lays the track for a ski jump isn't expected to make a very long jump but should make precise tracks down the carefully prepared inrun, leave the takeoff at just the right point, and touch down near the mid point of the landing area to test the condition of the hill for the competitors who follow.

I don't believe that anyone present that day had ever seen Otto on jumping skis, but because it was such an implied challenge, he was allowed to make the attempt. I was covering the Winter Sports Carnival for the *Oregon Journal,* so I was on the judges' stand taking pictures. To the wonder of the Nordic fans and the delight of Otto's friends he laid an arrow-straight track, sprang smoothly from the takeoff, and held his body still as he sailed some 150 feet to a steady landing with one knee not quite touching the ski. He absorbed the touchdown with a quick telemark crouch then finished the outrun with a smooth Arlberg turn instead of running on into the hay bales piled at the end to slow his speed, as most of the Nordic skiers would do.

The applause was mixed, as might have been expected in a year when Germany had just occupied Austria and a Nazi invasion of Norway seemed imminent. But from then on it was clear that there were two kinds of skiing on Mount Hood – Nordic and alpine.

Sun Valley had opened in 1936, and in 1939 Friedl Pfeifer, another Hannes Schneider protege who had become director of Sun Valley Ski School, asked Otto Lang to join him there as co-director. Otto had made a host of friends while operating ski schools at Mount Hood, Mount Rainier and Mount Baker, so he was loathe to leave, but he explained his decision in his autobiography, *A Bird of Paradise*.

It had been a good and productive three winters for me in the Pacific Northwest but I knew that the future of these three places [Mount Rainier, Mount Baker and Mount Hood] as destination resorts was dubious and that only Mount Hood with its Timberline Lodge had a chance in succeeding as a year-around attraction.

HANNES SCHNEIDER ESCAPES TO AMERICA

In 1939 Hannes Schneider, who was an ardent Austrian nationalist, was jailed by the Nazis and released only through the intervention of Harvey D. Gibson, chairman of New York's Manufacturers National Bank and owner of the Cranmore Mountain Development Corp. in North Conway, New Hampshire. That is how Schneider was able to follow his many disciples already teaching in American ski schools and become head of the school at Mount Cranmore Resort.

I skied in New England that winter and rode Mount Cranmore's touted "Skimobile," which I found much less exciting than Ole Haugen's handmade sled on the Multorpor jumping hill, but the Skimobile drew thousands of New England skiers to North Conway and had been the catalyst that brought the famed Schneider to America.

PUCCI'S GLADE

Before World War II Emilio Pucci had been a student at Reed College and had selected a beautiful open meadow just below Timberline Lodge to give ski lessons to fellow students. The area soon became known as "Pucci's glade." Few of us realized then that he was a member of the Italian nobility – his full title was Marchese Emilio Pucci di Barsento – and because he had little in common with other Mount Hood skiers, there developed a certain diffidence among us.

Pucci became a fighter pilot in the Italian Air Force in World War II, suffered at the hands of the Allies as a captive after Italy surrendered, and survived to establish the renowned fashion house that bears his name. When Timberline Lodge celebrated its 50th anniversary in 1987, Emilio Pucci designed a commemorative scarf for the occasion and flew directly from Rome to take part in the ceremony.

I found him to be a delightful, debonair aristocrat who, when we skied together that anniversary weekend, spoke fondly of his time as a student and volunteer ski instructor at Reed College 50 years before, calling it a humbling experience that changed his life. He was pleased that the fast new chairlift serving Pucci's Glade was called the "Pucci Lift."

27 PRESIDENT ROOSEVELT
DEDICATES TIMBERLINE LODGE

Timberline Lodge nearing completion in late 1937. The tall hemlock tree from which I took this photo was later cut to improve the view from the Lodge.

In September 1937 just as crews were hoping to have Timberline Lodge ready to open for the 1937-38 ski season, Oregon Senator Charles McNary dropped a bombshell. President Franklin D. Roosevelt was coming to Oregon to inspect Bonneville Dam; could FDR and Mrs. Roosevelt have lunch at Timberline on Sept. 28 and dedicate the lodge

then? The answer had to be "Yes," for never again would there be such an opportunity. But could Timberline Lodge be ready in time?

Much of the handmade furniture, hand-hooked rugs, draperies, bedspreads and interior ironwork was completed and waiting in WPA workshops in Portland, so it could be trucked to the lodge in time. But could the WPA revise

200 George Henderson—Lonely On The Mountain

construction schedules enough to complete every part of the project that would be visible to the president's party?

NO OPERATOR YET

Even if that could be accomplished, there were no bed linens, no dishes or tablecloths, no stoves or other kitchen equipment, and no food. The Forest Service owned the lodge but until a private operator was selected, there was no one for it to turn to for the monumental task of readying the lodge for occupancy.

DAN LONDON TO THE RESCUE

That is when Dan London, manager of the Multnomah Hotel in Portland and later manager of the St. Francis Hotel in San Francisco, came to the rescue. He assigned his assistant manager Bob Lindquist to prepare a luncheon for some 100 guests and to transport it, along with an entire hotel staff, to Timberline early on dedication day.

The organizational ability and leadership displayed by Lindquist during Roosevelt's visit served him well. Forty years later when I called on him in Seattle, he had become chairman and CEO of the entire Westin Hotels chain.

FROM FIRE LOOKOUT TO PRESS BOX

I probably was the happiest ski bum in the West in 1937, for although it was the depth of the Great Depression, I had three skiing-related jobs. In winter I worked for the Oregon Winter Sports Association and wrote a weekly ski column for the *Oregon Journal*, and in the summer I worked for the U.S. Forest Service.

That was how I happened to be in the press box above the front steps of Timberline on dedication day, watching anxiously down the gravel road for the President's party.

When I had arrived early that morning

the lodge resembled the inside of an active Hollywood sound stage. It was bedlam! The scores of transplanted staffers were trying to find their places, set tables, make beds and fire up steam tables, while construction workers put on finishing touches and distraught Secret Service agents sought to assure security.

As the limousines of Roosevelt's motorcade wound up the mountainside on the East Leg Road, the cavalcade of empty cars and trucks that had carried hotel employees and equipment from Portland were barely out of site, scuttling down the older West Leg Road.

As FDR's car rounded the last breezy bend above Salmon River, the president was smiling broadly and waving from the back seat of an open touring car. The phaetons top was down and had been all the way from Portland, past Bonneville Dam and around the Mount Hood Loop Highway.

Sid Woodbury, president of the Portland Chamber of Commerce, was driving, and it was his Lincoln phaeton, so since the president did not complain about the chill, the other passengers – Senator Charles McNary and Governor Charles Martin – may not have had a vote.

There was an enthusiastic ovation by hundreds, but not thousands, of purposeful visitors as the cars pulled up to the lodge steps. The crowd was not huge because getting to Timberline that day had taken a bit of doing. Except for a limited official reception list, visitors had to leave their cars near Government Camp and ride up the unpaved construction road in buses or canvas-topped trucks. Many of the younger crowd had opted out of the mass transit system and walked up the ski trail.

The lodge looked much the same from the outside that day as it does now, except that the C.S. Price Convention Wing wasn't built until almost 48 years later. The site of the present Wy'east Day Lodge was a phlox-covered meadow, and there were no ski lifts or tows.

But as the president gazed up the mountain,

President Roosevelt getting out of his car at Timberline Lodge. I had not been present when others in the press corps had been told of the prohibition against taking photographs showing FDR's disability. The secret service agent in front of the President is pointing a warning finger at me saying, in effect, no pictures.

the only structures in sight were the two-story fire lookout on the summit, built in 1915, and Lone Fir lookout, at 6,800 feet in plain view just below where Silcox Hut now stands.

A CRIPPLED PRESIDENT

Most of the onlookers were surprised that the president was so badly crippled. Two aides had to lift him from the car and support him as he walked painfully up a temporary wooden ramp over the stone steps into the lodge.

I had not been present when others in the press corps had been told of the prohibition against taking photographs showing his disability. As a result one of the pictures I took that day shows the president being lifted from his car while one secret service agent is pointing a warning finger at me seeming to say, "No pictures," and another appears to have his hand on his gun. I already had clicked my shutter, and fortunately no one from the president's party asked me for my film. A copy of that image now hangs on the lodge balcony near the Ram's Head bar.

An honor guard of U.S. Forest Service regional officers and forest supervisors flank the lodge entrance as President Roosevelt, above, dedicates Timberline Lodge.

MIRRORS FLASHED FROM MOUNTAIN PEAKS

It may seem surprising that I remember just what the weather was like that day 68 years ago, but it was important that it be a sunny day. Someone on the dedication committee thought it would provide a dramatic touch for fire lookouts on various mountain peaks within sight of Timberline Lodge to give a demonstration of heliography – a communication technique long obsolete even then – by signaling the lodge with mirror flashes at a given moment during the dedication ceremonies.

This posed several problems. For one thing, in late September many lookout buildings had been closed and their shutters secured for the winter; for another, there was no assurance that the sun would shine that afternoon, even if so ordered by FDR.

Undaunted, the Mount Hood National Forest people set out to comply. I was working as a smoke-chaser for the Forest Service that summer, so I had been assigned to open up the lookout tower on Foreman's Point southeast of Mount Hood and to take part in the dress rehearsal a few days in advance.

The rehearsal went well, and to the surprise of most of the participants the event itself also went off without a hitch, although no one ever was really sure that Mr. Roosevelt was gazing south over the forest during the moments when the flashes occurred. I even have a photo of one of the flashes. Since Forest Supervisor Waha had arranged for me to have press credentials that day, another forest guard was manning Foreman's Point.

A FINE WPA PERFORMING ARTS PROGRAM

A gourmet lunch awaited the president and Mrs. Roosevelt and special guests, but since I was not among those, I watched and listened to some fine entertainment provided by WPA workers enrolled in various arts projects.

They performed outside in an amphitheater west of the lodge, where spectators sat on hand-adzed sections of cedar trees and looked out upon a stage made from native stone, with the blue-green Cascade Range providing a spectacular backdrop. The stage and seats are still there and cause snowy washboards at the bottom of the Magic Mile ski run in winter.

THE WPA SYMPHONY ORCHESTRA

Music hadn't been overlooked in the WPA's patronage. The fine Portland Symphony Orchestra, directed by Wilhelm van Hoogstraten, had been a casualty of the Depression, but the WPA Symphony gave employment to many of its musicians. We listened that day as they performed the Jubel overture by Weber and Fête Bohem by Massenet, the music seeming to reverberate between the glaciers on Mount Hood and those on Mount Jefferson.

The Federal Theater Project presented dances written for the occasion by the WPA Writers Project, including "Dance of the WPA Workers" and "Dance of the Flax Scutching Machine."

President and Mrs. Roosevelt were shown to their rooms, and after a brief rest, attended a reception and luncheon, which went off smoothly. Among the official party, only suave WPA Administrator E.J. Griffith was aware of the turmoil behind the scenes.

FDR delivered a succinct dedication speech from the stone parapet above the front entrance, while a uniformed guard of Forest Service officers stood on the stone steps below. A photo of that scene also has hung on the lodge balcony ever since.

THE MEN AND WOMEN OF WPA

The story of the lodge's dedication is part of the little-known lore of the building of

Timberline. It is part of the story of those hard working and mostly unheralded men and women on the relief rolls of the Works Progress Administration, who built the lodge in just 15 months – less than half the time it took to build the Wy'east Day Lodge some 40 years later.

Since then Timberline Lodge has found a place in history as a storehouse of seldom-duplicated craftsmanship and as America's only truly year-around ski resort. But the miracle of its construction is little remembered.

On the day the cornerstone was laid, the narrow unsurfaced road from Government Camp to what then was called the Mount Hood Hotel had just been opened by the incredible process of digging out the 20-foot-deep covering of snow bite by bite with a gasoline-driven power shovel. A photo of that remarkable job also is displayed on the lodge's balcony.

The site had been surveyed the previous fall, and the first loads of building materials were arriving, but it was early July before actual construction got under way. Yet in only four months the building's roof and exterior were closed in so that work could continue through the winter, and Timberline Lodge opened for business on Feb. 4, 1938, still only 20 months after the cornerstone was laid.

Those 20 months are a tribute to the skill, dedication and, in some cases, desperation of the men and women for whom a job, sometimes fighting sub-zero blizzards, was the margin of family survival in an era before there was unemployment insurance, Social Security, Medicare or food stamps.

Much has been written that is disparaging of WPA workers, but those of us who were closely involved with the Timberline Lodge project did not join in that criticism. These were not derelicts, nor were they people who had grown up expecting that a handout would be available if they could not fend for themselves. They were proud American working men and women, most of whom signed up for WPA jobs as a last resort and lost a little pride in the process. Most of them sought to regain some measure of that pride through their industriousness and the quality of their work.

PROTECTING THE MOUNTAIN'S FLORA

The Forest Service was sensitive to the need to protect the mountain's native plants long before the term "environmentalist" was popularized. Wooden barriers were erected only a few feet outside the Timberline Lodge building site, and once the snow pack began to thaw, no one was allowed to step beyond those perimeters. Thus many delicate grasses, mosses and mountain flowers that would have taken decades to regrow remained undisturbed.

28 A DAUNTING SALES JOB

E.J. Griffith (left), Mrs. Charles McNary, Jack Meier, Mrs. E.J. Griffith, and Senator Charles McNary in front of Timberline Lodge in early September 1938. When he was appointed head of the WPA by Roosevelt in May 1935, Griffith made a hotel at timberline his first priority. George Henderson photo courtesy of Friends of Timberline.

A MILLION DOLLAR WHITE ELEPHANT?

Timberline Lodge was in the national spotlight on dedication day, even rating a headline in the *New York Times*. But its future was bleak, for when the Forest Service invited bids for a permit to operate the resort, there had been no takers. The investment required to equip the lodge with everything from bedding and dining service to kitchen equipment – and provide start-up operating funds – was daunting to experienced hotel operators and beyond the means of neophytes anxious for the glamour of running a ski resort. Was it possible that the lodge might be locked up before it opened?

Oregonians just were not going to let that happen. Only a year earlier the Mount Hood Development Association had raised $20,000 in matching money to assure the lodge's construction by the WPA, but now with the building almost finished they were facing the specter of a white elephant on their mountain.

A CHECKERED FINANCIAL HISTORY

The concept of a hotel at the tree line on Mount Hood dated from long before it was embraced by the WPA as a make-work project. In 1930 and 1931 the Forest Service built a summer road from Government Camp to timberline. This stimulated mountain enthusiasts to incorporate the Portland Winter Sports Association, which later changed its name to the Oregon Winter Sports Association. Its avowed purpose was to "Make Mount Hood the National Winter Playground," and its annual Winter Carnivals attracted more than 10,000 enthusiasts to Government Camp on some winter weekends. Berger Underdahl conceived the idea of a statewide organization of outdoor clubs with one member of each club on its board of directors, and he was its first chairman.

Among leading advocates for a hotel at timberline were Cascade Ski Club life member E.J. Griffith and architect John Yeon Jr., who teamed up with a plan for a picturesque chateau at the 6,000 foot level overlooking the west bank of Salmon River Canyon, but their proposal languished for lack of money.

Then suddenly the same Great Depression that had precluded private investment breathed life into the dream of a hotel at timberline. In May 1935 President Franklin Roosevelt appointed E.J. Griffith to be the Oregon director of the newly created Works Progress Administration, and the first relief project that Griffith initiated was a hotel at timberline on Mount Hood!

A $20,000 CHALLENGE

But it wasn't to be that easy. The WPA had $250,000 on hand for the project but couldn't start building until $10,000 in matching money and an equal amount in pledges was provided by local sponsors. Because the building would need to be well under way before the next winter set in, the Oregon Winter Sports Association stepped up to the challenge. On Jan. 9, 1936, seven of its directors – Jack Meier, Berger Underdahl, James Mount, L.B. McNabb, Dr. Paul Dutton, Franz Drinker and Walter W.R. May – incorporated a new nonprofit corporation, the Mount Hood Development Association, to do the job, electing Meier chairman, Underdahl vice chairman and Mount secretary.

That fund-raising effort was a cliffhanger, but it received wide community support; the Portland Chamber of Commerce even underwrote the first $10,000 pledge. Newspapers published daily sales totals, as they often did to report progress of charitable drives. Some 2,000 $10, 20-year 4% bonds were authorized, and most were bought by individuals.

CIVIC SAVIOR – TIMBERLINE LODGE, INC.

The miracle of the resort's rescue from oblivion that first winter following the president's dedication almost parallels the miracle of its construction. Many of the same winter sports stalwarts who had raised the WPA matching money banded together again to create a new corporation, named it Timberline Lodge, Inc., sold stock, acquired the operating permit held by the Mount Hood Development Association, bought furnishings, and hired a manager and staff. On Feb. 4, 1938,

Rotary plow clearing Timberline Road during the winter of 1939-1940.

with the winter's worst blizzard raging outside, Timberline Lodge opened for business to a sold-out house.

Jack Meier was president of the corporation, and the directors were A.M. Cronin Sr., Forrest Berg, William Healy Sr., Harold Hirsch, Fred McNeil, Horace Mecklem Sr., James Mount, Robert Burns, Albert Bullier Sr., Fred VanDyke, Berger Underdahl, Boyd French Sr. and Ernest Swigert.

TIMBERLINE'S STORM WRACKED OPENING

For 24 hours before the opening, Carl Alt and his Forest Service road crew had used their one rotary snowplow and two push plows to keep the six-mile-long gravel road from the Loop Highway to Timberline passable. But late in the afternoon, as the last busload of guests started up from the highway, the road behind it was finally blocked by snow and the gate was locked.

I arrived at the highway junction shortly afterward and, finding the gate locked, was unloading my skis from the car, when Ray Atkeson pulled in beside me on his way to Timberline to photograph the festivities. Not only was Ray an outstanding photographer, but he was an expert mountain climber and skier.

Famed outdoor photographer Ray Atkeson at timberline on Mount Hood, May 1931. Jim Harlow photo courtesy of Anne Harlow Trussell.

We rubbed climbing wax on our skis, donned headlamps, shouldered packs and skied up the road, arriving at the lodge while the cocktail hour was still in progress. The blizzard lasted another 24 hours, with most celebrants savoring the adventure of two snowbound nights in such splendor.

A NO-BUDGET NATIONAL SALES CAMPAIGN

With the lodge completed, staffed and open for business, the challenge was to fill those luxurious rooms with paying guests. We watched with envy as the Union Pacific Railroad hired a cadre of well-known ski racers and instructors, designated them "Sun Valley representatives" and assigned them to appear before ski clubs, travel agents and transportation directors nationwide.

At Timberline skiers and sightseers, mostly from Oregon and Washington, overran the lodge on winter weekends, but with only 50 rooms and few midweek guests, revenue didn't even cover the cost of maintenance. The answer was to develop more midweek business, and that meant soliciting guests from beyond the Pacific Northwest.

William Temple was lodge manager. He hired me as publicity manager on a salary-sharing arrangement with the winter sports association. With no money for advertising, we would have to depend on personal solicitation and on creating newsworthy events that would generate publicity in newspapers and on the radio; there was yet no television.

SAM SLOCUM, PROMOTER

Have you ever heard of the Taft Redhead Roundup? If you had lived on the Oregon Coast or most anywhere else in Oregon or Washington in the 1930s, you surely would have, because Sam Slocum was that good a promoter. I do not know how Sam got mixed up with the enthusiastic young businessmen of Taft, Oregon, but it was a winning combination. It could have started on a dull day in the barbershop when someone looking out the window casually inquired, "Have you ever noticed how many redheaded people there are in Taft?" Apparently there were a great many, and Slocum took it from there. Here was a way for the tiny village tucked in among the coastal towns of Ocean Lake, Delake, Cutler Lake and Nelscott to establish its own identity. Before long the Taft Redhead Roundup was an annual event, with a redheaded queen and redheaded princesses who earned their crowns through button sales. (Note that the five towns no longer exist, because in 1964 they voted to merge under the name Lincoln City.)

When the Oregon Winter Sports Association directors first announced their goal in 1932 to "Make Mount Hood The National Winter Playground," they knew they would need a reliable source of income and chose the Taft Redhead Roundup as their unlikely role model for fund-raising. It was a good fit, with Sam Slocum continuing his summer promotion at Taft, then switching to Portland and Mount Hood in the fall for the Oregon Winter Sports Carnival queen contest.

SIX PRINCESSES TO THE RESCUE

Oregon Winter Sports Association president James Mount was a renaissance man, a retail-advertising executive whose hobbies were mountain climbing and skiing. In 1937, when faced with the problem of conducting a national advertising campaign for Timberline Lodge with no money, he came up with a creative proposal: Why not let the lovely queen and princesses of the annual Winter Sports Carnival become ambassadors to spread the story of Oregon's year-round skiing to the rest of the country?

The idea caught fire. Every outdoors club in Oregon had a member on the OWSA board of directors, and most of them volunteered to work on the campaign. Sam Slocum predicted that the plan would more than double the income from winter carnival ticket sales and pay for railroad fare for the courts and chaperones.

Portland ski clothing manufacturers Jantzen, White Stag and Pendleton agreed to outfit the courts in their latest skiing fashions, and passenger agents from Northern Pacific, Union Pacific and Southern Pacific railroads traveled several days ahead of each tour to arrange for receptions and public appearances.

Multnomah County Sheriff Martin Pratt notified his counterparts in other cities of the impending arrival of skiing royalty, and they were met by motorcycle escorts who swept them between appointments with sirens wailing. Newspaper coverage was awesome.

RECEIVED AT THE WHITE HOUSE

President Roosevelt's son James welcomed the first goodwill tour to the White House in 1937, soon after Timberline's formal

Jim Mount at old Timberline Cabin, February 1932. When he was president of the Oregon Winter Sports Association in 1937, Mount came up with the idea of using the Oregon Winter Court in a national campaign to advertise skiing in Oregon. Jim Harlow photo courtesy of Anne Harlow Trussell.

James Roosevelt, son of President Franklin D. Roosevelt, poses with the 1937 Oregon Winter Carnival Royal Court while acting as official host to Queen Rose Winkler (white uniform), and her princesses during their stay in Washington, D.C., in 1937. White House photo.

opening. After Washington, D.C., the skiing ambassadors campaigned in Philadelphia, New York, Montreal, Banff and Vancouver, B.C.

In 1938 I managed the tour led by Queen Margaret Griffith, which appeared in a dozen cities from San Francisco and Los Angeles to Houston, New Orleans and Chicago. Walter Reimers, director of ceremonies for the 1939 San Francisco Golden Gate Exposition, took us across the new San Francisco Bay Bridge and on a tour of Treasure Island. In Los Angeles the Junior Chamber of Commerce had a throne built of ice blocks to receive the court right in downtown Hollywood, then arranged visits to active sound stages.

When our train pulled into railroad stations, mayors or their representatives usually greeted us. In Houston we were met by Mayor R.J. Fonville and civic leaders and were guests of the Texas lieutenant governor at the opening of the renowned Houston Rodeo.

QUEEN FETED AT MARDI GRAS

In New Orleans the queen and court were VIP guests at the Mardi Gras and shared press and radio coverage with Rex, King of Carnival, and Comus, God of Mirth.

Photographers were delighted when the six ski-clothed members of the winter court stood

Basil Rathbone (second from right), Wendy Barrie and Richard Greene host the Oregon Winter Sports Carnival court on the Hound of the Baskervilles *set at 20th Century Fox Studios in Hollywood, March 7, 1939. Court members from left are Norma Cowling, Maryanne Hill, June Long, Crown Princess Dorothy Olivero, Queen Fern Lorenzini, and Mabel Jean Lee.*

side by side and unexpectedly threw open their white ski jackets to reveal sweaters bearing large blue letters that spelled out OREGON. It made fine photo ops, and local dignitaries wcrc glad to be on hand to share the publicity with "Oregon's snow queens."

In 1939 Queen Fern Lorenzini, Crown Princess Dorothy Olivero and Princesses Maryanne Hill, Mabel Jean Lee, June Long and Norma Cowling led the Winter Sports Ambassadors on a campaign down the West Coast concluding in Mexico City. The Multnomah County Sheriff's motorcycle drill team was in international competition with a similar Mexican team that year, and the chief of police of Mexico City arranged for the court to be escorted by the team during its stay.

LAGUARDIA PRESENTS KEYS TO NY

In 1940 New York City Mayor Fiorello LaGuardia presented Queen Claire Erickson with the keys to the city. She and Princesses June Wong, Dorothy Trachsel, Betty Schmitz, Louise Elieff and Dorothy White also made appearances in the Midwest and Florida, then spent three days in pre-Castro Havana as guests of the republic.

The 1941 court of Queen Dorothy Gast and Princesses Lucille Torrison, Margaret Lindsay and Dorothy Willis were competitive skiers, so after an exhaustive 2,000-mile goodwill trip through the Midwest, they spent a few days skiing at Sun Valley.

THE TRAPP FAMILY SINGERS

Weeks of train travel to promote the Winter Sports Association's goal, "Make Mount Hood the Nation's Winter Playground," was wearying work even for an eager 25-year-old, but the job had many perks. One was the luxury of staying in the nation's finest hotels free of charge. Before the prevalence of hotel chains, resorts and hotels of comparable quality would band together for sales promotion, and they provided complementary rooms to each other's sales representatives. Timberline Lodge was in the luxury category, so I was given free lodging at hotels such as the Waldorf Astoria in New York, the Fairmont in San Francisco and the Copley Plaza in Boston. That was how I happened to hear the Trapp Family Singers perform soon after they escaped the Nazis by fleeing on foot across the Austrian Alps.

One evening in 1940 when I was staying at the Copley on one of those sales trips, I returned to the hotel after dinner. In the foyer seven children and their parents, all attractively dressed in dirndl and lederhosen, were singing songs in German before a rapt audience of hotel guests. I had not heard of the Trapp Family Singers but found a leaflet that told of their travails in escaping the Nazis after Hitler invaded Austria. Support for the Family was voluntary that evening, although soon they would be receiving $1,000 a performance on national tours. I made a donation, and then lingered to visit with Baron and Baroness von Trapp. They were interested in hearing about skiing in Oregon, so I invited them to visit Timberline Lodge if their travels should take them to the Pacific Northwest.

Soon the family gained national prominence and Maria von Trapp became an American citizen. She wrote a best selling memoir and remodeled a rundown farm in Vermont and made it the family home.

FAST- FORWARD 20 YEARS

Twenty years later, in February 1960, I was awash with the memories of that evening in Boston as my wife Jan, and I watched a live performance of *The Sound of Music* in New York with Mary Martin in the role of Maria von Trapp.

I was enrolled that winter in the Advanced Management Program at the Harvard Business School in Boston, and Jan was alone in Portland coping with Donna, 6; Bonnie, 5; Heather, 3; and Randall, 2. It surely was time for her to have a break, and during the school's midterm recess she had flown to New York. We spent two nights at the Waldorf Astoria, had dinner at '21' and attended the play whose 1,443 performances would make it the most successful Broadway musical in history.

THE TRAPP FAMILY LODGE

Boston had a record snowfall that winter. We were in classes six days a week, but my roommate, Air Force General Bill Veal, a B-17 Flying Fortress pilot during the war, and another classmate, Baron Lars De Geer of Sweden, and I survived the icy highways on Sundays to drive 300 miles round-trip to Stratton Mountain, Vt., to ski.

The Sound of Music was still ringing in my ears when the school took another three-day break for Easter. I borrowed the General's Volkswagen and headed for the "Valley of the Inns" in northern Vermont, which was close to Mount Mansfield, famous for its state-of-the-art ski lift and challenging downhill racing trail. I had heard that the Trapp family had converted its farmhouse into a mountain lodge. I wanted to stay there, but it seemed to be a well kept secret, for when I arrived at Stowe it was

Timberline Lodge brochure from about 1940.

only by making local inquiry that I located the inn. The motion picture version of *The Sound of Music* had not yet been produced, and after 20 years family members had discontinued their concert tours and were devoting their energies to their lodge.

I finally found the inn, secluded among dairy farms and pastures, and was delighted to be greeted by Maria Von Trapp herself and shown to my room by one of the "children" – an attractive young woman in her late 20s. It had the look and feel of an alpine chalet all right – with wooden bunks and mattresses stuffed with straw. Baron George Von Trapp had died, but I quickly felt the warmth of the family toward one another and toward the guests. I was sorry to decline to join them in their Easter service, however; Mount Mansfield's call was overwhelming.

If the lodge reminded me more of the Cascade Ski Club clubhouse in Government Camp than of Timberline Lodge, the hospitality could not have been warmer. (Note: In 1965 the motion picture version of *The*

Sound of Music with Julie Andrews as Marie was released, and by 2005 the Trapp Family Lodge had grown into a 116-room, four-star resort with the youngest of the children, Johannes von Trapp, as president.)

TIMBERLINE LODGE: THE MOVIE

After several sales trips around the country describing to prospective visitors the wide open ski slopes awaiting them on Mount Hood and the handcrafted beauty of Timberline Lodge, I realized how much better the story could be told by a motion picture.

We soon determined that a professional movie such as the several that Sun Valley had produced was far beyond our means, so we decided to produce our own. We bought a 16 mm Bell and Howell movie camera for $50, Jack Meier loaned us his fine Cine Special home movie camera for telephoto shots, and we went to work.

I had never used a movie camera, but fortunately a Hollywood production company was at Timberline making scenes for a feature film that winter, and one of the cameramen coached me on basics of motion picture photography. With the help of Norman Dimick, a genius in the new art of copying Kodachrome film, we produced *Timberline Lodge 1940* for only a few hundred dollars.

Senator Charles McNary arranged for the picture to be shown to President Roosevelt in the fall of 1941, but when I arrived at the Senator's office on the appointed morning, he told me that our appointment with the President had been cancelled due to a diplomatic crisis with the Japanese. The Senator then gathered 50 or so other senators and their staffs for a showing in the Senate office building.

I was embarrassed when I turned on the projector and Mount Hood scenes flashed onto the screen but there was dead silence from the loudspeaker. It turned out that 65 years ago many Eastern cities were served only by direct current electricity, so an AC/DC converter was required to operate our sound equipment. The Senator was unruffled – he simply asked me to ad-lib the commentary, and since I had done the photography and written the script, that was no problem. It was the only time I have ever enjoyed the undivided attention of a roomful of senators.

The film was shown again later that day before the U.S. Forest Service Chief and 2,000 Department of Agriculture employees in the department's auditorium, where a theater - style projector brought full brilliance to the scenes. For several more weeks that fall I made calls on the travel industry in a dozen states, sometimes showing the film twice in a day.

Sixty years later Norman Dimick's son located the original film and sound track where his father had stored them in a bank vault. I had him reproduce them on VCR format and donated the master to Friends of Timberline. Prints are available for sale at Timberline.

29   THE 1939 OLYMPIC TEAM TRYOUTS

Dick Durrance in his winning slalom run in the 1939 Olympic tryouts in the Ski Bowl.

It was a daring gamble, but in 1937 Oregon winter sports enthusiasts decided that it was time for the world to recognize Mount Hood as a leader in competitive skiing. The Cascade Ski Club and the Oregon Winter Sports Association applied to the International Ski Federation, the National Ski Association (NSA) and the U.S. Olympic Committee for sanction to hold the 1939 national downhill and slalom championships and tryouts for the 1940 Olympic ski team at Timberline Lodge and in the Ski Bowl.

Fred H. McNeil (above) and I were named co-chairmen of the Oregon Olympic Commission by Governor Earl Snell.

President Franklin Roosevelt had dedicated Timberline Lodge, but it was many months from completion, and there were no bidders yet for the contract to operate it. Mount Hood had no ski lifts or tows. The Forest Service had plans to build a chairlift at Timberline, but it had not appropriated money for it. Otto Lang had opened ski schools at Mount Baker and Mount Rainier and hoped to open one at Timberline Lodge but not until the lodge itself opened. So although we couldn't guarantee any of those facilities, we did have one big advantage: We could guarantee snow.

There would be stiff competition to hold the events, but while many other ski areas could not count on having enough snow beyond February, if at all, the success of Mount Hood's Golden Rose Ski Tournaments each June put that fear to rest for us.

Most of the decision-makers in organized skiing were from New England, including NSA President Roger Langley, a Barre, Mass., school teacher. They could not conceive of the vast open slopes between Crater Rock and Timberline Lodge where we planned to hold the downhill races. To help them visualize the course, we had Ray Atkeson take a dramatic aerial photo of the scene and sent copies to the NSA along with an engineering profile.

Then to demonstrate that there was broad local support for bringing the Olympic event to Oregon, we asked Governor Earl Snell for his help. Recognizing how valuable the tournament could be to the state's tourism industry, he created an Oregon Winter Olympics Commission made up of civic leaders, skiing officials and competitors, and he named Fred McNeil and me co-chairmen. McNeil was an *Oregon Journal* editor, author, competition judge and founder of the Pacific Northwestern Ski Association, and I was a nationally ranked downhill racer and winter sports writer. To ensure success, the governor placed the well-funded Oregon Department of Tourism and Travel squarely behind us.

CLIMB EVERY MOUNTAIN

Even though we were confident there would be ample snow for the tournament, we still were faced with the fact that Mount Hood didn't yet have even one tow or chairlift serving the race courses, so we turned to the Forest Service for possible help. To assure that Timberline would become a well-rounded skiing complex, the Forest Service had planned to build both a day lodge and a chairlift in 1938. Although rumblings of war delayed the day lodge – for 42 years it turned out – the chairlift was a different matter.

HOW SILCOX HUT GOT ITS NAME

Here is the little-known story of how the Magic Mile was financed and why the upper terminal building came to be named Silcox Hut. The Depression was in full cry, and having appropriated some half-million dollars to build Timberline Lodge, Congress was in no mood to provide more for a mile-long chairlift.

Ferdinand A. Silcox, chief forester of the United States and the man for whom Silcox Hut was named, was an ardent supporter of Timberline Lodge and largely responsible for construction of the Magic Mile chairlift. USFS photo courtesy of the Forest History Society, Durham, North Carolina.

Fortunately F.A. Silcox, chief forester of the United States, made an inspection trip to Timberline in the fall of 1938 accompanied by Assistant Chief E.W.Tinker, Regional Forester C. J. Buck, Forest Supervisor A.O. Waha and WPA director E.J. Griffith. Money for the lift could come only from existing budgets, and a ski lift had low priority in a national forest managed "for the greatest good of the greatest number." Neither the Mount Hood National Forest nor the Forest Service's Pacific Northwest Region had enough money in their recreational budget to finance it.

After a tour of the lodge and a ride up to Lone Fir Lookout on the Snowcat, the Chief was so interested in the resort he decided to stay longer. I was then an assistant manager of Timberline and was one of the dinner hosts. It was a brilliant fall day, with Mount Hood's shimmering snowfields framed in the lodge's tall north windows, and as I freshened drinks during the cocktail hour, I pointed out the proposed location of the lift. There was no response from the chief.

The dinner and wine were excellent. As the convivial evening in front of the blazing fireplace progressed, Chief Silcox looked out at the moonlit slopes rising to the mountain peak and suddenly pronounced, "The chief's office could provide half of the money needed for the chairlift," and turning to Buck and Waha, added, "if the two of you could provide the other half from your own budgets." What could they say but "Yes"?

Forest Service engineers already had drawn up specifications for a chairlift similar to those at Sun Valley but using fabricated steel towers rather than the wooden poles. The lift would take racers a third of the way to Crater Rock, where the downhill race started. The Forest Service expedited the order, and there seemed to be ample time for the lift to be in operation before the tournament a year hence.

Cascade Ski Club president Boyd French Sr., with the financial backing of former OWSA president Berger Underdahl, had a permit to build a rope tow from the highway into the Ski Bowl and another up the back wall of the Bowl. Both tows would be in operation before our requested tournament race dates of April 1 and 2, 1939.

DURRANCE CHECKS THE COURSE

Skiing's governing bodies still hadn't decided what ski area would be awarded the national championships and tryouts, and we were becoming concerned. Then we got a break. Dick Durrance, captain of the Dartmouth Ski Team, was by far the finest American downhill and slalom racer, and his sister, Lisal, got a job as waitress at Timberline Lodge. Dick was working that summer laying out ski trails on newly developed Baldy Mountain at Sun Valley, and it was our good fortune that he came to Timberline one weekend to visit Lisal.

Dick hadn't brought his skis, because he

had no thought that we could still be skiing in September, but since he would be racing in the national championships and Olympic tryouts the next winter, he gladly accepted my invitation to borrow skis and look over our proposed course.

I explained to him that the usual practice of waxing skis with soft Klister for warm snow wouldn't work, because the wind had spread the snowfield with pumice dust picked up from the bare ridges. So we scraped the bottoms of our skis bare and coated them with a hard mix of paraffin and graphite that would resist adherence by the pumice.

IS THIS STEEP ENOUGH?

We shouldered our skis and reached the top of Triangle Moraine in a couple of hours, and as we strapped on skis and looked back down, I was happy to hear Durrance exclaim, "Wow – and they're wondering if this course will be fast enough?" It had been a heavy winter, and the hot summer sun had turned the Palmer snowfield into a vast expanse of sun cups much like moguls, some 2 feet deep and 8 feet from crest to crest.

I was used to bouncing down through sun cups in late summer, but it was a revelation to watch Durrance tame them with his new "dipsy-doodle" technique, holding his hips nearly level while his knees absorbed the shocks. That foretaste of summer skiing on Mount Hood might have helped him to win the national combined downhill and slalom championships the following April.

DATES APPROVED

Final approval for the tournament to be held on April 1 and 2, 1939, was received not long after Durrance's visit.

The skiing world's eyes were on Mount Hood that weekend as America's best amateur men and women Olympic team hopefuls,

Cascade Ski Club racers Lin Bowman (left) and Boyd French Jr. make a practice run down Alpine Trail near Timberline Lodge.

and many other fine racers classified as "FIS Amateurs," (for Fédération Internationale du Ski) faced off on the Crater Rock run and on the nearly sheer undulating slopes of the Ski Bowl. (Note: "FIS amateur" referred to ski teachers and others who made money skiing but did not ski for money prizes. They were not amateurs under Olympic rules.)

Timberline Lodge and Government Camp inns housed most of the competitors and journalists, but thousands of spectators crowded into resorts along the highway or commuted from Portland.

The weather was nearly perfect. It had been a heavy winter with more than 4 feet of snow in the bowl and 20 feet at Timberline, but most important, the skies were clear, and there was little wind either day. We had consulted many years of Mount Hood climbing reports kept by the Mazamas as well as weather bureau records before setting the race dates for April. We knew that, despite careful planning, the odds of having two warm, almost cloudless spring days for the competition were no better than fifty-fifty, yet that was what happened!

"CLIMB EVERY MOUNTAIN" IT WAS!

The down side of that near record snowfall was that it wreaked havoc with our plans to have the latest in uphill devices in place for the tournament. Many of the top racers had competed the week before in the Harriman Cup races at Sun Valley, where four new

Ski Bowl on race day, April 1, 1939. Swiss skier Elsa Roth wrote, "We can confidently say without wanting to be merely polite, that the latter [the slalom course] was one of the prettiest, best prepared, and most cleverly laid out runs which we have ever seen."

American Elizabeth Woolsey (left), first in Olympic team tryouts and winner of the women's downhill.

Erna Steur (right), of Switzerland who won the women's open.

Both photos were taken April 1, 1939, in the Ski Bowl by Lynn Darcy and are provided courtesy of the Mazamas.

chairlifts served the courses on Baldy and Dollar mountains. In contrast, at Timberline Lodge the steel towers of the new chairlift soon to be christened by Crown Prince Olav of Norway lay under snowdrifts that had halted construction in early November. That meant that skiers had to climb more than 3,000 vertical feet from Timberline to reach the starting gates of the downhill races.

The story in the Ski Bowl was similar. Neither the new tow that would take skiers from the highway into the bowl nor the planned extension of the original tow to the top of Tom Dick and Harry Mountain was completed.

Weather and snow conditions were near perfect for the slalom races in the Ski Bowl on Saturday. The manager of the U.S. Women's team, Mrs. Alice Damrosch Wolfe, had asked that we equalize the difficulty of courses for men and women, so slalom course setter Otto Lang simply decided that men and women would run the same course. It began on a cornice near the top of Tom Dick and Harry Mountain, with forty pairs of gates swinging racers down the undulating canyon to finish on the bowl's level floor 900 vertical feet below. There were 73 men and 34 women racers making two runs each.

Friedl Pfeifer, head of the Sun Valley Ski School, won the men's open division, while Dick Durrance won the amateur and was first in the Olympic team tryouts. Erna Steur of Switzerland won the women's open, and another Swiss, Doris Friedrich, the women's amateur. American Elizabeth Woolsey was first in the Olympic team tryouts, won the women's downhill by a wide margin, and was third in the women's combined.

To the surprise of many, the course held up splendidly for two runs each by 107 competitors. That was due to the work of old-time ski jumper Corey Gustafsson, whose hill maintenance team had foot-packed it top to bottom like a jumping hill, abetted by the fact that much of the north-facing bowl remains in shadow most of the day.

The slalom course on Ski Bowl was a pleasant surprise to those skiers visiting Mount Hood for the first time. Swiss skier Elsa Roth's enthusiastic praise in her article "Reflections On Our American Tour" in the *American Ski Journal* reflected what many felt after the race was over: "We can confidently say without wanting to be merely polite, that the latter [the slalom course] was one of the prettiest, best prepared, and most cleverly laid out runs which we have ever seen."

FRIEDL PHEIFER CALLS A STRIKE

The downhill races on Sunday didn't go off quite as smoothly. I was among the first to reach the men's downhill starting gate at 9,500 feet elevation just below Crater Rock, and there the tournament's first crisis developed. Austrian Friedl Pfeifer, who had won the slalom the day before, was seated on his skis, squinting down the unpacked course marked by a dozen pairs of blue flags that faded from sight at the finish line three miles below. No doubt the three-hour climb made by racers and officials alike had darkened his mood.

"Too dangerous," he declared, "Vee vill start down zare!" and pointed to the ladies' starting gate 500 vertical feet lower.

The day had dawned bright and clear, but an ominous cloud cap hung over the summit, and by race time it was cold and windy at the starting line. The official starter District Ranger Harold Engles, who had backpacked a tent and radios all the way up from Timberline, was awaiting word from Race Committee Chairman Fred VanDyke, who was on the radio at the finish line 3,500 feet below.

Dick Durrance – who had won the amateur slalom title the day before and placed second to Pfeifer in the open division – made no comment but continued to wax his skis. He and Pfeifer had had differences before. I thought that with the weather deteriorating

Friedl Pfeifer at the start of the downhill race course on Mount Hood, April 2, 1939.

At the Timberline Lodge national tournament banquet on April 2, 1939, Roger Langley (left), president of the NSA, congratulated Dick Durrance for winning the Bass Silver Boot for All American Skier Of The Year. Durrance was the new national open and amateur combined champion.

rapidly, most of the racers would rather start right away, but that could mean losing Pfeifer and perhaps some others.

Chief of Course Boyd French Sr. was on the radio at the women's start, and according to a later account by Fred McNeil, "There was some excited palavering on the short wave by members of the race committee [McNeil was one of them] resulting in the decision to move the men's start down [to the women's start]."

Who knows what the outcome would have been if the start had not been lowered? It was a tough call, but when Engles received the decision on the radio, I drew a deep breath and told him and his officials to load up their equipment and follow. Awash with adrenaline, I pointed my skis straight down that controversial upper schuss, barely managing a clean stop when I reached the women's start, which then became the men's start too.

FRIEDL PFEIFER FAILS TO FINISH

After all that fuss Friedl Pfeifer failed to finish the downhill race! Fred McNeil wrote, "Friedl Pfeifer fell too far back to get back for a time worthwhile." Instead he skied off the course and didn't cross the finish line at all.

Despite the softening snow near the finish the first three finishers in the open division, Austrians Toni Matt, Hannes Schroll and Peter Radacher, were only split seconds apart. Dick Durrance was only 5 seconds behind them and won not only the amateur downhill and amateur slalom championships but also the amateur and open combined championship and was first in the Olympic team tryouts.

"FINEST IN AMERICAN SKIING HISTORY"

Newly inaugurated Oregon Governor Charles Sprague was chairman of the awards banquet that night, at which NSA president Roger Langley presented to Dick Durrance the Bass Trophy for All American Skier of the Year. When Elsa Roth, manager of the Swiss women's team, was introduced, she commented, "The slalom was one of the best I have ever seen. There is seldom such a beautiful race."

In the 1939-40 *American Ski Annual* Roger Langley reported, "Everyone agreed with Miss Roth that this was an unusual race, a ski day in history. For the field of competitors assembled, weather, snow conditions, race course, and the capable manner in which it was conducted, the tournament was praised by competitors and spectators alike as the finest in American skiing history."

FROM RACE OFFICIAL TO RACER

Two weeks later I was at Camp Muir, 10,000 feet high on Mount Rainier, waiting for my number to be called to start in the legendary Silver Skis Open Championships. Twenty-nine racers had qualified for the event, billed as "America's most wide open and toughest downhill race."

Standing nearby with the other contestants were Peter Radacher from Sun Valley and Arthur Schlatter from Switzerland, who had finished third and sixth in the open division of the national championships at Mount Hood; Reidar Anderson from Norway, who had just won the national Class A jumping championship in St. Paul; former world jumping distance record-holder Olav Ulland; and past Silver Skis champions Hjalmar Hvam and Don Fraser.

It was the first race I had entered that year, and I had hoped that Friedl Pfeifer would be there too, but he wasn't. It had galled me two weeks earlier to have to cut off the critical top schuss of our national championship course on Mount Hood as a result of Pfeifer's complaint, even though for the past three years we had successfully held the Golden Rose Race over the same course from Crater Rock to Timberline. I was nursing that grudge when I decided to enter the Silver Skis, which was among the most hazardous courses in that era of reckless downhill racing.

SKIERS HAD TO PACK THE COURSE

At 8 a.m. the racers met with Otto Lang at the finish line of the race in 5,200-foot-high Edith Creek Basin near Paradise Inn, then ski-tramped up 500 vertical feet of unbroken snow on Alta Vista to the snout of Nisqually Glacier. From there we climbed ice-crusted snowfields to the starting line at 10,000-foot-high Camp Muir below Rainier's summit.

After a long winter the warm spring sun seemed to draw rocky ridges right up through their mantles of snow. Lang was head of the ski school at both Mount Rainier and Mount Hood and was course setter for both the Olympic tryouts and the Silver Skis that year. As he pointed out the barely half-dozen control flags. I recalled that the Instructions to Competitors had proclaimed, "Control gates are few permitting racers to plunge from Camp Muir to Edith Creek in a series of downhill runs." Even more than speed would be the need for dexterity in dodging the bare ridges and rock outcrops.

As I stood at Camp Muir with Cascade Ski Club teammates Olaf Rodegard and Hjalmar Hvam, looking down the course, I wondered if my legs were in tough enough condition to carry me down that 3.16 miles. So I asked Hjalmar how he kept his speed in control in such a race. With an excited grin he replied, "George, when I begin to feel tired in a race, I just say to myself, 'Faster, faster,' and then I won't fall down!"

It was good advice. During the race while skiing almost 60 mph, I had to lift one ski and then the other to avoid patches of bare rock, and I realized that to hesitate would be to court disaster. By relaxing muscles and skiing unchecked, I reached the top of the final schuss into Edith Creek Basin feeling that my elapsed time might be as fast as any, but a dozen yards before the finish line the course leveled abruptly. My knees could no longer absorb the shock and I tumbled headfirst toward the gates. Both skis stayed on, and I was unhurt, but I lost both poles. Even after scrambling furiously across the finish line on all fours, my time of 5:38:2 was 13th overall and 10th among the amateurs. Peter Radacher of Sun

George Henderson (left), and Hjalmar Hvam at Timberline Lodge at start of a race on Nov. 21, 1937. Hvam's advice to George for staying in control during the Silver Skis race was just to say to himself "Faster, faster." George Henderson photo courtesy of Friends of Timberline.

Valley won the open in 4:54.1, and Bob Blatt of Stanford was first amateur in 5:02. Sixty-six years later I continue to speculate on how many seconds that fall added to my time.

Sadly, Sigurd Hall of Seattle Ski Club, who finished 3 seconds faster than me that day, was killed in the same race the following year when he crashed into exposed rocks.

A few weeks later my self-confidence was restored, when I finished third behind Bob Blatt as he won the Golden Rose downhill race from Crater Rock to Timberline.

OLYMPICS CANCELLED BY WW II

The fierce rivalry for selection to the American ski teams was for naught, because the 1940 Winter Olympic Games scheduled for Norway were cancelled by the start of World War II in Europe. The next opportunity for Olympic class ski competition wasn't until 1948 when the Winter Games were held in Garmisch-Partenkirken, West Germany. In the interim Gretchen Kunigk, of Tacoma who had won a place on the 1940 team eight years earlier, again won a place on the 1948 team. By then she and 1936 U.S. Olympic team member Don Fraser were married and living in Vancouver, Wash. To the delight of American skiers, Gretchen won the women's slalom – the first American ever to win an Olympic gold medal in skiing.

Virginia Bowden (left), Skit Smith Babson, and Gretchen Kunigk on Mount Hood, March 20, 1938. Ten years later Gretchen, then Mrs. Don Fraser, won a gold medal in the 1948 Winter Olympics, the first American, man or woman, to do so. Al Monner photo.

30 Norway's Skier Prince

Crown Prince Olav of Norway at the microphone dedicating the new Magic Mile chairlift on Mount Hood, May 21, 1939. Princess Martha is at right front. Friends of Timberline photo.

I surely didn't plan to challenge Crown Prince Olav of Norway to a downhill ski race when he visited Timberline Lodge, but that's the way it turned out.

It was May 21, 1939, and the Crown Prince and Princess Martha were guests at Timberline, where the prince had agreed to dedicate the new Magic Mile chairlift. They were the first royalty to visit Portland since 1926, when Queen Marie of Rumania made her never-to-be-forgotten visit to dedicate the Maryhill Museum in the Columbia Gorge.

Oregon had a large population of first and second generation Norwegians who thought of Prince Olav as almost their king-to-be and who had responded enthusiastically to the royal visit. Both the *Oregonian* and *Oregon Journal* published special color sections welcoming them, and there were both official and informal receptions statewide.

Thousands drove to Timberline on a day of sunshine mixed with May snow showers to take part in the dedication and were pleasantly surprised by the warmth of the royal family as they mingled with onlookers. Princess Martha was a charming person who became a favorite of President Roosevelt after Norway was invaded by the Germans a year later, and she and the family often were White House guests. As I recall, two of the royal children, Prince Harald (later King Harald V) and Princess Ragnhald, were on hand too.

A CHAIRLIFT SANS CHAIR OR LIFT

While Sun Valley's chairlifts used wooden telephone poles for towers, in order to conquer Timberline's 20-foot-deep snows, the new lift had been heralded as the world's first to be built with fabricated steel towers. But when the crown prince strode toward the dedication site, nary a chair nor a cable was in view.

A year earlier the Forest Service had appropriated $100,000 to build a chairlift to help assure that Mount Hood would be awarded the 1939 national downhill ski championships. Winter had halted construction before a single tower could be raised. Concrete bases had been poured in the fall, so it was decided to position the bottom tower on its base and ask the prince to tighten up the bolts with a ceremonial wrench (only in America!).

The crown prince smiled wryly as he was handed a silver-plated oversized wrench with which he tightened a huge bolt, fastening steel to concrete and completing the ritual.

THE PRINCE SCHUSSES THE MILE

We knew that the prince was an accomplished ski jumper who had competed on the renowned Holmenkollen hill in Oslo, so we had skis ready for him and for his aide de camp, Major Nicole Ostgaard, president of the International Ski Federation, and for his

Crown Prince Olav (left), and his Mount Hood host, Boyd French Sr., President of Cascade Ski Club, ready for a ski run on slopes above Timberline Lodge. Photo courtesy of Margie French Simmons.

military aide, Captain Nils Raam.

The chairlift was still unfinished, so a Snowcat patterned after the original invented by WPA worker Ira Davidson was used to transport the royal party to the upper terminus of the new lift, a mile above Timberline.

Here is the news story of our ski run back down, which was carried on the front page of the May 22, 1939, *Oregon Journal*.

TIMBERLINE LODGE, MAY 22. − Sunday I skied with the crown prince. Not any ordinary crown prince, oh no! But the crown prince of skiing, and incidentally of Norway too. But after all, aren't the two nearly synonymous, at least to skiers?

Yes I skied with the crown prince, or rather after him, and let me say − if you ever try to get a story from the crown prince of Norway while skiing − you'd better take a couple of years to train or you'll report, 'He started. The snow behind his swishing skis (they're shees to him) was beautiful. Later I asked about the run.'

But not so your Journal Ski Scout. True the prince started schussing from where we were a half mile or so above Timberline Lodge and took us all by surprise. His aide de camp and his military aide who always are by his side were taken by surprise too and had he fallen there would have been neither aid nor aide to help him.

But after a couple of very superior sort of check turns by which your reporter hoped to impress somebody and at the same time to be on hand to see his royal highness mangle a snow bank, he began to realize that H. R. H. had no intention of checking or falling.

About the time your Ski Scout saw his cherished interview disappear over a gosh-awful cornice he figured it was time to put two ski tracks into one for the general purpose of sneaking up on royalty.

We had ridden up on the Snowcat and of course behind the conveyance was a long ribbon of well packed and slightly iced snow. So says your writer to himself, 'If Prince Olav gets away I might as well resign so why not borrow a little on the old

accident insurance and follow him?' So saying we stepped into the cat track. Whish! You skeptics on the sidelines can say what you want about May snow − I tell you it was way too fast for comfort because of that icy track.

I hereby officially take my ski cap off to Prince Olav of Norway. He has the spirit of a real ski racer. What was below Timberline he had no way of knowing but it was fun so why not take a chance? There you have Prince Olav. But it is no wonder that King Haakon of Norway has such grey hair! What papa wouldn't with such a daredevil, though grand, person as a son?

WITH A LITTLE BIT O' LUCK

The story of that high speed schuss might not have had so happy an ending, had it not been that when we skied off the cat track, the surface quickly changed to corn snow, which allowed a gentle finish.

I then realized that Prince Olav was a Nordic skier, competent in cross country and jumping but without experience in downhill racing. The speed of our schuss was comparable to that on a jumping hill inrun, and there was no way that he could have safely turned or checked in the icy cat track.

AN AWKWARD MOMENT

I was privately proud of Prince Olav the next day when he and Princess Martha arrived at the Broadway Theater for a formal reception by city, state and federal officials. The prince had been excited over our ski run the day before, and we had made another run together. I learned then what a down-to-earth person he really was.

So I was taken aback by the scene on the theater stage when I arrived at the reception that evening. The Broadway was an ornate movie house, decorated in Roaring Twenties style with its deep-carpeted foyer lined with high-backed red and gold upholstered chairs.

E.J. Griffith, head of the WPA, greets Crown Prince Olav of Norway and his wife, Crown Princess Martha, upon their arrival in Portland.

Portland theater impresario Ted Gamble had placed two of those throne-like chairs in the center of the stage, and in them were seated Crown Prince Olav and Princess Martha in evident discomfort.

As I accompanied a late-arrival to the stage, the crown prince broke the tension by calling out, "My skiing companion, what a sunburn!" and reached out to shake my hand.

TWENTY-SEVEN YEARS LATER

Twenty-seven years later – in 1966 – King Haakon VI had died and Crown Prince Olav had become King Olav V of Norway, and I decided it was time to try to renew our acquaintance. I was no longer a sports writer for the *Oregon Journal* but had become a vice president of the First National Bank of Oregon with plans for a business trip to Europe, so I

boldly cabled the king seeking an audience. To my delight there came a response from an aide that "His Majesty remembers with pleasure skiing at Timberline Lodge and commands you to come to the palace..." on the Friday I planned to be in Oslo.

Here are excerpts from a letter I wrote to my family February 13, 1966, reporting on the resulting trip to Sweden and Norway.

GREETING FROM KING OLAV

Dear Family

Well – on Friday I said 'Hello' to the King of Norway for all of you. I had made calls on correspondent banks that morning then returned to the hotel to pick up the gift I had brought for the king and took a taxi to the palace. It is located in a beautiful park-like setting on a gentle hill in the center of Oslo, but as it was well below zero with about four feet of snow everywhere, I could only see barren trees flanking the palace itself.

A few snappy soldiers guarded the entrance, but they didn't even ask my name or business as I went in. A butler met me at the front door and led up a great open stairway to the second floor where I was greeted by a brightly uniformed army colonel who is military aide to the king.

THE THRONE ROOM

The Colonel ushered me into the throne room and left me alone with the king who stood to extend a warm handshake.

He hasn't changed a great deal in the 27 years since his visit to Oregon – is a little heavier but still cordial, outgoing and inclined to quick, almost nervous chuckles. We talked Common Market, "England will surely join, but not for a year or a year-and-a-half, and when England joins, Norway must follow"he said.

We discussed Norwegian exports and he said that aluminum production, which in Norway is based on hydroelectric power, is the nation's principal export but of course that hasn't a market in Oregon. Handcrafted furniture, knitted goods, metal gift items and the like seem to have the most potential for trade between our two countries.

The king doesn't know just how Norway will continue to expand its exports after all of the hydroelectric potential has been developed.

(We just boarded the beautiful electric express train, which then glided in from the cold darkness. It is about 25 degrees below zero here at the moment so writing may soon get rough).

Back at the palace – I asked King Olav when he would visit America again, and his reply was like something out of Camelot. He said, "I don't know, really. I'd like to come again very much, and I'd like to see Oregon again for there are so many friends of Norway in Oregon. But it's hard to make plans very far ahead these days. You know, the King of Belgium was in Denmark recently and planned a longer stay, but his parliament just resigned and he had to rush home.

"You know, they are talking of abolishing the King in Sweden," he continued with a laugh to indicate that such a thing could never really happen. "The Social-Democrats are almost to lose power here in Norway, so I don't know just when I may be able to travel," he averred.

Then we talked skiing a little and I showed him a color photograph of the fine new double-chair ski lift which had replaced the single-chair lift he had dedicated a quarter-century before. He smilingly reminded me that there had been only a single tower in place at the time of his visit.

Then we talked about our children. He told me his "little boy" from 1939, Crown Prince Harald, is now about 40, and was just elected commodore of the Royal Norwegian Yacht Club. He said that is a great honor and goes only to excellent sailors and he felt that the crown prince had to be even better than most commodores in order to have the Norwegian sailors select him, for they wouldn't want anyone to think they'd played favorites.

'FROM YOUR FRIENDS IN OREGON'

I presented him with an Oregon thunder egg mounted on a myrtlewood base inscribed, "From Your Friends in Oregon." He agreed to sign an autograph for our family but said, "I only give my signature to friends; I never even sign letters."

Then we talked skiing a little and finally I got around to telling him about the leadership of our bank in financing international trade. He was surprised to learn that we have deposit and loan relationships with several Norwegian and Swedish banks, partly due to the substantial number of Norwegian Americans in the Pacific Northwest. He commented that the name of our president, Ralph Voss, is Norwegian.

By then I had been there a half-hour and King Olav hadn't indicated any impatience but as I left there were several others waiting in the anteroom. The audience ended in time for me to get to Kristiana Bank of Kreditasse for a real Norwegian smorgasbord lunch with smoked herring and aquavit with the bank's officers.

OSLO, NORWAY, TO LESJOEFORS, SWEDEN

Meanwhile Lars de Geer, a classmate at the Harvard Business School Advanced Management Program, had cabled me in London saying that he would send a car from his town in Sweden to pick me up in Oslo on Friday evening. It turned out to be a six hour drive from Oslo to Lesjoefors over narrow, icy roads, with the temperature colder than 30 degrees below zero. It was a Pontiac sedan and the Swedish driver was not accustomed to the American car so I drove halfway, which meant driving at night for two hours on the right side of the road then switching at the Swedish border to the left side. That change was the only indication of a border – no customs or immigration – easier than crossing the border from Oregon to California.

We arrived in Lesjoefors at nearly midnight but Lars was waiting up with cheese, dark bread, herring and beer. It was 42 degrees below zero when we arrived – the coldest day in the coldest winter in memory I was told.

Lars is a Swedish baron and his wife Birget is also of Swedish nobility. They own the whole darned town of four or five thousand population including a steel mill, wire rope plant, spring manufacturing plant and a sawmill. In their beautiful home up here in forested central north Sweden they have a formal dining room with walls lined with paintings of eleven generations of de Geers, the first of whom came to Lesjoefors in 1690 and started Sweden's steel industry.

Lars also has factories in Finland, Belgium, Peru and Africa. He even has a major contract for steel for San Francisco's new Bay Area Rapid Transit system.

BANDY AND A 40-MILE SKI RACE

On Saturday morning Lars rousted me out early to watch molten steel being poured at the mill then took me on a three-hour tour of woodlands and logging operations. It was 40 degrees below zero out in the woods but fortunately I had brought the same warm clothes that I wear on winter trips to Fairbanks, Alaska.

We had lunch with Lars' father, a former member of the Swedish Parliament, and with Torstin Tiniare, a sports writer who had come from Stockholm to cover a cross-country ski tournament and a bandy championship that were being held in Lesjoefors that weekend. I learned that bandy is a Scandinavian-Russian version of ice hockey played on an outdoor rink like a football field.

I was really impressed when Lars told me that he was entered in the 40-mile ski race on Sunday. We had skied together in Vermont during our time at the business school and he hadn't shown racing skill but cross country skiing was very different.

On Sunday he went to the race course early and the sportswriter and I followed with Birget in her cozy warm Cadillac. There were 400 starters of all ages and darned if they did not take off with the thermometer at 32 degrees below zero. We divided the day between standing in the cold watching Bandy matches and driving from point-to-point along the racecourse to assay Lars' progress. 'Our' Lesjoefors team beat Filipstad 7 to 2 and by golly, Lars won a prize. He finished in the top 25 percent, and he's not trained much this winter. Then back to the de Geers' authentic Swedish sauna to take away our chills. Lars seemed full of pep, all sauna-ed and dressed for a black tie dinner at the mansion.

We said good-bye there, and I'm riding on to Stockholm by train with Torstin Tinaire. We are due there at 11 PM, and the journalist, who is 77 and tells me that he has attended and reported every Olympic Games from 1908 to 1964, insists that I come home with him for wine and cheese, 'and see a real Stockholm home,' and meet his wife before I check in at the hotel tonight. I'll not be this way again soon, so of course I accepted.

A FIFTY-YEAR RECORD COLD

When I made my first call on Monday my Swedish banker host told me that it was the first time in many years that Stockholm harbor had frozen over. Love, George.

31 THE STORMY STORY OF HOOD'S SUMMIT SHELTERS

Veteran Mazama climber Don Onthank standing beside the storm-torn lookout on Mount Hood's summit on June 16, 1940. Don Onthank photo.

A QUARTER-CENTURY ON THE PEAK

It only took a Forest Service crew one day to remove the remnants of the ruined second floor cupola on the historic Mount Hood fire lookout on Sept. 16, 1940, but the lower floor clung so tenaciously to the mountaintop that it did not collapse until 1945.

The venerable landmark built in 1915 and 1916 by legendary mountain guide Elijah Coalman had survived sub-zero blizzards, raging winds and broiling sun for a quarter-century at the most exposed point in the state of Oregon. By the time it was abandoned in 1934, so much of the ground beneath it had eroded that two years later Ranger Harold Engles reported, "One-third of the foundation is resting on thin air."

By then more than 150 other lookouts

on lesser peaks were providing superior fire surveillance, but the old lookout had become such a haven for climbers that it was decided to replace it with a new kind of shelter designed by Forest Service engineers.

I was on the crew that Engles rounded up that August to tear down the old fire lookout and build the new climber's shelter. Plans called for an igloo-like edifice half-buried in the soft pumice soil with few windows, a round roof and a single wind-sheltered doorway. I do not remember how many climbers it was intended to accommodate.

THE ILL-FATED 1933 HOSTEL

That was the second time that the Forest Service had set out to build a climber's shelter on Mount Hood. Both attempts failed, thwarted by the mountain's unstable geology, inhospitable weather or the fortunes of war.

The first attempt to build a shelter had been in 1933, when construction was begun on an impressive hostel on a flat table of talus rock extending out from the base of Steel Cliff on the east side of the mountain's crater. The building was 30 by 27 feet, had bunks for 32 climbers, a kitchen and a 250-square-foot assembly room. In an article in the November 5, 1933, *Oregon Journal,* editor Fred H. McNeil reported, "The building's 2-foot-thick walls of basalt and concrete and its corrugated iron roof will be strong enough to resist the wildest storms that rage about the peak."

It was a disaster!

In winter the crater fills to overflowing with ice and snow except for areas near Crater Rock, where hot gasses from volcanic fumaroles keep the rock and earth warm year-around. In summer a lake usually forms in the crater, surrounded by a glacial moraine underlaid with permanent ice that is the beginning of White River Glacier. Rocks falling from Steel Cliff on the east bound right into the lake.

That lovely hostel, which was completed in 1934, barely survived two winters. In the first winter a heavy load of ice damaged the roof and ice and snow cracked the walls with constant freezing and thawing. It is also possible that boulder bombardments from Steel Cliff damaged the walls. By 1936 it was beyond repair.

1940 – THE BOLD NEW PLAN

The attempt to build a new shelter on the summit began in July 1940 with a crew assembled by the Forest Service regional

Harold Engles on Zigzag Mountain.

engineers. That crew had ample equipment but little experience working on glacial peaks, and after moving much of the building materials to the top of the Magic Mile chairlift, the logistics defeated them, and they suspended work. That was when Ranger Engles challenged our group of a dozen or more Mount Hood denizens, with years of experience on Mount Hood, to finish the job. The crew included Gary Leech, holder of the south side climbing route speed record; Ralph Day Jr., who had made the 80-mile ski trip down the Skyline Trail with me four years before; Boyd French Jr., a top downhill ski racer; and Jack Ferrell, a radio expert who had manned several remote summer lookouts. Others I remember were Edison Mills from Sandy, Lew Hayes, Fred Tolley, George Lasher and Tom Murphin.

I was the forest guard at Toll Gate near Zigzag, and Boyd French Jr. was the lookout at Lone Fir Rock a few hundred feet below Silcox Hut, which was at the top of the Magic Mile ski lift. One of our assignments was to climb the mountain regularly to maintain the "lifelines" – fixed safety ropes strung each season down the Chute on the south side climbing route and down Cooper Spur on the north side. Of course Boyd and I became part of that summit construction team, and Boyd's wife, Laurie, took over as lookout at Lone Fir.

HAROLD ENGLES, INDOMITABLE MOUNTAINEER

Harold Engles had come to the Mount Hood National Forest in 1936 from the Darrington Ranger District in Washington, where he was known as a man who never asked others to do a job that he wasn't willing to do himself. He had built lookout cabins on mountain crags where only skilled rock climbers had gone before and the stories of his strength and endurance were enhanced at Zigzag District Ranger, where he led midwinter searches for lost climbers and manned the starting gate near the top of White River Glacier for the 1939 national downhill ski championships. He took personal charge of the new summit project.

Boyd and his father had designed and built rope tows in the Ski Bowl, so Engles assigned him to devise a similar system to haul material up Mount Hood. A 10-year-old Ford car engine was converted into the equivalent of a lightweight logging donkey to power a high-line cable, and soon we had almost two tons of lumber moving into the crater.

Fourteen-foot-long 2-by-6-inch rafters were hard to fasten to the highline and often fell off halfway to the top of the relay, and someone would have to climb up or down and clear the line. Once after handling that chore, daredevil Gary Leech tied himself to the haul-back and insisted that Boyd use the engine to pull him back to the top of the relay. Although it was a hazardous stunt, Gary made it safely, and I copied his ride once while Boyd took my picture hanging from the line. The crew

George Henderson riding the high line used to haul building materials up Mount Hood.

then decided to carry the rest of the rafters up by hand. We made several climbs up those thousand vertical feet with one end of a 14-foot rafter on one man's shoulder and the other end on another's.

Packer Win Hull loaded tents, stoves, food and utensils on a string of pack mules and gentled them above the steep headwall of White River Glacier and into the crater, where we set up a base camp using the broken walls of the destroyed 1933 hostel as tent frames.

LIFE IN A VOLCANO'S CRATER

The crater soon looked like a circus, with lumber being high-lined from below, packer Hull riding his horse and leading the sure-footed mules across the glacier, part of our crew backpacking tools up the Chute, and others on top excavating for the shelter.

Most of us slept in the fire-crew-sized canvas tents, but Boyd had a special problem. His wife, Laurie, had no difficulty handling the lookout duties at Lone Fir, but she would not turn in for the night until she received a reassuring radio call from her husband in the crater. She was very firm about that, and unfortunately the radios of the day couldn't always overcome the high-mountain static, so more than once I watched Boyd pull on boots

and parka, step out of the warm tent and make his way 3,000 feet down to Lone Fir for the night then climb back in the early dawn. Often he was the only one of us who could coax the little ice-encrusted donkey engine to start each morning.

The circus had its fireworks too, particularly at night during the frequent thunderstorms, when it seemed as if we were in the midst of cloud-to-cloud lightning, and an eerie blue glow pulsated inside the tents.

SUCCESS ONLY A WEEK AWAY

By Sept. 16 all the construction material was in a cache near Crater Rock, and from there the loads were to be high-lined up the final 1,200 feet to the summit. Rigging that final lift was a feat in itself. The donkey engine had pulled itself into the crater beside the cache, but the quarter-inch steel high-line cable still had to be strung to the top by hand, threaded over a tripod and anchored to boulders beyond. Gary Leech had his heart set on making a ride from the crater to the summit when the rigging was done. (Note: Mount Hood summit registration books are archived in the library of the Mazamas, to whom I extend thanks for making the original pages available for review.)

Forest Service fire crew tents in the crater on the south side of Mount Hood. One of the tents was set up inside the remains of the Crater Rock Shelter. George Henderson photo courtesy of Oregon Historical Society, OrHi 88240.

SEPT. 16-22, 1940 – THE FINAL WEEK

On Monday morning, Sept. 16, I made a photo of Engles and several of the crew assembled in the crater beside the donkey engine before the highline to the summit was rigged. That picture is reproduced here along with a picture taken on the summit on Sept. 22 by an unidentified photographer showing the highline tripod in place and the cupola atop the lookout partially dismantled.

One of the crew members who signed the summit register Sept. 16 made the following entry: "Began to take down the old summit lookout cabin in preparation for construction of a new one."

With the excavation finished it would take only a few days to finish the new shelter, because the lumber was pre-cut and would be high-lined up in orderly bundles ready to be bolted together.

THE STORM THAT CHANGED MOUNT HOOD HISTORY

But that was not to be. The first major storm of the winter was imminent, and Ranger Engles regretfully decided to close down the job for that year. Here is the closing entry in the summit register that day.

"September 22, 1940. Pulled up cable for haul-back. Set up tripod for haul-back and anchored sky-line tripod. We have just finished pulling a 1/4 inch steel cable from the crater and the east ropes [lifelines], and now to hoist the south ropes. Frankly we feel pulled to pieces. We are nailing on the lookout's storm windows for the winter."

That crew of tough modern mountain men led by the indomitable Harold Engles had overcome countless mind-boggling odds, but when the weather turned dangerous, they had judiciously accepted defeat.

The following year was a frantic period of undeclared war climaxed on Dec. 7 by the Japanese attack on Pearl Harbor. There was no time for even a thought of the lonely lookout cabin, shorn of its cupola and clinging to the top of Mount Hood.

Engles was transferred back to Darrington, and construction was never resumed. When I last climbed the mountain 45 years later the overachieving little engine and hard-won cache of materials were still languishing in the crater, and in 2005 Zigzag forest ranger Bruce Haynes told me that they were there yet.

Summit shelter construction crew standing by donkey engine in Mount Hood Crater. Shown from left Ralph Day Jr., probably Fred Tolley, George Lasher, Gary Leech, Boyd French Jr., and Harold Engles. I made this photo on Monday morning Sept. 16, 1940. George Henderson photo courtesy of Harold Engles.

Forest Service crew on the summit of Mount Hood pulling up the haul-back cable, probably on Sept. 22, 1940. Photographer unknown. Photo courtesy of Harold Engles.

FEW CLIMBERS REACHED THE SUMMIT DURING WW II

The Mazamas' summit registers show only 580 signatures during all five years of World War II. By contrast, from 1,500 to 2,000 had signed the register each year during the 1930s.

After the war, on June 23, 1946, I volunteered on a Forest Service crew that packed a new 1,500-foot-long lifeline up the mountain. We strung it from near the big crevasse to the summit, providing a fixed rope for climbers as had been done each year before World War II. I do not recall seeing any vestige of the old lookout that day.

32   BONNEY BUTTE – 1942

HARD LUCK ERIC

"Hard Luck Eric" he was called.

Eric Gordon was the ranger on the Barlow District, with headquarters at Dufur, which is about as far east of Mount Hood as you could be and still be in the National Forest. He hated winter. At least, he hated the kind of winter that skiers loved. Winter to him meant fighting snow-laden winds and sub-zero temperatures in order to provide feed and water for the bands of sheep and herds of cattle and horses that ranged over the high desert that he was there to protect. Seldom was there a winter when nature did not visit upon the district at least one disaster, if not to the livestock then to the rolling acres of wheat, so other rangers had tagged him Hard Luck Eric.

Ranger Gordon did not like mountains either. But the Barlow District contained fine stands of yellow pine, and because mountains with lookouts on top provided the best fire detection, there were several on the district.

In November 1942 an unseasonable rain had laved the thirsty high desert, and most of the lookouts had been closed up for the winter. But Ranger Gordon knew how quickly a dry east wind could turn moist grassland and underbrush tinder-dry, so he had told the lookout on 5,600-foot-high Bonney Butte to leave the cabin open for a possible quick return if the weather cleared.

That was a hard-luck decision!

The rain soon turned to snow, making the road to the top of the butte hazardous. It was decided to delay sending anyone to close up the lookout until there was a break in the weather, but that break never came. Seen from a distance, the lookout with its shutters propped open seemed almost to be welcoming the storm and daring the wind to drive open its unprotected windows and door. There would be little chance of the Osborne Firefinder and related detection and communications equipment surviving six months of winter unprotected. Even the cabin and tool house, with its cache of firefighting equipment, were at risk.

Hard Luck Eric had another kind of problem; not a man on the Barlow District staff would admit to even owning a pair of

A Forest Service L-4 style fire lookout cabin with shutters open, similar to the cabin on Bonney Butte that had been left unattended in November 1942.

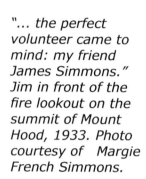

"... the perfect volunteer came to mind: my friend James Simmons." Jim in front of the fire lookout on the summit of Mount Hood, 1933. Photo courtesy of Margie French Simmons.

skis, much less to being capable of undertaking the lookout rescue mission. He decided to ask for help from Ranger Harold Engles on the neighboring Zigzag District.

(Note: There were virtually no female employees in Forest Service field posts 60 years ago, but that changed in the next 25 years. In 1975 my daughter Donna was the lookout on Flag Point on that same Barlow District. She was a qualified mountain climbing guide, and if a similar problem had arisen, then she would have been quite capable of resolving it.)

Harold Engles liked both snow and mountains and was sympathetic, but he wasn't

sure that he could help. Most of those from his staff who would have been capable of the task were in the military or committed to wartime jobs. Shortage of experienced manpower had even forced him to shut down work on the new climber's shelter being built on top of Mount Hood. Then Engles thought of me. I had enlisted in the Army Air Corps on Dec. 9 and was working for the Forest Service until I was called up for flight training. Engles estimated that two experienced skiers could do the job in three days, so he asked if I knew of anyone who might be willing to join me on a volunteer basis.

George Henderson on the south side of Mount Hood in 1939 with the type of gear he and Jim Simmons used to ski to the top of Bonney Butte in 1942. Friends of Timberline photo.

GOOD LUCK ERIC

Ranger Gordon's sobriquet should have been changed to Good Luck Eric right then, for the perfect volunteer came to mind: my friend James Simmons. He was a past president of the Mount Hood Ski Patrol, a Mazama and a member of the Forest Service Reserves. We had been skiing and climbing companions for many years. He had just enlisted in the Army Signal Corps and was to report for basic training at Camp Kohler that month and then go to Officers Candidate School.

The opportunity for a skiing adventure before leaving civilian life was irresistible, so Jim accepted my invitation.

A MIGHTY LONG DAY

It was mid-December, and a heavy storm was just tapering off, so we got ready in a hurry. Jim left his car in Zigzag and rode with Engles to where the snowbound loop highway joined Highway 26. I met them there and left my pickup. Engles then took us up Timberline Road to the big horseshoe bend where the road first overlooks White River Canyon, about three miles below the lodge.

We had planned to start at dawn, but after all that shuffling it was mid-morning before we donned skis, shouldered packs and skied boldly over the edge of the road grade – only to sink hip-deep into a snowdrift!

After breaking free and sliding and poling for two miles down the canyon in knee-deep powder, we reached the snow-choked highway bridge that provided the only way to cross rowdy White River. We must have wondered then whether the two or three miles we had saved by driving partway up Timberline Road had been worth it.

BEFORE MOUNT HOOD MEADOWS

The bulk of mile-high Bonney Butte rose before us, and we knew we must circle it and traverse Bennett Pass before climbing the peak's steep east face. From the bridge, three miles of steady climbing under a hot sun took us to the pass, where we arrived sweat-soaked in the early afternoon.

It would be 35 years before there would be a road from Bennett Pass to near Umbrella Falls where Mount Hood Meadows ski resort would be built.

A FIRE-RAVAGED LAND

Bonney Butte looked to be about five miles away. As we ate a quick lunch, a close look at the map showed that the route from the pass to the lookout wound for 10 miles though a starkly beautiful land of towering white snags thrusting through a 6-inch blanket of snow, where trees and underbrush had been burned down to mineral earth by an intense forest fire a few years before.

We made good time for several miles as the trail climbed from the 4,600-foot pass toward 5,400-foot-high Bonney Meadows, but then the sun dropped behind the butte, and the temperature plummeted toward zero. The snow began to freeze, and soon the skis were breaking through 6inches of hardening crust with every step, and in another mile the crust froze so hard that we seldom broke through. We realized then that we were in for trouble!

At Bonney Meadows the road forked, and the way to the top seemed to soar upward in the bright moonlight. In summer it would be a narrow shelf contoured along the butte's steep face, but it had drifted so full of snow that only a border of white snags outlined its course.

After being thawed by the afternoon sun, the snow had frozen, turning the hillside into a grotesquely tilted skating rink. We took off our skis and tried to kick steps in the crust, but it was so hard that we would have needed to wear crampons or cut steps with an ice axe in order to climb the slope in our boots, and we had neither.

Like most Mount Hood skiers we'd had lots of experience skiing on icy slopes, often carrying an injured skier on a toboggan, but never where the penalty for a fall could be so extreme. Once a person fell here he would slide until the slope flattened or he hit something. The hillside ended in piles of rocks and broken logs, so hitting something nasty was certain. Metal skis hadn't been invented yet, but our wooden skis had metal edges that allowed us to side-step up or side-slip down on the crust.

The lookout was still a steep mile ahead, so we could either continue on our skis or stay at Bonney Meadows and try to build a fire and bivouac in the open, hoping that a warm sun would allow us to reach the lookout the next day. We had no camping gear, because we had planned to spend both nights in the lookout.

STEEL EDGES AND STEELY NERVES

We held a chilly conference, but with Jim and me there really was no doubt about the decision; we'd been in tight spots together before. Jim led off, testing the grip of his edges on the ice, and as he gained confidence began pushing with his poles and sliding gently

The steep traverse on the way to Bonney Butte, circa 2000. In 1942 forest fires had denuded the area. When we crossed it on sheer ice we described it as "a grotesquely tilted ice rink." Cross country skiers in later years labeled it the "terrible traverse." Klindt Vielbig photo.

forward with each upward step. As I followed I saw that his skis left no mark on the ice. Then it was my turn to take the lead, and I stepped around him, careful that our heavy backpacks not touch and throw one of us off balance. I had been happier to follow, for then I kept my eyes only on his skis, but as trail maker I kept glancing down to our left and imagining the speed at which I would crash into the rocks below if I lost my footing.

After an hour of nerve-frazzling progress, we knew that we were nearing the lookout when the roadway made a turn at the edge of White River Canyon. I shudder still as I recall the 3,000-foot fall that would have resulted from a single slip of a steel edge there.

AGONY TO ECSTASY

A few minutes later we were expelling long-pent-up sighs of relief as we unstrapped our skis in front of the half-buried lookout cabin. There was a snowdrift 10 feet deep between it and the garage, but its windows seemed intact. Our Forest Service key opened the padlock, and with a hammer and pry bar from our packs we soon broke the door loose from its coating of ice.

Inside there were only a few ridges of snow extending across the floor from where the wind had found openings around the door. Before he left, the lookout had brought in an armload of dry wood and a bucket of now-frozen water, so we fired up the little stove. By the time the moon had set beyond White River, we were basking in the essentials of a good life: a sturdy shelter, hot tea, warm food and a warm glow from having succeeded in a difficult endeavor.

As we stoked the stove and slid into our sleeping bags, clothes and all, we must have shuddered to think what it would have been like to bivouac in the snow at Bonney Meadows.

Patching up the storm-battered lookout was a daunting task. It was almost 8 o'clock the next morning before the last bright stars were winked out by the predawn light and we could assess the damage. The telephone line had been broken somewhere along the way, so we had no way to report our arrival. All of the cabin's shutters were still attached by one or more of their hinges above the windows, but the shutter that should have covered the front entrance was nowhere in sight.

Before the lookout left he had covered the Osborne Firefinder with a canvas tarp that was still in place, so if we could close and secure the shutters, the most important detection and communications equipment should survive the winter. However the door to the nearby garage and tool shed stood open, with its cache of tools partly buried in snow.

ANOTHER WORRY FOR HARD LUCK ERIC

In a moment of compassion for Ranger Eric Gordon, I remembered that rangers were held personally responsible for such equipment until it was either worn out, broken or destroyed in a fire, and I wondered how he would account for the loss of fire tools if they were blown off a mile-high lookout in winter.

The hammer and pinch bar that we had brought would not go far in doing the restoration, so we used skis and our hands to dig out shovels, carpenter tools, hinges and nails. As we worked we warmed up quickly, and a glance at the thermometer hanging near the front door showed that the temperature was fast moving up toward the freezing mark.

One person can close up a lookout cabin unaided when all the hinges and latches are in working order, but it took us both just to lift some damaged shutters into position. Then one would hold the shutter with numbing hands while the other attempted to latch it with freezing fingers or, more often in this case, to spike it expediently to the frame.

We could not duplicate the missing shutter for the front entrance, but from a sheet of three-quarter-inch plywood in the garage, we made a one-time substitute and stored it inside the cabin for the night. By then the short seven hours of daylight was fading, so we dug the garage door clear of snow and closed it, brought in a supply of firewood, rationed our remaining food, and made ready for an early start home in the morning.

The cold snap had broken during the day, as the east wind gave way to a warm western front that would soften the crusted snow, thus assuring that we would be able to escape on skis from our icebound mountaintop aerie.

ANOTHER VERY LONG DAY

Twenty miles of skiing in uncertain weather lay ahead, so at dawn the next day we closed the door, snapped shut the padlock, nailed the makeshift shutter tight over the doorway, and threw the switch that grounded the telephone line to the cabin's heavy copper lightning protection system. Then we shouldered packs and pointed our skis back down the steep east face of Bonney Butte that had been so frightening two nights before.

There hadn't been any new snow since we arrived, so from Bonney Meadows to White River we did little trail-breaking, although the road grade was seldom steep enough to slide without poling. We crossed the bridge at noon and ate lunch on the go, for gusty winds and a darkening sky foretold another storm.

FIVE MISERABLE MILES

The final five miles turned out to be tough duty. Because we had begun the trip from partway up Timberline Road, the last stretch of the return trip from White River to Highway 26 where I had left my pickup was through 6-inch-deep unbroken snow. We were two very weary skiers when we reached the highway well after dark and drove to Government Camp to enjoy the luxury of dinner in front of the blazing fireplace at Battle Axe Inn.

I think that we both were a little let down by the casual manner in which rangers Engles and Gordon and our families received our enthusiastic reports on the expedition.

They had expected no less!

HAWAIIAN RENDEZVOUS

It was more than a year before Jim and I saw each other again. He was stationed at Hickam Field in Hawaii and was about to receive his captain's bars in the Army Signal Corps. Because my hopes of becoming a pilot in the Army Air Corps had been dashed, I had joined the Merchant Marine and made a trip to the South Pacific on an ammunition ship, then taken a crash course in radio engineering and Morse code and become chief radio Officer on a tanker carrying aviation gasoline from California to Pearl Harbor.

We had rendezvoused at the Royal Hawaiian Hotel on sun-drenched Waikiki Beach, and as he drank fresh pineapple juice and I sipped Scotch whiskey, we swapped stories about the disparate turns our lives had taken since that frigid ski trip to Bonney Butte.

It was a brief reunion, for it doesn't take long for a tanker to pump out its cargo, but on that trip and two more on the same ship, S/T Battle Rock, I carried bundles of mail between Jim and his wife, Margie, that otherwise would have taken a month or more each way. Although I could never be sure of the ship's next port, Margie guessed it right on my last trip to Hawaii and baked a chocolate cake for Jim, which I delivered to him at his barracks.

Scotch whiskey was hardly available at any price in the States then, but although Jim was a non-drinker he was eligible to buy a bottle of liquor a week at the Officers PX, so in turn he presented me with a prized farewell gift – a fifth of Scotland's best!

Ernie Pyle. Oregon Historical Society photo, OrHi 105575

33 ERNIE PYLE LEARNS TO SKI – 1942

Ernie Pyle was the most widely read U.S. war correspondent in World War II. His daily column appeared in about 200 newspapers in the United States in 1942, including the *Oregon Journal*, sometimes appearing beside my weekly "Ski Scout" column. Estimates put the number of people who read his articles at 14 million. I was therefore awestruck one day in February 1942 to receive a phone call from the writer himself.

Could this be the same Ernie Pyle whose dispatches written in London air raid shelters during the Battle of Britain in 1940 had conveyed so poignantly the meaning of all-out war? Indeed it was the same writer, but he had shifted back from war reporter to his traditional role of whimsical observer of everyday Americans at work and play.

To my surprise, he wanted to write a lighthearted story about learning to ski at Timberline Lodge and asked me to make the arrangements. Of course I could not turn down an opportunity to bring the lodge to the attention of 14 million Americans – it was my job – but the timing surprised me, since just two months earlier the Japanese had bombed Pearl Harbor, and America had gone to war. He wanted to come to Portland in a few days, and I agreed to meet for lunch at the Congress Hotel and then drive him to Timberline for a week of ski lessons.

On the phone I did not mention that I had recently broken my ankle for the second time while scouting a new ski area at Spout Springs in the Blue Mountains near Walla Walla and that I was in a walking cast. Here is how he reported our meeting in his column "Traveling," also known as "The Roving Reporter."

PORTLAND, Ore. [Feb. 3, 1942]: Let it be known that henceforth – at least for a week or ten days – the author of this column shall be referred to as Ernst Otto Sven Pyle, familiarly called 'Swish' by his intimates.

No, I am not turning Quisling or Nazi spy. It's just that for an interlude my talents will be devoted to the slipping and sliding pastime of skiing, so, of course, I must have an Old World name. The 'Swish' refers to my here-he-comes-there-he-goes aspect (I hope).

I have been planning this winter sports spasm for three years – and managing to sneak out of it every year before this. You know me: I'm a tropical beachcomber at heart. I like to be hot, and to heck with the tang and exhilaration of frosty mornings and snowy slopes. But this winter I got trapped. The Japs cut me off from my idyllic winter among the Balinese maidens.

I'd never had on a pair of skis in my life. Now that the time is nigh, putting on skis is the one thing in this world I do not wish to do.

But the Timberline Lodge people saw that I was cornered, and threw their hooks into me. It was come up and ski, or else. My ski debut was all set for two weeks ago, on my way north. They almost got me then. But at the last minute I phoned and said I had to see about a bomber in Seattle right quick. It was a close shave.

I thought of going back south by way of Kansas City and El Paso, in what could be called a wide arc around Mt. Hood. But that would have taken too much rubber off my last set of tires. And I figured they'd catch me sooner or later, anyway, so maybe I might as well ski before my bones got even more brittle.

So I drove back through Portland. I stopped there for a last deep breath. For two days I've been down in Portland (ah, sweet Portland, only 65 miles away!) trying to muster up the courage to come up here and face my Armageddon.

JAPS DIVE BOMBING ON SKIS

The thing actually became a horror to me. Last night I had nightmares of Japs ... diving out of the skies at me - not in planes, but on skis. I saw the thing was getting out of control. I knew it was now, or the booby hatch for me. So here I am.

I have not yet been on skis. I'm working into it gradually. Until yesterday noon, my fear was largely devoted to the prospect of people laughing at me. But now I have a tangible fear.

For yesterday noon George Henderson came in to my hotel in Portland to have lunch with me. Mr. Henderson is connected with Timberline Lodge in a promotion way. Mr. Henderson is a young and handsome man of the athletic type, and one of Oregon's better skiers himself. And Mr. Henderson arrived at my door – get this straight, mind you – Mr. Henderson arrived at my door with his left leg in a cast. Yes, he broke it skiing!

It was the second break in two years for Mr. Henderson's leg. He seemed to think nothing of it at all. He says practically everybody who skis has broken a leg.

Mr. Henderson's arrival was my first contact in a long, full and pleasant life with anybody who had ever been on skis. It was my initiation to the true skier's attitude toward the subject of life and limb. So sorry to have met you, Mr. Henderson. Drop in again after your next break. Or perhaps we'll see each other in the morgue. Good-bye Mr. Henderson.

Tomorrow at 10, I face my doom.

On the following day at Timberline he met his "doom" in the form of Swiss-born Martin Fopp and Norwegian native Olaf Rodegard – champion racers who headed the Timberline ski school in 1942. They must have been daunting figures as he stood with skis and poles gathered in his arms awaiting his first ski lesson. But his irrepressible humor showed through in the columns he wrote for the next week. He also accurately described what it was like for a raw beginner to learn how to ski.

SECOND DAY...

TIMBERLINE LODGE, Ore., Feb. 5, [1942] – The second day on skis – that takes will power for a man with muscles as soft as mine. This morning I tried to think where I might have been yesterday. My impression was that I had been lynched. I felt exactly as if I had been beaten to death with sticks, stones and a blunt instrument. If I'd had sense I'd simply have built a big fire in the fireplace in my room, put on house slippers and settled my sobbing tendons deep into a couple of pillows for a good forenoon of groaning.

But no! I've taken this stuff to heart about France going soft and England going decadent and Americans getting so mechanically dependent that a fellow can't tie his own shoe.

I have to gird up my reluctant sinews and charge out there to the hillside again and plug around on those damn clapboards just to help restore the old tradition that America is peopled by stalwart and hardy men.

There's no use going into detail about today's skiing. It was ... a bad imitation of yesterday's awkwardness. It can be told briefly as follows:

1. I got my ski pole caught in the snow, ran my left leg into it, took off about three inches of skin, and the blood was ... soaking through my pants.

2. To avoid running into a woman, I sat down real quick and twisted my left ankle so badly it made me feel sick and I had to sit there awhile.

3. Another time, and for no purpose I've been able to figure out, I suddenly sat down with great force and determination right on the back of my ski. Skis are not soft like snow. The exact point of my anatomy which came into contact with the

Champion racer Olaf Rodegard, Ernie Pyle's instructor and co-director of Timberline ski school in 1942. Ralph Gifford photo courtesy of Mount Hood Museum and Cultural Center.

ski is not usually mentioned in polite society. But whatever you wish to call it, it was destroyed all to pieces, as the Japs say. I'm sure it's much worse than George Henderson's leg. He can at least limp.

Despite these temporary setbacks, I am learning a great deal about skiing. Not learning how to do anything, of course, but learning a lot of little facts you could put in an encyclopedia. For instance:

Even though the day is cold, you actually do keep warm skiing, and you don't have to bundle up much. If I say that, you know it's true, for I'm the coldest man on earth.

Skiing is mighty hard work. Another novice plodding up a hill, steaming and grunting, said, "If we were doing this for wages, we'd quit."

ONLY TEACHERS STAY UPRIGHT

Falling down is nothing to be ashamed of. Everybody falls down. I think the only people up here who don't spend an important portion of their day flat on the snow are the teachers.

Skis are the awkwardest things. Mine are six and a half feet long, and I'm convinced five feet of them are superfluous and an impediment to the usual fine grace of my movements.

The main trouble with trying to learn to ski when you've reached my palsied status in life is that you just can't relax and throw yourself around. I'm all rigid as a bar of steel when I start down a slope. The way to ski is to float like a flag in the wind.

AN OLD MAN AT FIVE

Another trouble is that my joints are too stiff. They've always been stiff. I couldn't run fast or turn handsprings as a boy. I was an old man at 5.

In skiing you have to twist your legs and your body and frequently spraddle out like a ballroom dancer. Why, today I had my legs stretched out so wide I couldn't even see my feet, and Olaf kept yelling, "Wider! Wider!" If I had got any wider you would have heard a ripping noise and all Pyle would have been divided into two parts.

But what balls me up worst is that in skiing you must balance yourself just the reverse of what instinct tells you. You must lean toward the OUTSIDE of a turn, instead of toward the inside, as on skates or a bicycle.

I've been trying to tell Olaf this is all wrong, but he's stubborn, and I can't seem to teach him anything. I've even given him numerous personal demonstrations, proving that no matter which way you lean on a turn you fall down. But he just shakes his head.

So tomorrow I'm going to let the other skiers fall where they may, and I'm going to ride up on the ski-lift and have a look over the country. My skis, however, will remain right down in the locker room, where they'll be safe.

TIMBERLINE LODGE, Ore. [Feb. 7] – It would be hard to visualize, to a Floridian for instance, how deep the snow is up here. It's even hard to believe it yourself. For when we ski out through the trees to our practice slope, the snow is hard on top and you imagine it's just a few inches deep, since it follows the contour of the ground.

Yet this snow we daily cross is more than six feet deep. And that's shallower than the average depth. Usually it is 10 feet or more.

You stand beside what apparently is a small bush, not as high as your waist, and actually it is a tree much higher than your head. Most of it is down under the snow.

It gets down to zero up here. But during my visit, it has been only a little below freezing. The sun has been bright and the far-off mountain panorama magnificent – although you wouldn't dare mention that in print on the day it happened, because of censorship.

I have a green-eyed jealousy of the people who are capable of going up on the ski lift and skiing back down. That would be an accomplishment. But it's something that will not happen to me this trip. I can't even grapple with our little 50-foot practice slope. And it's actually about two miles down the Magic Mile...

On weekends they keep a doctor up here, and the ski patrol is on the prowl constantly. With 2,500 people skiing all over the place, a good portion of them novices, somebody is bound to get hurt. And somebody always does. The ski patrol brings them in on stretchers.

SAFE ENOUGH FOR GRANDPA

But perhaps I'm scaring you. I would feel practically criminal if I deterred anybody from this exhilarating sport.

Skiing is indeed insidious the way it gets into people's blood. Practically everybody who works around this great lodge either can ski or is learning. They're not all young, either.

The hotel manager skis, the bus driver skis, the waitresses ski, the busboys ski, the clerks in the ski-shop ski, the forest rangers ski. Even Jack Ferrell, who is in charge at the top of the ski-lift, skis all the way down from work every evening, instead of riding the chairs down. And the instructors actually ski for fun in their off-hours.

The lodge ran out of guest stationery this evening, so I went around the public writing desks trying to gather up a few scraps to write on.

At one desk I found two sheets, on which some young man had been trying to start a letter home. He apparently just gave up and left his efforts there. Here is what he left:

Dear Folks. Dear Mom Pop ... Rah! Benson! ... Mt. Hood National for ... Dear Folks, Po ... Popin ... I sure am stove in, in answering you I really ... Dear Folks ... There'll always be an Eng...

Apparently, he just collapsed at that point, from being so stove in. I know just how he felt. I'm stove in too. Dear Folks. Dear England. Dear Timberline. Dear Popin. Dear Me.

TIMBERLINE LODGE, Ore. Feb. 8 – Skiing is hard work. The altitude is high and exercise violent. You use a great many muscles you never knew you had. Long-unused muscles get mighty sore.

"Perhaps I'm scaring you." Evertt Darr and Ralph Weise of the Mount Hood Ski Patrol bringing in an accident victim at Timberline about 1940. Al Monner photo.

Skiing consists about as much in being in good condition as it does in skill. My skill at the present writing is hidden under some obscure bushel.

So you can imagine what a pitiful, broken thing all this violent skiing exercise has made of me. Even standing real still in the lobby the first few days was a bodily agony.

FINALLY THE ACHES ABATE

But fortunately I kept right at it and didn't let my tortured muscles get "set." I kept them working. And now at last I'm beginning to get conditioned. Finally the aches have begun to abate; my wobbly ankles have strength in them now; I throb with such new inner energy that I stand before a mirror and twitch my arms, admiring myself.

A soft fellow really does begin to feel strong after a few days of this. Skiing would add years to the health of any office-sitter. I'm aware again that I've got something in my wrists and shoulders besides soup. Even my shiny scalp feels muscular.

You see some of the oddest skiing outfits up here. As in golf, the swankiest outfits usually don't belong to the best skiers. You can ski in almost anything. This morning I saw one boy (a good one, too) skiing around .. in a grotesquely long overcoat. And a girl skiing in shorts, her legs bare.

But I was anxious to get sunburned, for I've lost all my good New Mexico cowboy color. So I skied with my sock-cap pushed way back on my head, in order to get lots of sun. And so far I haven't burned even faintly. I still look like a hothouse flower.

"We're still out on that same little slope, still trying to ... make stem turns." A ski class, March 1939. Ralph Gifford photo courtesy of the Mount Hood Museum and Cultural Center.

TIMBERLINE LODGE, Ore., Feb. 10. – These last few days, while dwelling on other things, we've somehow neglected my personal skiing. I mean neglected it in this column. But I've been right out there every day, laboring conscientiously.

The days are building up now, and it'll soon be time to leave. And so far I haven't learned how to do a thing. We're still out on that same little slope, still trying to find out how to make 'stem turns.'

I still can't force myself to lean OUT on a turn – and when I do accomplish that violation of scientific balance I always fall on over in that direction. I still get the tips of my skis crossed, which is comparable to having no legs at all. I still find my ankles so weak I can't hold the skis out in a turn. I still get to going in the wrong direction and have to sit down quick to keep from running into somebody.

HE'S NEVER 'OUT'

Maybe I could learn some day. I'm not sure. Certainly I can't be accused of not persevering. I'm known around here as the guy who's always down but never out.

One of the girls in our threesome class disappeared, leaving only one girl and myself. We are both tenacious students. We always show up at class time, to plague Olaf with our ineptitudes, and we even stay out and practice after he's gone.

For days I didn't know this girl's name, or where she was from, or anything about her. Finally it occurred to me that maybe I should get her identified, just in case of accident or something.

So after rolling down the same hill together for several days, we at last met in the Lodge, shook hands, and introduced ourselves. Her name was Maureen Jackman. Mine was Ernst Otto Sve – oh to hell with that, you know my name.

Maureen is from Spokane. She's just a kid. She went one year to college, and then got a job as telephone operator in Spokane last summer. She loves to telephone-operate.

She got a week's vacation after six months.

Maureen says she's sore from head to foot from her falling down bruises. But being young, her muscles don't bother her a bit. It's the opposite with me. My hide is wrinkled and tough and I don't bruise easily. But oh those tendons of mine. Ouch!

Maureen has never before been away from home on a big trip. She doesn't know beans about traveling, so that gives me a chance to show off and help her out with little things —such as telling her how much to tip, and that there are cabs in other cities besides Spokane, and that New Mexico is in the United States. I don't think she believed it, though, when I said I'd been in England.

In a way, I feel badly about Maureen's vacation. It has always been my assumption that girls who spend their hard-earned money for ... a jaunt to the ski-bowls, did it in a kind of romantic hopefulness. But there are no detached young men at Timberline just now. In fact the paucity of Greek gods is so extreme that Maureen has had to wind up her first big worldly vacation with an old goat like me as her only social companion. I can't dance, sing, swim, ski, skate, carry on a conversation or tolerate moonlight. I'm not even rich. I don't see how Maureen can bear it.

HAPPY AS A LARK

Yet she seems happy as a lark, intrigued with everything that happens, profoundly serious about her skiing, and wonderfully glad she came.

The other instructor took us on for a while this afternoon, to give poor Olaf a little respite from his ordeal. This other one is named Martin Fopp. He is a Swiss, and he's a noted racing skier. He and Olaf both speak perfect English and are very nice people. [Note: A few weeks later I took Martin Fopp to Yosemite to race in the U.S. Nationals and he won first place in the Downhill.]

Both Olaf and Martin are small men. They say short people make the best skiers. Olaf has already been in the Army, but was let out because he was over 28. He's expecting his recall any day now. He'll be in the Ski Troops when he re-enters.

A great many Oregon skiers have gone into the Ski Troops. Practically any good skier can get into the outfit, they tell me. If you're of draft age and not bad on skis, the way to go about it is to have your local ski club write to the National Ski Patrol in New York City recommending you. The Army has given the Ski Patrol the job of attesting to the ability of ski volunteers.

TIMBERLINE LODGE, Ore., Feb. 10, – There is one trouble with learning to ski, as far as writing about it is concerned. That's the fact that your mood changes so often. When I came up here I thought I'd just clown through the whole thing, make only a half-hearted attempt at skiing, and try to be funny about it in the column.

SKIING NOT FUNNY – BUT FUN

But it really isn't funny at all. You get very serious about it, and all of a sudden.

After that you go through a whole cycle of determination, elation and disgust. After you've been doing fairly well for a couple of days, the beginner usually has a bad relapse. Everything goes wrong.

Right there's the critical time. A great gloomy disinterest in skiing comes over you. You get cynical. Most people of my character quit right there.

That's where I was this morning. I hadn't even put on my ski clothes when some friends arrived from Portland at noon and found me sitting before the fireplace.

"How do you like skiing?" they shouted.

"I think it is asinine," I said. "You go ahead and ski, and I'll be packed and ready when you come in."

"Oh, no," they said: "you're going up the ski lift with us and ski down the Magic Mile."

"DON'T BE INSANE"

"Me ski down the Magic Mile?" I said. "Don't be insane."

But they insisted and so we rode the lift to the top. One of our friends took off. Then the other. Then the others. That left me all alone. Again came that terrible panicky feeling. But I gave a shove. My last bridge was burned.

I guess that first straight run must have been 50 yards, and at the bottom you either had to turn or smack into a hillside. So do you know what I did? I turned! And me a guy who can't make turns. It was several seconds before I realized what I'd

"Me ski down the Magic Mile? ... Don't be insane." Jack Ferrell unloading a skier arriving at the top of the Magic Mile chairlift in 1940.

done. It was a queer feeling.

We worked down the mountain slowly. Suddenly we looked at our watches, and saw that it was almost time to leave for Portland. The veteran of our party said that it was still half a mile to the bottom.

And with that he dug in his ski-poles, gave himself a push, and shot straight down the mountain. We had to follow.

It was that last half mile which finally made a rabid, raving ski enthusiast out of me. For I personally skied that last half mile without stopping and without falling down; skied all the turns, and made them with passable grace; hurdled small ice ridges without losing my balance; finally felt the magnificent rush and rhythm of the thing.

We dashed up to our rooms to change clothes. My friends waited for me in the lounge. I didn't appear and finally they came to my room.

They found me on the floor, fainted dead away. In my hand was clutched a folder which I'd picked up while dressing. It described the various ski runs

at Timberline. And under the heading "Magic Mile" was the following warning:

"A 20 per cent grade. For intermediate and expert skiers only!"

A TREMENDOUS TRIBUTE

Following his exuberant run down the Magic Mile Ernie Pyle concluded his Mount Hood reports with this column.

PORTLAND, Ore. [February 12, 1942]: The skiing is over, and I'm sorry. For now I'm nuts about it. The whole 'feeling' of the thing came all of a sudden, just as they said it would.

You stumble along for days, getting more and more discouraged, and then like a flash, comes that marvelous feeling of release.

The skis, instead of being shackles, suddenly become something to help you and speed you along. I think this week has taught me a few things more than just how to stand up on skis.

I've discovered, for one thing, what a completely exerciseless life I ordinarily lead. Why, after the agonies of sore muscles had finally worn off, I felt better than I'd felt in years.

I learned also that you can do things when you're face to face with the necessity for doing them. For instance, the instructors said I undoubtedly learned more about skiing in that one trip down the mountain yesterday than I would have in two months of practicing on our safe little slope. That's because you can do things when you have to.

But I'm not sure that should be set up as a standard theory of life. For instance, if you couldn't play the piano, yet HAD to sit down and play the piano in order to save your life, could you do it? Of course you couldn't. Well, it was a good theory while it lasted, anyway.

But most important of all the things I learned is that a person works hardest, fights best, plays more gaily, even is braver, when he has companionship.

In the last two years – due to the urgencies of war living and the illness of That Girl and some other things – I have learned what it is to be alone. I have at last come to know the terror of being afraid by yourself – either in the vain little torture of embarrassment, or in the gigantic fright of thinking you are about to die.

NO MAN CAN STAND ABSOLUTELY ALONE

Today, at last, I know that no man except a freak is able to stand absolutely alone. I know that if I am to be bombed to death, I want somebody with me. If I am rollicking in the snow, it is no fun at all unless some friend is beside me to fall down with me grotesquely so that the two of us can laugh together.

My odd skiing interlude was saved by the arrival of two people I knew and could be natural with – E.J. Griffith, who is administrator of WPA for Oregon, and Mrs. Dexter Keezer, whom I have known for half my lifetime. With them beside me, I finally relaxed and laughed and threw myself around – because it was fun to ski with friends.

This Anne Keezer is quite a fellow. Her husband is president of Reed College out here and has just been given an important job in Washington …

Annie Keezer is a whirlwind of animation, exaggeration and headlongism. She sews and knits and skates and skis and rides and reads and entertains and takes charge of things all over the place, because she has to let her spirit out into something. The best yarn that ever happened isn't half as good as when Anne finishes telling it.

All of which is just a build-up to what happened on our final afternoon of skiing. We were plunging down Timberline's famous "Magic Mile." Anne was skiing ahead of us, turning and exploring the white mist of falling snow.

And suddenly Anne disappeared, as though she vanished into thin air.

What happened was that Annie had simply skied right over a 20-foot precipice. She flew a vast distance through the air, lit on her head, and wasn't hurt at all. She said she had no sensation of falling, and when she got her head out of the snowdrift couldn't think where she was.

I'm disgusted that I can't stay around to hear Annie tell it to other people. I'll bet by the tenth telling she will have fallen half a mile, broken her back and discovered gold in the snowdrift. Annie is wonderful.

WAS PYLE ALSO CAMPAIGNING FOR E.J. GRIFITH?

There is one question about Ernie Pyle that still perplexes me after 63 years. Had Pyle timed his visit to Oregon so that it might assist his good friend E.J. Griffith in his campaign for the U.S. Congress?

I was Griffith's press agent for that campaign. I knew that a key ingredient was to point out to voters his success in battling the Depression through jobs created by the WPA.

In his Feb. 13 column Ernie Pyle writes that he spent an additional week in Oregon writing stories about the WPA Art project.

PORTLAND, Ore., Feb. 12 – Since the WPA has always captivated me as a phenomenon, a social force, a doer of good deeds, and a possible haven for myself in some future private storm, I dropped around today to see what the WPA was doing for its country now.

Or more specifically, to see what the Art Project under WPA was doing. For I have been curious about how sculpture and hand-weaving and murals could help save America from the Japs.

Well, they're helping all right. The Art Project of Oregon's WPA is hard at work on defense. In fact it's doing nothing else. It isn't making shells or planes – but it's making the men happy who shoot the shells and pilot the planes.

The Art Project, you might say, has gone into the business of making life bearable for some of our armed forces. At the moment it is head over heels furnishing and decorating the new Tongue Point Naval Air Station.

The Art Project has made the furniture for all the public and many of the private rooms –280 pieces, chairs, tables, beds, lamps, ash trays, even a crap table.

Oregon's art project is unique. No other state has put its art craftsmanship to such practical use. They've really created a renaissance out here.

The Art Project fished out carpenters from the WPA rolls, and made delicate cabinetmakers out of them. It took foundry workers and trained them into ironwork-Cellinis. It took guys like me whose fingers were all thumbs, and made fine upholsterers of them. It took ordinary housewives and set them to weaving unusual drapes...

BUILT AND FURNISHED TIMBERLINE LODGE

Then with all this newly developed talent it started making things that were both useful and beautiful. It built and completely furnished Timberline Lodge. It decorated the University of Oregon's medical school.

It is just winding up a magnificently beautiful job of refurnishing the Governor's mansion at

Juneau, Alaska.

Five years ago it had to ... beg for projects to work on. Today it is so flooded with requests that it has a hard time choosing which to do.

If the war goes on long enough, the Art Project visualizes the day when it will fold up altogether because there'll no longer be anybody to do the work – everybody will be in actual defense work. That would be a fitting climax to a job spectacularly well done. [Note: E.J. Griffith narrowly lost the Democratic primary race in April. See the next chapter for more on my involvement.]

1944 – ERNIE PYLE AWARDED PULITZER PRIZE

Ernie Pyle's often lighthearted and always sensitive reporting style belied his traumatic personal life. Upon his return from reporting the Battle of Britain in 1940, his wife and travel companion was suffering from mental illness, and he withdrew temporarily from reporting on the war.

That was when we knew him at Timberline Lodge, but soon afterward he returned overseas, took part in the Allied invasions of North Africa and Italy, and won the Pulitzer prize "for distinguished war correspondence in the year 1943." He then covered the Allied landings on Normandy. His last assignment was the Battle of Okinawa – the bloodiest campaign in the South Pacific.

When I read that Ernie Pyle was killed by a Japanese machine gun bullet on the small island of LeShema near Okinawa on April 17, 1945, I recalled a paragraph he had written on Feb. 12, 1942 commenting on his week at Mount Hood learning to ski at Timberline.

"The most important thing I learned was that a person works hardest, fights best, plays more gaily, even is braver, when he has companionship. I know that if I am to be bombed to death, I want someone with me."

Ernie Pyle died in the company of his beloved infantrymen.

34 LONELY ON THE MOUNTAIN

The start of all-out war between Japan and the United States. Pearl Harbor with the battleships West Virginia and Tennessee engulfed in smoke, Dec. 7, 1941. U.S. Navy photo.

TIMBERLINE LODGE JUST BARELY SURVIVED WORLD WAR II

When Japanese bombers shredded America's Pacific Fleet in Pearl Harbor on Dec. 7, 1941, they also shredded Timberline Lodge's expectations for its greatest ever season.

A HEARTRENDING HOMECOMING

I returned from a six-week Eastern sales trip on Dec. 6 bursting with enthusiasm; the ski season was well under way, Timberline was sold out for the Christmas and New Years holidays, and the Portland Day trail race would soon kick off the racing season, but when I awoke the next morning the radio was reporting that the Japanese were bombing Pearl Harbor.

Timberline's business momentum had been building steadily in the four years since President Roosevelt dedicated the lodge. The glamour of the Olympic tryouts and the stunning success of the nationwide goodwill campaigns by the Winter Sports Carnival royal courts had kept Mount Hood in the public eye and attracted visits by artists, writers and foreign dignitaries.

Norway's Crown Prince Olav had inaugurated the Magic Mile, Sir Arnold Lunn, inventor of slalom racing, had sanctioned the Far West Kandahar ski classic while at Timberline, and renowned Austrian ski instructor Otto Lang had established one of the first American Hannes Schneider ski schools at Timberline.

Journal editor Fred McNeil chronicled that progress on Dec. 20, 1942.

VANDYKE NAMED MANAGER

Fred VanDyke, Portland business man of Swiss birth and background who had been a winter sports leader for years, was installed as manager in the autumn of 1940 and his first large endeavor was to launch an intensive campaign for business. George M. Henderson, young sportsman, became [was] promotion manager and his extended trips through Eastern and Central states put the lodge on the maps of the national travel agencies. Bookings of large parties from such centers as New York, Boston and Chicago were listed for the first time, and the summer of 1941 saw the enterprise well out of the 'red.'

The Forest Service meanwhile had added the [mile-high] mile-long chairlift, extending up the mountain to the 7,000-foot level. Intended primarily for the convenience of 'down hilling' skiers, it became even more popular with summer tourists, and receipts from this were greater because of more midweek business in the warm months, than from the big weekends with the skiers.

Back East again last fall [1941] the story of the resort and of Mount Hood in winter and summer was told hundreds of times in scores of cities with the outstanding motion pictures that Henderson had spent almost a year in taking. Results were almost immediate. Bookings that would have utilized the hostelry's capacity for the entire summer of 1942 were made. The lodge at last went on the 'big-time' travel circuit.

SUDDENLY A WORLD AT WAR

But suddenly that hard-won reputation lost its meaning when America was plunged into the savage two-front war. Gasoline and tires were rationed, hotel staffs were fragmented by calls to military service, some resorts were taken over by the armed services, some closed for the war's duration, and still others refitted their ballrooms and public spaces into low-priced dormitories.

Timberline Lodge stayed open for the 1941-42 season then closed "for the duration" on Sept. 8, and the Forest Service suspended the operating permit with the understanding that it would be taken up again within six months after peace was declared.

E.J. GRIFFITH FOR CONGRESS

I was living at Timberline Lodge and expected to continue my job there until the end of the 1941-42 season, but in February, manager VanDyke called me in to tell me that former WPA Administrator E.J. Griffith was going to run for the United States Congress and wanted me to be his publicity director. He asked VanDyke if Timberline would give me a leave of absence. Of course Timberline acquiesced, and I savored the challenge.

It was my first and last political campaign and a real education. E.J. Griffith would have been a fine U.S. representative, and I did my best to help him get elected, but Oregon politics were brutal in those New Deal days, and the urbane, soft-spoken ex-WPA administrator was outclassed in the infighting.

A MISTAKEN POLITICAL STRATEGY

It should have been an easy win, but we lost the election, not from lack of publicity but from a miscalculation in strategy. Griffith was running against Tom Mahoney in the May 15, 1942, primary election for the Democratic

Congressional candidate E.J. Griffith (right), former Oregon WPA administrator, is greeted by Democratic National Committeeman Oscar Ewing at campaign luncheon in April 1942. Oregon Historical Society photo, CN 010923

nomination for Congress from the 3rd District, a seat held by Republican Homer Angel.

Griffith's name was synonymous with WPA, and there was scarcely a voter who hadn't benefited in the past several years from some project for which he had been responsible. But he was so confident of winning the primary that he ignored fellow Democrat Mahoney, his competitor for the nomination, and campaigned mostly on his qualifications to beat the incumbent Angel in the November general election.

Our campaign's newspaper and radio coverage was exceptional. America had been in the war for only three months, and the country was ill-prepared for an armed invasion of the Pacific Coast which many considered imminent. War and defense news claimed the headlines, but I succeeded in finding a war angle

for almost every story without compromising the strict secrecy of many projects in which Griffith had been involved.

Portland's new WPA-built international airport was off limits for most photographers, but when an Air Corps general landed the first four-engine DC-4 there, I was allowed to photograph our candidate on the tarmac welcoming the general.

Tongue Point Naval Air Station near Astoria was a classified storage and distribution facility for Navy petroleum, but I was allowed to take a picture of Griffith inspecting the site with Lieutenant-Commander George Hasselman, who was responsible for defense of the Oregon Coast. Two days later I got a picture of the candidate inspecting Columbia River navigation aids with Army Colonel C.R. Moore, the district engineer responsible.

Of course we made much of Griffith's principal role in bringing Timberline Lodge to Oregon and in assuring its national prominence through its dedication by President Franklin D. Roosevelt.

OUTCLASSED IN THE INFIGHTING

Meanwhile the really meaningful campaigning was under way within the Democratic party between the CIO-supported Mahoney and the more moderate American Federation of labor-backed Griffith. The bitterness of that split was reflected in the following article in the April 17, 1942, *Oregon Labor Press*.

The International Woodworker, *official paper of the rebel and dual labor movement in the Northwest, made a shameless effort to besmirch labor-endorsed E.J. Griffith for the Democratic nomination to Congress. The following CIO officials must assume responsibility for the scurrilous, lying attack ... It is assumed, however, that the author of the vicious and untrue story who mutilated the picture of the President of the United States in order to misrepresent and lie about Griffith, is a former employee of the Works Progress Administration who was discharged because of neglect of duty and drunkenness.*

Griffith was widely admired by Republicans, but of course they had no voice in the Democratic primary. I will always think that E.J. Griffith would have won handily if he had made it onto the general election ballot.

Griffith had been a member of the War Shipping Board during World War I, and after defeat in the 1942 primary election he established the Griffith Transportation Company, an international trading firm. I returned to the Forest Service in the summer of 1942, continuing to write a weekly "Ski Scout" column for the *Oregon Journal* but changing its name in summer to "Mountain Breezes."

TIMBERLINE – A NAVY BASE?

After Timberline closed to the public, talks began with Navy Department officials of possibly turning the lodge into a therapeutic center for combat-weary seamen. The suggestion was put forward by Lieutenant Commander Hasselman, commandant of the Tongue Point Naval Base and a longtime booster for Timberline.

According to a Dec. 10, 1942, article by *Oregon Journal* editor Fred H. McNeil, an agreement was made for manager Fred VanDyke and his wife, Anna, to operate the lodge and ski lift for the Navy beginning on Oct. 1. The building was kept staffed and in readiness for the Navy takeover for two months until "legal difficulties intervened and the agreement was ended on November 30," McNeil reported.

WINTER'S FIRST GREAT STORM

As a result of those delays, the first winter storm struck before the chairlift was dismantled or other preparations made for winterizing the resort. The Forest Service owned the building and the chairlift, so no matter who might be held responsible for the damage, it was up to Ranger Harold Engles to gather what men he could to begin clearing the roof and digging free a mile of half-buried cable, towers and chairs. I was a member of that crew.

A WORLD AFIRE

America had been at war for six months, and things were not going well. Japan had overrun the Pacific Rim except Australia and New Zealand, and the United States was girding to defend Hawaii and the west Coast against an expected Japanese invasion. Germany had swept Allied armies off the European continent and had driven deep into Russian territory on Operation Barbarossa.

FATHER JOINS THE WAR EFFORT

Wymond had joined the Merchant Marine in 1936 and after the war began had survived two trips as bos'n on Liberty ships in convoys carrying munitions, food and aircraft for the British through Halifax, Nova Scotia, to Murmansk, Russia, under almost constant attack by German submarines and bombers. According to the U.S. Naval Historical Center, "Ships leaving the United States for Northern Russia (in 1942 and early 1943) had less than one chance in three of returning safely."

Because I provided the only support for our parents, I had been deferred from the draft. Father was 75 and had not had a job for 10 years, but with the growing labor shortage he decided he might get work as a carpenter in the shipyards. One day in 1942 he headed for the employment office but was told that he couldn't make an application without a Social Security number. The Social Security system hadn't been established until 1936. He had never needed a number before, but he promptly applied for one, giving his age as 65 instead of 75. He soon received a number and went to work installing radar antennas atop the masts of minesweepers being built at the Albina shipyards. He continued to work until he was 80 (70 by Social Security records), and after that he was eligible for retirement benefits.

FOREST RANGER TO AIR FORCE TRAINEE

Since Father was making more money in the shipyards than I was in the Forest Service, our parents no longer were dependent on me. Although my job was classified as "necessary to the war effort," Forest Supervisor Waha, a veteran of the First World War, agreed to release me, and I set out to enlist in the Army Air Corps for pilot training. (The Air Force hadn't yet been separated from the Army). I was 27, in good health, and had yearned to learn to fly ever since Wymond and I made our first flight with a barnstorming pilot on a Montana prairie when I was 8 years old.

But those hopes were dashed when I showed up at the Army recruiting office in Portland and found that because I hadn't been to college, I wasn't eligible for pilot training, and anyway I was past the preferred age.

Since it was unusual for a potential recruit to be seeking to have his draft deferment cancelled in order for him to enlist, the recruiting sergeant proposed an alternative – the Army Civilian Pilot Training Program (CPT) – which allowed otherwise qualified inductees to attend civilian flight schools, then after completing pilot training to go on active duty as glider pilots, flight instructors or ferry pilots. It looked like a perfect fit, and on Dec. 9, 1942, I enlisted in the Army Air Force, expecting to be quickly assigned to a flight school but continuing to work for the Forest Service in the meantime.

TIMBERLINE'S MIRACLE SURVIVAL

Weather in the fall of 1942 was deceptively mild, but when winter did arrive, it was with a vengeance. Timberline Lodge engineer Arthur A. "Mitch" Mitchell had maintenance of the heating, lighting and fire protection systems inside the building well in hand, but the chairlift and lodge exterior were being battered by the fierce storms. Chairs and cable were sheathed with so much ice that their weight had torn off sheaves and buried many chairs.

Snow had drifted 20 feet deep on the lodge's east wing, and as the building cooled, snow clung to the roof until the ridgeline was dangerously deflected. By New Years the Lodge was facing serious structural damage, and in time the weight of snow might have moved it from its foundations.

Engles wanted to relieve the east wing of as much of its snow load as possible even before more men and equipment could be assembled, and he remembered a scheme that had worked on a snow-covered barn when he was a boy. He phoned Zigzag and asked Assistant Ranger Amos Smelzer to bring up a roll of barbed wire, and he had us stretch a long piece along the comb of the roof where the snow was deepest. With half of us at each end we began sawing the barbed wire back and forth like a tug-of-war until our "saw" surfaced several feet below the top, releasing a sizable slab of snow that slid off the roof in a small avalanche. The technique was imperfect, but combined with lots of backbreaking shoveling, enough snow was cleared off in two days to bring the roofline partway back to normal.

Engles then took two of us with him to see what could be done about the Magic Mile. It was a frightening experience. Before we realized what a tremendous strain the chairlift cables were under, we dug one of the chairs loose from the snow. It came out with such force that at the top of the cable's spring, the attached chair broke away and flew 50 yards through the air, burying itself somewhere in Salmon River Canyon. Later an experienced ski lift crew managed to drop the cables from the towers and stow the chairs in the lift house. The Zigzag Civilian Conservation Corps camp had been disbanded in June 1942 and converted to a work camp for wartime conscientious objectors. Those crews were a great help in the snow removal jobs on both the lodge and the Magic Mile.

HOLDING DISASTER AT BAY

After the building and chairlift were dug out, snow closed the road from Highway 26, leaving the lodge standing lonely on the mountain, six miles and 2,000 feet above Government Camp, 30 miles from the nearest electric power lines, with backpacking on skis the only way to transport supplies or mail. Fuel oil for electric generators and boilers had been delivered during the summer.

Keeping the building structurally sound, heated in winter, and protected from fire and the ravages of weather year around depended upon chief engineer Mitch Mitchell, Colonel Hartwell W. Palmer and two assistants whose dedicated efforts went unheralded in the midst of the fearful war.

I spent a week as a relief engineer at the lodge that February and learned what a dreary place the beautiful building could be when the temperature was barely above freezing, the building's lights were on only for a few hours most days, and only the engine room and kitchen areas were used for living quarters.

The lodge had a modern fire protection system with water sprinklers in every guest room, while in the east wing attic and other unheated spaces there was a frost-free compressed air system with fused sprinkler heads, which in case of fire would melt, releasing the air pressure and allowing water to rush out and douse the blaze.

Power for heat and light, for the air compressor, and for the two-mile-long water pumping system depended on a 50-kilowatt, four-cycle diesel engine with a 35-kilowatt backup, which were run only a few hours a day, and a 5-kilowatt portable generator to supply light at other times. Engineer Mitchell pampered those engines as though they were members of his family, because an error in calculating any of the power sequences could have resulted in frozen pipes, loss of fire protection or worse.

COLONEL PALMER EXPLAINS THINGS THE CAVALRY WAY

Usually one of us on Engles' staff skied up on weekends to bring supplies and to keep an eye on visitors who came up the Blossom and Alpine trails and sought shelter around the building. Colonel Palmer found one such group starting to build a warming fire against the lodge foundation. They probably learned

Clearing rime ice from the Magic Mile cable; I'm on the right. Just after this photo was taken, the cable – partially relieved from the weight of ice – released itself instantaneousy and catapulted the chair past me and into Salmon River Canyon. Ray Atkeson photo courtesy of Friends of Timberline.

some new words from that veteran of 46 years in the U.S. Cavalry.

Summer added more burdens, for when the road was free of snow, a surprising number of sightseers used their precious gas rations to drive to the lodge and were disappointed that it was not open for visitors. Then Colonel Palmer's years of experience as a wrangler and tour guide were invaluable.

When my week as relief engineer ended that winter, I was happy to return to backpacking supplies to the lodge and to servicing Army Aircraft Warning Service lookouts. I recall once when there was a particularly large load to carry, Engles joined me, and as we plodded up the six-mile road on skis we each insisted that we had the heaviest share. When we reached the Lodge we weighed the packs, and Engles won; he had 104 pounds, and I had only 100.

Ole Lien and George Lasher were among other Forest Service workers who were Mitch's assistants. Colonel Palmer, who served the lodge in so many capacities between 1937 and 1956, was in his 80s when he retired.

Power for heat and light at Timberline Lodge came from a 50-kilowatt, four-cycle diesel engine and a 35-kilowatt backup. Friends of Timberline photo.

AIRCRAFT WARNING SERVICE

The Japanese had devised clever schemes to try to set West Coast forests on fire, including twice launching a small firebombing seaplane from a submarine The seaplane dropped its bombs on Oregon forests and was successfully retrieved by the submarine, but no forest fires were ignited. They also sent thousands of incendiary balloons into the jet stream over Japan that were carried across the ocean to the Pacific Northwest in three or four days. The only known fatalities on the U.S. mainland from enemy action during World War II occurred May 1945 when one of those balloons landed near Lakeview, killing a woman and five children who were on a church picnic.

Among the least-known guardians of America's security during the war were the Army Aircraft Warning Service lookouts located inland from the West Coast. They were staffed by dedicated men and women who perched in towers high above the forests day and night, fine weather and foul, and watched and listened for enemy aircraft.

Radar was just being perfected but was not available to the AWS. Ironically one of the few American radar installations in full operation on Dec. 7, 1941, was near Diamond Head overlooking Pearl Harbor, and it did provide early warning of the Japanese arrival 30 minutes ahead of the attack but was given no credence by those in command.

Supplementing the Army Aircraft Warning Service lookouts were the Forest Service Reserves – volunteer men and women, mostly older members of outdoor clubs such as the Mazamas, Trails Club and Crag Rats, who undertook extensive training to prepare themselves to carry out the duties of observers and fire fighters on a temporary basis.

THE HICKMAN BUTTE CAPERS

Ranger Harold Engles, Assistant Ranger Amos Smelzer, fire guard George Lasher and I were responsible for maintaining and servicing several of those Aircraft Warning Service lookouts, including the one on Hickman Butte at 4,400 feet elevation inside the Bull Run

Retired cavalry officer Colonel Hartwell Palmer and Kenny VanDyke, son of lodge manager Fred VanDyke, conducted Timberline Trail rides in the summer of 1941.

water reserve and about 15 miles from the Zigzag Ranger Station. There was a summer road to the top, and in the fall we had helped a middle-aged couple get settled for a winter of watching in the winterized fire lookout cabin. By early December 2 feet of snow had closed the access road and left drifts 4 feet deep around the tower.

Then one bright, cold morning the lady aircraft observer phoned in a panic to tell us that she had to get to town right away to preside over the imminent birth of a grandchild. She couldn't ski but had brought a pair of snowshoes when they came to the lookout and now was planning to use them for the first time; she wanted us to bring a truck to the bottom of the butte to meet her. She didn't realize what a frightening prospect that was. The blizzard had been followed by several warm days, then a cold snap had turned the surface of the snow to an icy crust.

BEWARE OF MOTHER BEAR WITH CUBS

When I told her that we would try to get her down the following day, I suddenly was reminded of a Forest Service adage, "There is no fury like that of a mother bear separated from her cubs." The lady was adamant. She seemed not even to hear me, and as we spoke on the phone she was continuing to bundle up for the trip. George Lasher and I finally realized that if we didn't hurry up and help her get down that morning, we might well end up having to organize a search party for her that night. We gathered rescue equipment and almost as an afterthought piled a ski patrol toboggan and a pair of crampons into the truck. The snow level was above 2,000 feet, so the truck with only a light load and a single-blade push-plow came to a stop about two miles from the butte and 1,000 feet shy of the top.

Hickman Butte in the Bull Run Water Reserve was manned day and night during World War II by Army Aircraft Warning Service lookouts watching and listening for enemy aircraft. Mount Hood shown in the distance, September 1963. Forest Service photo courtesy of Zigzag Ranger District.

It was our fond hope that our quarry hadn't gotten far from the lookout, because once she got down among the trees she could easily miss the snowbound road. But there was no such problem. Although the lady had been determined to conquer her snowshoes, even the most skillful snowshoer would have been daunted that day. Not only was the snow like an ice rink, but her snowshoes were the long heavy style favored by Alaskan trappers for deep snow.

She had finally given up and decided to walk, but her slick-soled boots slipped, and she slid down the steep mountainside until becoming becalmed on a flat ledge about 500 feet below the summit where Lasher and I spotted her, fortunately unhurt.

I was able to traverse up the mountain on sharp steel-edged skis, and Lasher strapped on the crampons and pulled the rescue toboggan right up to the frustrated observer. We secured her on the toboggan, and while I straddled the front wearing skis, Lasher rode the brake in back, and we soon were off the ice and made our way to the truck before dark.

Was it a boy or a girl? Honestly, I don't remember the rest of that story.

SAD DEMISE OF THE ZIGZAG COVERED BRIDGE

Some old-timers may remember the quaint covered bridge that once spanned the Zigzag River just east of the ranger station, but few ever knew the story of its demise.

It happened on a frosty morning a month later with two feet of new snow on the ground. With a load of supplies ready to be taken to Hickman, we thought of the big Forest Service FWD rotary snowplow formerly used on Timberline Road that was in temporary storage right there in the Zigzag shops. George Lasher had operated it before, so we yielded to the temptation to use it to open a few miles of the Hickman Butte road that day.

He fired up the rotary and we started for the lookout. As we approached the bridge across the Zigzag it seemed to grow smaller, and I got out and walked ahead to guide the plow to the center. We knew that in summer the bridge carried loaded logging trucks safely, but still we crept across carefully. Then just as we reached the far side, the top of the plow's cab hit the bridge's last overhead support, which fell across the windshield.

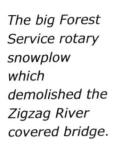

The big Forest Service rotary snowplow which demolished the Zigzag River covered bridge.

A SHUDDERING COLLASPE

As George tried moving the plow gently back and forth, the whole roof structure shuddered then collapsed like a house of cards. Fortunately the rotary was undamaged, and the roadway across the bridge seemed solid, so with the help of a crew from the ranger station we cleared away the debris, leaving only memories of what I believe was the last covered bridge along the route of the historic Barlow Road.

The rotary then made short work of opening the road to the base of Hickman Butte, and that night we backpacked the last of the supplies to the lookout by moonlight.

If there was any trouble over our unauthorized use of the rotary plow I didn't hear about it, but the main stringers of the bridge must have been reinforced earlier to carry log trucks, for I was told later that covered bridges depend upon their sides and roof trusses for much of their strength.

Suddenly it was summer. It had been seven months since I enlisted in the Army Air Corps, and now instead of a call to report for flight training, I received a letter saying that the Civilian Pilot Training Program was cancelled, and I could either remain in the Air Force as a private or request an honorable discharge.

AN HONORABLE DISCHARGE

I wondered if there might be a third option: the Merchant Marine. Portland and Vancouver shipyards were launching several new cargo ships and tankers a week, so I took the Air Corps letter to my draft board and found that in fact there was a greater need right then for men to sail the new ships than for men to fill the draft quota. Wymond believed that with a little coaching I could handle the duties of an able seaman, but he knew that it would be difficult to get Coast Guard certification without first spending months at a War Training Service school.

FELLOW KIWANIAN LENDS A HAND

I had been vice president of the Portland Downtown Kiwanis club and remembered that fellow Kiwanian Harold C. Jones had been in the Coast Guard in World War I, so I asked him for advice. It was my good fortune that he had been recalled to active duty in Portland as a commander in the Coast Guard, and he quickly determined that the only rating in the deck crew of a merchant ship for which there was no War Training Service school was ship's carpenter. He arranged for me to be certified for that job based on my experience in the Forest Service, and he endorsed the papers to allow me also to sail as able seaman in case of an emergency.

On July 10, 1943, I received an honorable discharge from the Army Air Corps. On July 16 I signed on as an able seaman aboard the new Liberty Ship S.S. J.D. Ross, which had just been completed at Oregon Shipyards in Portland.

A week later, as the ship was crossing the Columbia River bar to begin a six-month cruise carrying ammunition and F4U fighter planes for Marines in the South Pacific, I cast a lingering look back up the river at Mount Hood and thought of Timberline Lodge waiting there, lonely on the mountain.

S.S. J.D. Ross on her maiden voyage from Oregon Shipyards. On July 16, 1943, I sailed on her to the South Pacific with 10,000 tons of ammunition and a deck load of fighter planes.

Timberline Lodge, "Lonely On The Mountain." I took this photograph of the west portal in 1938, several years before the swimming pool was built at the west end of the building.

EPILOGUE

Richard L. and Molly Kohnstamm. Photo Art photo courtesy of Friends of Timberline.

TIMBERLINE LODGE ALMOST CAME A CROPPER

Timberline Lodge almost came a cropper in the years right after World War II. The proud building had fallen into disrepair, and many of its handcrafted furnishings were in tatters. Finally in February 1955, the Forest Service cancelled the operator's permit, and the lodge was closed.

That was the lowest point in its checkered financial history, but it also was the beginning of 50 years of enlightened management by Richard L. Kohnstamm, who took over the operating permit that May. His R.L.K. and Company invested private funds in chairlifts, a swimming pool and other permanent improvements, even though he had only a short term lease. Then as he proved his management skill, the Forest Service appropriated money to

270

The Henderson cabin at Government Camp, November 2005. James M. Simmons Jr. photo.

build a new east wing and a separate day lodge to serve burgeoning crowds of day users.

In 1975 mountain devotees formed the nonprofit Friends of Timberline, dedicated to preservation and restoration of the building and its artifacts. Now in 2005, with Dick Kohnstamm chairman of R.L.K. and Company and his son Jeff president and area operator, the lodge's future is bright indeed.

GOVERNMENT CAMP'S REVIVAL

Meanwhile Government Camp, the cradle of Mount Hood skiing, is undergoing a rebirth comparable to that of the late 1920s, when highways were first opened for winter travel. Similarly Mount Hood Meadows on the mountain's east side is enhancing its fine network of lifts and trails by installing the most advanced snow-making equipment.

NINETY WONDROUS YEARS

In 1946 Father helped us build a cabin at Government Camp similar to the cabins that he built for our family at Pablo and Hayes Creek, Mont., and Headquarters, Idaho, so many years ago. We enjoy watching the seasons change as we peer through the cabin's often frost-rimed windows.

Recently I celebrated my 90th birthday there.

Index

A

Adamson, Linny ii
American Ski Journal 221, 224
Amick, Don 194
Anderson, Andy 182
Anderson, Reidar 224
Atkeson, Ray
  George Henderson skiing with to Timberline Lodge's
     opening 207
  photos by
   George Henderson skiing v
   Magic Mile covered in ice 263
  photo of at timberline 208
  photo of Olympic tryouts downhill course 216

B

Babson, Skit Smith, photo of 226
Baldwin, Jack 182
Barrie, Wendy, Hollywood actress, photo of 211
Bass Silver Boot for All American Skier of the Year
     223–224
Battle Axe Inn 96
  operators Ma and Pa Villiger 96
  photos of 97
bear rugs from 1904 St. Louis Fair 19–20
Becker, Max 179, 182
  photo by 180
Beckey, Fred, Yocum Ridge climb 185
Bennett, Jack, photo of after Cathedral Ridge climb
    183
Big Eddy, Clackamas River, photo of passenger train
    160
Black, Randi ii
Blackwood, E.C., photo of Government Camp and
    Mount Hood 188
Blatt, Bob 226
Blue Box Pass, naming of 157–158
Blue Box telephone, photo of 157
Bonneville Dam Chronicle 149
  reproduction of 150
Bonney Butte
  photo of Terrible Traverse 243
  winter ski trip to summit lookout 239–245
Bowden, Virginia, photo of 226
Bowman, Lin, photos of
  after Cathedral Ridge climb 184
  skiing with Boyd French Jr. 219
Boyer, Tim, photo of American white pelican 80

Bradbury, Joe 194
Bradley, David, "Two Boards," poem 187
Bradshaw, Orin, manager at S.H. Kress 125, 132, 134
Breitenbush Hot Springs 137, 147, 172
Breitenbush Lake 167
Breitenbush Lake Guard Station 143–144, 161
  photo of 143
British Ski Year Book 190
Buck, C. J., Regional Forester 217
Buhler, Wilfred 184
Buhtler, George 194
Byrd, Admiral Richard E., photo of 77

C

"Custer's Last Stand," painting by Edgar S. Paxson 44
  reproduction of 45
Calkin, Ralph, Wy'east climber 177, 185
Calverley, George 150
Cascade Ski Club 215
  clubhouse
   new clubhouse 102–103
   photo of 103
  description of early facilities and events 98–99
  founding of 95
  jumping hill on Multorpor Mountain
   first built 95
   photo of 99, 100
Cathedral Ridge, Mount Hood
  climb of 183–184
  photo of 184
Chainsaws, early 159
Clackamas Lake Ranger Station 139–140, 164
Clearwater Timber Protective Association, Idaho 63,
    65–66
Clear Lake Butte Lookout 163
  photo of 162
Clermont, Indiana 9, 10, 36, 92–93
Cloud Cap Inn area as a destination ski resort 181–182
  photo of group surveying site for a destination resort
    181
Coalman, Lige 177
  built Government Camp Hotel 98
  Christmas with 122–124
  photo of at Spirit Lake 123
Contents, Table of vi–vii
Cramer, Harriet Park, photo of Lige Coalman 123
Crater Lake 83–86
  1928 first visit 83
  1938 second visit rim to lake on skis 84–85
  1949 third visit in an airplane 85–86
Crater Rock Downhill Run, photo of ii: *See also* Golden Rose Ski Race

Crater Rock Shelter, Mount Hood 132
  history of 234
  photo of 236
Crookham, Arthur, Oregon Journal City Editor 137, 151
Cruikshank, Pharmacist Magill's Drug Store 81–82, 87–88
  photo of 87
Curtiss JN4-D Jenny, photo of 60

D

Dail, Bob and Cooper Spur climb 130
Dana, Marshall, Oregon Journal Editor 137
Daniel, Joe, Lakes District Forest Guard 158
Darcy, Lynn, photos by
  Betty Woolsey, American amateur skier 220
  Erna Steur, Swiss skier 220
Darr, Everett, Wy'east climber 116
  photo of 251
Davidson, Ira, inventor of the Snowcat 194
Day, Ralph Jr.
  1936 Skyline Trail ski trip 137
  1940 Mount Hood shelter construction crew 235
  photos of
    at Blue Box Pass 139
    at Breitenbush Guard Station 143
    on Park Ridge 146
    sliding into Jefferson Park 145
    starting descent from Park Ridge to Jefferson Park 135
    summit shelter construction crew 237
Dean, Wade and Glacier Mining Company 130, 132
Dedication of book to Henderson children iii
Dennis, Paul, Forest Guard Clackamas Lake 139, 164
  photo of he and his wife at Packer's Cabin 140
Desiata, Gary, photo by of Summit toboggan slide 96
Diamond Match Company 63
Donlan, Crissy 48
Donlan, Ed, Ben Henderson's business partner 26, 29, 43
  photo of his Missoula home 49
Durrance, Dick
  checks Olympic tryouts downhill course 218
  differences with Friedl Pheifer 221
  first in Olympic tryouts amateur slalom 221
  photos of
    on Ski Bowl slalom course 215
    receiving Bass Silver Boot award 223
  wins Olympic tryouts amateur downhill 224
Durrance, Lisal, sister of Dick Durrance 218

E

Eagle Creek Trail by candle light 104
Eddy, Ralph, photos by

Battle Axe Inn 97
  cars on a busy weekend at Government Camp 95
  Magic Mile 195
Enebo, Delores, Queen of the 1936 Oregon Winter Sports Carnival 152
  photo of in bathing suit 153
Engles, Harold, Zigzag District Ranger
  1936 George Henderson first met 161
  1937 ski Skyline Trail 169, 171
  1938 Timberline Trail 177, 179–180, 182
  1939 Olympic tryouts 221, 223
  1940 Mount Hood summit shelter construction 233–237
  photos from
    of summit shelter construction crew 237
    of USFS summit shelter construction crew working on top of Mount Hood 238
  photos of
    at Abbot Pass on skis 169
    on Zigzag Mountain 234
    summit shelter construction crew 237
Equipment
  homemade headlamps 103–104
  homemade pack boards 114
  homemade skis by Father 102

F

Faircourt, Maxine 132
Ferrell, Jack 235, 250, 254
Fire fighting 163–165
FIS amateur, definition of 219
Flathead Indian Reservation 8, 31–32
Flathead Lake 8, 30–31
Flu epidemic, 1918 10: *See also* Influenza, Spanish
Foreman's Point Lookout 203
Forest History Society photo 217
Frank, Aaron, and Cascade Ski Club clubhouse 103
Frankland, James, USFS Regional Engineer
  photo of laying cornerstone for Timberline Lodge 155
Fraser, Don 194, 224, 226
French, Boyd Jr. 84, 120, 156, 184
  and wife Laurie 235–236, 236
  Lone Fir Lookout 124, 235
  photos of
    skiing with Lin Bowman 219
    summit shelter construction crew 237
  Ski Bowl rope tows 192–194
  summit shelter construction crew 235
French, Boyd Sr. 103, 190, 207, 223
  Cloud Cap Inn permitee 181–182
  photo of
    skiing with Crown Prince Olav 228

president Cascade Ski Club 182, 218
  Sir Arnold Lunn 190
  Ski Bowl 181, 192–194, 218
French, Donal 120
French, Laurie, wife of Boyd Jr. 235–236
French, Margie: *See* Simmons, Margie French
Friedrich, Doris 221
Friends of Timberline, photos from
  George Henderson with camera ii
  George Henderson with Hjalmar Hvam 225
  George Henderson with skis 241
  Griffith, Meier and McNary 205
  Magic Mile covered with ice 263
  Movie, 1940 214
  Prince Olav dedicating Magic Mile 227
  Richard L. and Molly Kohnstamm 270
  Timberline Lodge power generators 264

G

Gamble, Ted 230
Gano, Ward, Forest Service project engineer for Timberline Lodge
  photos of
    looking up forty-foot snow tunnel 151
  search for Timberline Lodge's water supply 150–151
Geer, Lars de 232
Gifford, Ralph, photos by
  Battle Axe Inn 97
  ski class at Timberline 252
Gilbert, "Gil" 158
Glacier Mining Company and Wade Dean 130, 132
Golden Rose Ski Race ii, 153, 155–156, 216, 224, 226
Government Camp: *See also* individual alphabetical listings for some entries
  Battle Axe Inn 96, 97
  George Henderson's first visit 95–104
  Government Camp Hotel 98
  Hill's Place 98
  Mt. Hood Hut 96
  photos of
    Battle Axe Inn exterior and lobby 97
    Cascade Ski Club Clubhouse 103
    from Tom Dick and Harry Mountain 188
    Government Camp Hotel 98
    Multorpor ski jump 99, 100
    Summit toboggan slide 96
    Swim covered with snow 101
    winter crowd 95
  Swim 98
  toboggan runs 96
Government Camp Hotel 98
  photo of 98
Graham, Grace 194

Graham, Joe and USFS telephone box construction 157
Griffith, E.J., Timberline Lodge advocate 154, 217
  appointed head of Oregon WPA by Roosevelt 206
  campaign for Congress 258–260
  photos of
    at Democratic candidates luncheon 259
    at Timberline Lodge 205
    laying cornerstone for Timberline Lodge 155
    shaking hands with Crown Prince Olav 230
Guatemala, Father's visit to 10
Gustafsson, Corey 221

H

Haack, Reinhardt 169
  photos of
    at Abbot Pass on skis 169
    crossing Olallie Lake on skis 170
    on top of Park Ridge 171
Hackett, Bill 120
Hall, Sigurd and Silver Skis Race 226
Halling, George, Rose Festival Association President
  photo of in Multnomah Stadium 155
Hannigan, Steve, Sun Valley promoter 152
Harlow, Jim, Wy'east climber, photos by
  Jim Mount at old Timberline Cabin 209
  Ole Lien, 1931 118
  Ray Atkeson at timberline 208
Harrison, Hal, Breitenbush Lake Forest Guard 161, 165
Haugen, Ole, Multorpor cable sled 187
  photo of 188
Hayes, Lew 235
Hayes Creek, Montana, logging in 8, 53–60
Hays, Jim, Union Pacific public relations 181
Headquarters, Idaho 63, 63–64
Henderson, Ben Wymond, aka Father
  birth 11
  cold baths to promote health 28
  early partnership with Ed Donlan 93
  first car, Jackrabbit Apperson 22–23
  geography book from elementary school 11
  gold prospecting in North Cascades 14–15
  Henderson, Montana, named for 93
  Henderson cabin, Government Camp 271
  homemade skis 102
  Jobs
    1926 for Weyerhaeuser Company 63
    1927 building Headquarters, Idaho 63, 65
    1928 as a millwright in Klamath Falls 76
    1930 real estate agent 107
    1942 carpenter at Kaiser Shipyards 261
  Great Depression's effects on 107–109

joyful years in Portland 105
marriage to Verlinda Miller 9, 109
Montana first move to 12–16
Montana second move to 25–42
Mount Hood climb 122–123
Pablo lumber mill fire 51–52
parents of 12
photos of 13, 23, 39, 70, 102
Portland visit 17
San Francisco visit 18
social security 261
St. Louis Fair visit 19
winter chute logging 8, 53–55, 59–60
Yellowstone Park
   first visit 15
   second visit with family 32
Henderson, Bonnie Lynn
  Crater Lake hike 86
  Dedication of book to iii
  photo by of Cascade Ski Club Clubhouse 103
Henderson, Clark
  in Montana 12–14
  photo of in Missoula 13
Henderson, Clint, photo of sons with George and
    Wymond 106
Henderson, Darcy Verlinda
  Crater Lake hike 86
  Dedication of book to iii
  Hawaii water slide 33
Henderson, Donna Cate
  Crater Lake hike 86
  Dedication of book to iii
  Flag Point Lookout 240
Henderson, Dr. Lawrence 48–49
  teaching George and Wymond Arlberg technique 44,
    46, 50
Henderson, George Miller
  Admiral Byrd 76–77
  alone 52
  birth 10
  bootlegging 55
  Boy Scouts 76, 78
  Cascade Ski Club
    Frank, Aaron, donation for new clubhouse 103
    weekly progress photos of new construction 103
  Christmas with Lige Coalman 122–123
  co-chair Olympic tryouts 216
  first airplane ride 61–62
  first camera 132, 138
  Government Camp first visit 95–104
  gymnastics 107
  health

    1918 flu epidemic 10
    adhesions 38–39
    appendicitis 38
    broken arm 57
    broken leg 248
    cold baths and showers 28
    nearly drowning 77
    scarlet fever 56–57
    tick fever 56
  hikes
    Eagle Creek to Wahtum Lake by candle light 104
    Mount Defiance 115
    Spirit Lake country 111–114
  jobs
    1926 as a teamster, Headquarters, Idaho 71–74
    1927 odd jobs, Lewiston, Idaho 76
    1928 as a disc jockey, Klamath Falls 82
    1928 at Magill's drug store, Klamath Falls 81–82
    1929 four jobs a day in Klamath Falls 87–90
    1930 hauling sawdust, Portland 108
    1930 selling Christmas cards, Portland 108
    1933 counselor and coach, YMCA, Portland 108
    1933 S.H. Kress and Company, Portland 125
    1934 first job as a photojournalist 130, 132
    1935 quit S.H. Kress and Company 134
    1936 Bonneville Dam Chronicle 149
    1936 Publicist, Winter Sports Association 151–156
    1936 Red Cross fundraising 149
    1936 USFS forest guard 156, 157–168
    1936 window displays for Meier and Frank 149
    1937-1942 Journal "Ski Scout" column 193
    1938 manager of Royal Court tour 210
  learning to drive 58
  learning to swim 77
  Mount Hood climbs
    1933 first climb 115–121
    1933 second climb with Father and Aunt Jenny
      121–122
    1933 third climb 122
    1934 Cooper Spur 130
    1934 with Ranger and George Riggs 132
    1938 Cathedral Ridge 183–184
    1939 Yocum Ridge 184–185
    1946 to install lifelines 124
    1986 last climb 124
  panning for gold 66–67
  pets
    Lucky 167
    snowshoe rabbit 35–36
    snowshoe rabbit, photo of 36
    Tippy 69–70
  photos by ii, 100, 102, 117, 120, 126, 129, 131,

133, 136, 139–144, 149, 151–154, 160, 166,
    169–172, 173–174, 179, 181, 183, 184, 186,
    191, 195, 197, 199, 201, 202, 205, 207, 215,
    216, 220, 222, 223, 225, 230, 234, 236, 237,
    239, 265, 267, 269, 271
photos of v, 8, 21, 25, 28, 39, 53, 82, 83, 89, 106,
    120, 124, 126, 235, 241
playing Indian 55
poem by 113
Preface by v
schools
    Grant High School 107
    Pablo, Montana, elementary school 36–38
    photo of Pablo, Montana, public schools 37
    Willamette University 111
ski lessons, first 44, 46–47
stealing Wymond's sled 56
Henderson, Heather Ann
    Dedication of book to iii
Henderson, Milton Moon 12
    photo of 12
Henderson, Randall Wymond
    Dedication of book to iii
    home-made airplane 23
Henderson, Sarah Legg 12
    photo of 12
Henderson, Verlinda Miller, aka Mother
    angel food cakes 39
    birth 9
    family of 21–22
    marriage to Ben Wymond Henderson 9, 109
    photos by ii
    photos of 9, 23, 24, 39
Henderson, Ward 48–49
Henderson, Wymond Donlan: *See also* Henderson,
    George Miller
    1918 Flu epidemic 10
    birth 10
    photos of 8, 21, 39, 53, 106, 115
    signature in Mount Adams summit register 128
Henderson Cabin at Government Camp 271
    photo of 271
Henderson Family moves
    1920 from Indiana to Pablo, Montana 23, 25–26
    1922 from Pablo, Montana to Missoula, Montana 43
    1927-1 from Missoula, Montana to Headquarters,
        Idaho 65–66
    1927-2 from Headquarters, Idaho to Lewiston, Idaho
        75
    1928 from Lewiston, Idaho to Klamath Falls, Oregon
        79
    1929 from Klamath Falls, Oregon to Portland, Or-
        egon 91–94
    1930 new Portland home 105
Henderson home
    Indiana, photo of 24
    Pablo, Montana, photo of 24
Hermann, Mike
    Larch Mountain hike 116–117
    photos by
        Mount Adams summit lookout 129
        Swim covered with snow 101
Hermanson, Howard iv
Hiatt, Terry, Yocum Ridge climb 185
Hickman Butte Lookout, photo of 266
Hill's Place 98
Hill, Maryanne 98, 102, 189, 211
    photo of 211
Hotel English 9
Hughes, Bill 194
Hughes, Ed, Mazamas president 156
    photo of holding Mazamas Cup 155
Hull, Win, USFS packer 158, 179–180, 236
    photo of on horseback on Timberline Trail 179
Hvam, Hjalmar
    bridge between ski factions 196
    Crater Rock Downhill Run ii
    Golden Rose Race ii
        and Mazamas Cup 155
        promotional ski jump for in Civic Auditorium 153
        winner of 156
    photos of
        1935 riding Ole Haugen's cable sled 188
        1936 jumping over the Rose Garden 154
        1936 testing Crater Rock Run i
        1937 with Arnold Lunn 191
        1937 with George Henderson 225
    Silver Skis Race 224–225

I

Ijames, Curtis, Wy'east climber
    climbing advice 121
    equipment rental 116
    photos by
        Jim Mount skiing at timberline Mount Hood ii
        skiing at timberline before ski lifts 187
Illumination Rock ii
Indianapolis 9
Indianapolis Speedway 9
Indians: *See* Warm Springs Indians
Influenza, Spanish 10: *See also* Flu epidemic, 1918
International Ski Federation 215

J

Jackrabbit Apperson
    Ben Henderson's first car 22

photo of 23
Jefferson Park 135, 137, 138, 148, 171
   first ski descent into 144–145
   photos of
      looking down into from Park Ridge 135
      Ralph Day schussing into Park 145–146
Johnson, Otis J., Clackamas Lake District Ranger
   1935 Skyline Ski trip 136–137
   photo of on skis 137
Johnsrud, Ken 126–127
June, William, Vice President of Portland General
      Electric 127

K

Kerr, Muki ii
Kohnstamm, Jeff 271
Kohnstamm, Molly
   photo of 270
Kohnstamm, Richard L., R.L.K. Inc. 270–271
   photo of 270
Kunigk, Gretchen
   1940 Olympic team 226
   1948 Olympic team 226
   photo of 226

L

Lang, Otto 101, 224
   brings Arlberg to Oregon 196
   course setter Olympic tryouts slalom 221
   move to Sun Valley 198
   nordic - alpine standoff 196–198
   photo of 196
   ski schools 196, 216
Langille, Doug and Will 124
Langley, Roger 216
   photo of presenting Bass Silver Boot to Durrance
      223
Largest log cabin in the world, photo of 17
Lasher, George 159, 235
   photo of, summit shelter construction crew 237
Leech, Gary 177, 235–236
   photo of, summit shelter construction crew 237
Lewis, Hank iv, 116, 120
Lewis, Ray, last Mount Hood lookout 119
Lien, Ole 118, 120
   photo of 118
Lill, Jim 181
Lindquist, Bob, Multnomah Hotel assistant manager
      200
Litchfield, John, Sun Valley ski school director 181
Little Crater Lake 168
logging
   photo of finished lumber drying 27
   photo of Ponderosa pine logs 27
   winter chute logging 8, 53–55, 59–60
      photo of 53
   with High Wheels 29–30
   with horse team and sleigh, photo of 28
   with steam locomotives 30
London, Dan, Multnomah Hotel manager 200
Lookouts: *See also* separate alphabetical entries plus
      Mount Adams and Mount Hood Lookout
   Bonney Butte 239–245
   Clear Lake Butte 163
   Flag Point 240
   Foreman's Point 203
   Hickman Butte 264–266
   Peavine Mountain 164
   photos of
      Clear Lake Butte 162
      Hickman Butte 266
      L-4 style 239
      Mount Adams 129, 131
      Mount Hood 120, 233, 238, 240
   RHO Mountain 164
   Sisi Butte 165
   West Pinhead Butte 164
Lorenzini, Queen Fern, photo of 211
Lunn, Sir Arnold
   invents slalom racing 190
   photo of with Hjalmar Hvam 191
   sanctions Arnold Lunn Downhill and Far West Kan-
      dahar 190
   visits Timberline Lodge 190
Lymph, Jerry 150
   photos of
      in forty-foot tunnel 151
Lynch, Everett, Clackamas Lake District Ranger 157,
      165, 166
   1936 Skyline Trail ski trip 137, 138, 141
   1937 Skyline Trail ski trip 169
   photos by
      George Henderson with modified pack 138
      Henderson and Day on Park Ridge 146
      Mount Jefferson from Park Ridge 135
      Ralph Day sliding onto Russell Lake 145
   photos of
      1936 at Blue Box Pass 139
      1936 at Breitenbush Lake Guard Station 143
      1936 at Warm Springs Guard Station 141
      1937 at Abbot Pass on skis 169
      1937 crossing Olallie Lake on skis 170

M

MacCluer, Malcolm, photo of 120
Macnab, Barney 116
Magic Mile chairlift 194, 235, 250, 253–255, 258, 262

chairlift not finished for Olympic tryouts 221
dedication of 227–228
funding for 216–218
photos of
   clearing the ice from in winter 263
   Crown Prince Olav dedicating 227
   from the bottom looking up 195
   from the top looking down 254
Magill, Lloyd, owner of Magill's Drug Store 81–82
Mansfield, Dick 128
photo of 129–130
Maps
   Idaho panhandle 64
   North America in 1846 11
   Timberline Trail, Mount Hood 178
Martin, Governor Charles 200
Matt, Toni 224
Mazamas 120, 132, 219, 233
   Mazama Cup 153, 156
   photo of held by Ed Hughes 155
   photos from
      Betty Woolsey 220
      Erna Steur 220
      Mount Adams summit lookout 129
      Mount St. Helens and Spirit Lake 126
   summit register entries from 120, 122, 128, 184,
      236, 238
McCoy, Elwood 128
photo of 129
McCoy, Keith, from White Salmon iv, 59
   Mount Adams climb 128–130
   photo of 129
McFadden, Bernarr, renowned health advocate 14
McJury, Russ, Wy'east climber 120, 177, 185
McNary, Senator Charles 199–200, 214
photo of 205
McNeil, Fred H., Oregon Journal Northwest Editor
      103, 137, 181, 207
   co-chair of Olympic tryouts 216, 223
   news articles by 223, 234, 258, 260
   photo of 216
Mecklem, Horace Jr. 184
   photo of after Cathedral Ridge climb 183
Mecklem, Janet 184
Meier, Jack 154, 206–207, 213
   photos of 152, 205
Merritt, Dixon Lanier, "The Pelican," poem 79
Miller, Aunt Jennie climbs Mount Hood 121–122
Miller, Grandpa
   75th birthday 39–40
Miller, Grandpa and Grandma, photo of 22
Miller, Uncle Carl

photo of 33
the ticktack caper 33–34
Mills, Edison 235
Mills, Jack iv
Monner, Al, photos by
   Gretchen Kunigk 226
   Mount Hood Ski Patrol 251
Morton, Richard, Chief pharmacist Magill's Drug
      Store 81–82
Mount, James A., Wy'east climber
   board member of Mount Hood Development Asso-
      ciation 206
   board member of Timberline Lodge, Inc. 207
   created national advertising campaign for Timberline
      Lodge 209
   first Mount Hood ski circuit 177
   photos of
      at base of First Gendarme, Yocum Ridge 186
      at old Timberline Cabin 209
      front cover, skiing at timberline on Mount Hood ii
      with Jack Meier and Berger Underdahl 152
   President of Oregon Winter Sports Association 209
   Yocum Ridge climb 185–186
Mountain, John 122
Mount Adams
   climbs 128–132
   lightning strikes lookout 128, 130
   photos of
      diamond drill for sulphur mining 129
      horses on summit 131
      lookout 129, 131
   sulphur mining 129–132
Mount Hood ii
   Crater Rock Shelter
      history of 234
      photo of 236
   history of the lifelines 124
   Mazamas summit registers 120, 122
   photos of
      Cathedral Ridge 184
      Yocum Ridge 186
Mount Hood Development Association, formation of
      and board 206
Mount Hood lookout
   history of 233
   photos of: *See* Lookouts: photos of
   replacement of 233–238
Mount Hood Museum and Cultural Center photos
   Olaf Rodegard 249
   ski class at Timberline 252
Mount Hood Ski Patrol 116, 251
   photo of 251

Mount Jefferson 135, 138, 143, 148, 161, 171, 182, 203
  photos of ii, 135, 146, 162, 172
Mount Sentinel, Montana, photo of 46
Mount St. Helens
  climbs 125–128
  photo of 126
Multorpor Mountain 95–96, 98, 188
  photos of Cascade Ski Club's jumping hill
    from the bottom showing crowds 99
    skier coming off class A takeoff 100
    skier coming off class B jump 197
Munro, Sarah ii, iv
Murphin, Tom 235
Musser, Lloyd ii, iv

N

National Downhill and Slalom
        Championships: *See* Olympic tryouts, 1939
National Ski Association 215
Nile River Yacht Club 116
Notson, Bob, Oregonian City Editor 130, 132
Nudelman Brothers 157

O

Olallie Butte photo of 144
Olallie Lake 161
  photo of 166
Olallie Lake Guard Station 143, 161, 164
Olallie Meadow Ranger Station 142
Olav, Crown Prince
  at the Broadway Theatre 229
  George Henderson visits in Norway 230–231
  photos of
    dedicating Magic Mile 227
    on skis with Boyd French Sr. 228
    shaking hands with E.J. Griffith 230
  schussing the Magic Mile 228
  visit to Oregon 227–230
Olympics (1940 and 1948) 226
Olympic tryouts (1939) 215–224
Onthank, Don 233
  photo by 233
Oregon Department of Tourism and Travel 216
Oregon Historical Society Photos
  E.J. Griffith 259
  Ernie Pyle 246
  Forest Service camp in Mount Hood crater 236
  Multnomah Stadium ski jump 156
  Ole Haugen's cable sled 188
Oregon Winter Sports Association 151, 157, 208–209, 215
  advertising campaign for Timberline Lodge 209
  incorporation and formation of 206

Timberline Lodge promotion 151–153
Oregon Winter Sports Carnival
  and James A. Mount 209
  and Sam Slocum 208
  Queens
    1937 Rose Winkler 210
    1938 Margaret Griffith 210
    1939 Fern Lorenzini 211
    1940 Claire Erickson 211
    1941 Dorothy Gast 211
  Queen Contest modeled on Taft Redhead Roundup 208
  Royal Court as ambassadors of Oregon's year-around skiing 209–212
    1937 tour including the White House 209–210
    1938 tour including San Francisco and Mardi Gras 210–211
    1939 tour including Hollywood and Mexico City 211
    1940 tour including New York City and Havanna 211
    1941 tour including Midwest and Sun Valley 211–212
  photos of
    1937 Court at White House 210
    1939 Court at 20th Century Fox Studios 211

P

Pablo lumber mill
  destruction by fire 51–52
  photos of 25, 51
Pacific Crest Trail: *See* Skyline Trail
Pacific Northwestern Ski Association 216
  founding of 95–96
Palmer, Colonel Hartwell 262–263
  photo of 265
Paxson, Edgar S., painting of "Custer's Last Stand" 44
  reproduction of 45
Pearl Harbor 237, 245, 247, 257, 264
  photo of Battleships West Virginia and Tennessee 257
Peet, Bob 55, 57
  photo of 58
pelican, American white 79–80
  photo of 80
Perry, Jack, Mount Adams horse packer 130, 132
  photo of on horse on Mount Adams 131
Pfeifer, Friedl 198
  calls a strike during Olympic tryouts 221–222
  falls on Olympic tryouts downhill course 223
  photo of at Olympic tryouts 222
  wins Olympic tryouts open division slalom 221
Phlox Point Guard Station 150–151

Poetry
  "God's Great Memorial" by George M. Henderson
    113
  "The Pelican" by Dixon Lanier Merritt 79
  "Two Boards" by David Bradley 187
Ponderosa pine, photo of 27
Porter, "Shorty" 138
Preface v
Pucci, Emilio 198
Pyle, Ernie 247–256
  photo of 246

R

Radacher, Peter 224, 225
Raddon, Sam, Oregon Journal Sunday Editor 137
Ranger, the climbing dog 117–118, 121, 132
  photos of climbing Mount Hood 117, 133
Rankin, Ed 184
Rathbone, Basil, Hollywood actor, photo of 211
Red Box at Warm Springs Meadow 165: *See also* Sisi
    Butte Lookout
Riggs, George 157
  Christmas with Lige Coalman 122–123
  Mount Defiance hike 116
  Mount Hood climbs 115–121, 122, 132
  photos by
    abandoned miner's cabin 110
    summit of Mount Margaret 112
  photos of
    July 1933 on summit of Mount Hood 120
    while chairman of Cascade Ski Club's Rose Festi-
      val Committee 156
    with Ranger on Mount Hood 133
  plan to finance new clubhouse for Cascade Ski Club
    103
  Spirit Lake country hike 111, 114
  YMCA counselor Camp Collins 108
Riley, Frank Branch 120
Rodegard, Olaf
  photo of 249
  Silver Skis 225
  ski instructor at Timberline Lodge 248–253
Rogers, Homer 120
Roosevelt, James, photo of with Royal Court 210
Roosevelt, President Franklin D. 108, 125, 214, 227
  and disability 201
  appoints E.J. Griffith head of Oregon WPA 206
  dedication of Timberline Lodge 199–204
  photos of
    dedicating Timberline Lodge with honor guard 202
    getting out of his car at Timberline Lodge 201
Rope tows: *See also* Ski Bowl and Skiing
  how to ride 194

Roth, Elsa, and Olympic slalom course 220–221, 224
Rouse, Willard F., secretary of NE YMCA
  photo of on top of Mount Margaret 112
  Spirit Lake country hike 111
Rowan, Bob 194

S

S.S. J.D. Ross, photo of 268
Scheiblehner, Leo, Yocum Ridge climb 185
Schlatter, Arthur 224
Schneider, Hannes 44, 196, 198
Schroll, Hannes 224
Section Seven 34
Sheppard, George 182
Silcox, Ferdinand A.
  and Magic Mile funding 217–219
  photo of 217
Silcox Hut, how it got its name 216–218
Simmons, James
  meeting with in Hawaii 245
  photo of 240
  ski trip to Bonney Butte 240–245
Simmons, Margie French 120, 245
  photos from 228, 240
Sisi Butte Lookout, metamorphsis from Red Box 165
Skiing: *See also* Magic Mile and Ski Bowl
  1935 Skyline Trail 136–137
  1936 Skyline Trail 135–148
  1937 Skyline Trail 169–172
  Arlberg technique 44, 100–101, 196–198
  Crater Lake, from rim to lake 84–85
  downhill and slalom explode 194
  nordic-alpine standoff 196–198
  Ole Haugen's cable sled on Multorpor 187
    photo of 188
  Otto Lang ski schools 216
  races
    1934 first slalom races on Mount Hood 190
    1936 Olympics 194
    1939 Harriman Cup at Sun Valley 221
    1939 Olympic tryouts 215–224
    1939 Silver Skis 224–226
    1940 and 1948 Olympics 226
    Far West Kandahar 193
    Golden Rose ii, 153, 155–156, 216, 224, 226
  rope tows
    first in Ski Bowl 192
    how to ride 194
    on Multorpor Mountain 194
    second in Ski Bowl 193–194
    Sweden rope tow in Ski Bowl 194
  world's first slalom race 190
Ski Bowl 181, 189, 189–190, 193–194, 215, 235

and Olympic slalom tryouts 218–221
  photos of
    French's second ski tow 193
    Mount Hood's first engineered ski tow 192
  rope tow not finished for Olympic tryouts 221
Skyline Trail 165–167: *See also* Skiing Skyline Trail
Slocum, Sam
  Oregon Winter Sport Carnival queen contest 208
  Taft Redhead Roundup 208–209
Snell, Governor Earl 216
Snowcat
  invention by Ira Davidson and use of 194
  photo of on Mount Hood 195
Snowplow, rotary
  destruction of Zigzag covered bridge 266–267
  keeping Timberline Lodge road open 207
  photos of
    clearing Timberline Lodge road 207
    plow which demolished covered bridge 267
Spanish Influenza: *See also* Flu epidemic, 1918
Sperry, Midge photo of Otto Lang 196
Sprague, Governor Charles 224
Steele, Foster, Assistant Supervisor Mount Hood National Forest 150, 157, 165
  1935 Skyline Trail ski trip 136–137
  1936 Skyline Trail adjustment 167–168
  1936 Skyline Trail ski trip 137–148
  1937 Skyline Trail ski trip 169, 172
  biography of 136
  broken leg 146–148
  hut-to-hut skiing in Oregon Cascades 136, 172
  photos of
    at Blue Box Pass 139
    at Breitenbush Guard Station 143
    at Clackamas Lake 136
    at Clackamas Lake Packer's Cabin 140
    at Warm Springs Guard Station 141
  photo by of Otis J. Johnson 137
Steur, Erna 221
  photo of 220
Sun Valley 198, 218, 219
  invents the chairlift 193–195
  Steve Hannigan promoter of 152
Swim
  desription of 98
  hot water or hot air? 101
  photo of covered in snow 101

T
Temple, William, Timberline Lodge manager 208
Terry, Tom 169
  photos of
    at Abbot Pass on skis 169

crossing Olallie Lake on skis 170
    on top of Park Ridge 171
Thomas, Jeff ii, 185
  photos by
    beaded gloves and bag 175
    Clear Lake Butte Lookout 162
Timberline Cabin 117
  photo of 115
  site of first slalom races on Mount Hood 190
Timberline Lodge
  1935 Griffith and Yeon advocates for 206
  1936 cedar shakes for 190–191
  1936 early financial history 205–207
  1936 laying cornerstone 154
  1936 search for water supply 150–151
    photo of tunnel 151
  1937 President Roosevelt dedicates 199–204
  1937 Sir Arnold Lunn visits 190–192
  1938 ski school 196–198
  1940 advertising brochure 213
  1942 closure by World War II 257–258, 260–262
  1942 Ernie Pyle writes about 247–256
  1942 Navy base 260
  1955 closure 271
  1987 fiftieth anniversary 198
  managers
    Fred VanDyke 258, 260
    Jeff Kohnstamm 271
    Richard L. Kohnstamm 270
    William Temple 208
  photos of
    before completion of headhouse ii
    Delores Enebo in bathing suit on future site of 153
    during Roosevelt's dedication 202
    from tree 199
    power generators 264
    west end in winter 269
    with Bowman, Bennett, Mecklam and Henderson 183–184
    with Griffith, Meier and McNary 205
    with Lunn and Hvam 191–193
  promotion of
    1936 by staging a ski tournament 151–156
    1937-1941 by Royal Court 208–210
    1940-1941 by George Henderson 258
    1940 with a movie 213–214
Timberline Lodge, Inc.
  organization of 206, 207
  original board members 207
Timberline Trail, Mount Hood 177–182
  Engles decision to change original route 177
  map of 178

photos of
    Henderson at Upper Sandy Guard Station 180
    Waha, Walters and Hull above Zigzag Canyon 179
Tinker, E.W. 217
toboggan runs, Government Camp 96
Tolley, Fred 235
    photo of, summit shelter construction crew 237
Tolls, Leveritt 128, 132
Trapp Family Singers 212–213
Trussell, Anne Harlow 118, 208, 209

U

Udelius, Arne, Hood River Crag Rat 181
    photo from 181
Ulland, Olav 224
Underdahl, Berger 193, 206–207, 218
    and Oregon Winter Sports Association 206
    and promotion of Timberline Lodge with a summer
        ski tournament 152
    photo of in Royal Rosarian white uniform 152
United States Forest Service
    campfire permits 161
    chain saw testing 159
    guard training camp 159–161
        photo of at North Fork Guard Station 160
    photos by
        Blue Box telephone 157
        Ferdinand A. Silcox 217
        Hickman Butte 266
        laying Timberline Lodge cornerstone 155
        mules carrying phone line 158
        passenger train at Big Eddy, Clackamas River 160
    telephone line 158–159

V

VanDyke, Fred, Timberline Lodge manager 103, 190,
    207, 221, 258
VanDyke, Kenny, photo of 265
Vielbig, Klindt photo of Terrible Traverse 243
Villiger, Ma and Pa 96

W

Waggener, L.A. "Bud," Mount Hood Forest Engineer
    137, 138, 141–144, 146
    photos of
        at Blue Box Pass 139
        at Breitenbush Lake Guard Station 143
        at Warm Springs Guard Station 141
Waha, A.O., Mount Hood Forest Supervisor 137, 177,
    179, 203, 217, 218, 261
    photo of on Timberline Trail 179

Walters, Stanley, Parkdale District Ranger 179
    photo of on horseback on Timberline Trail 179
Warm Springs Indians 173–176
    hunting black bear on Zigzag Mountain 176
    photos of
        beaded gloves and bag 175
        building a sweat lodge on Zigzag Mountain 174
        encampment on Zigzag Mountain 173
        with bear skin 174
        picking huckleberries on Zigzag Mountain 174
Warm Springs Meadow and Guard Station 140–141
    photo of guard station in winter 141
Waterfall, the elusive 35
Webb, Bob, Oregonian ski columnist 181
Weeman, Roy 169, 171
    photos of
        at Abbot Pass on skis 169
        crossing Olallie Lake on skis 170
        operating radio 170
Weise, Ralph, Mount Hood ski patrol 251
Werner, Morton A. 184
Weyerhaeuser Company 63
White House photo 210
Winkler, Queen Rose, photo of 210
Wolfe, Mrs. Alice Damrosch 221
Woodbury, Sid, president Portland Chamber of Com-
    merce 200
Woolsey, Elizabeth 221
    photo of 220
WPA Symphony Orchestra 203

Y

Yellowstone Park
    Father's first visit 15
    Father's second visit, with family 32
Yeon, John Jr., architect 206
Yocum Ridge, Mount Hood
    attempt to climb 184–186
    photo of 186
Young, Del, Yocum Ridge climb 185
Young, George 107
    Mount Hood climb 116–119
    photos of
        on summit of Mount Hood 120
        on top of Mount Margaret 112
    Spirit Lake country hike 111–112, 114

Z

Zigzag covered bridge, demise of 266–267

ISBN 141208233-1

49989766R00160

Made in the USA
San Bernardino, CA
10 June 2017